Praise for *Farewell, Fred Voodoo*

"Excellent and illuminating . . . a love letter to—and a lament for—Haiti, a country with an already strange and tortured history that became even more tragic, interesting and convoluted in the months after the earthquake. . . . [Wilentz] brings to Haiti empathy and her great skills as a narrator. . . . It's Wilentz's honesty about her own role in Haiti and that of so many other American visitors to that country that ultimately distinguishes her book most from other works that cover similar terrain."

—*Los Angeles Times*

"Unlike many commentators on Haiti, Wilentz genuinely likes and is stimulated by the Haitians themselves, and, in between despairing observations, in both *The Rainy Season* and *Farewell, Fred Voodoo*, she manages to capture the beauty of Haiti, physical and spiritual, something that foreigners writing about the place rarely do. . . . Writing in a marriage of memoir and critique, Wilentz's true strength is in honestly documenting the Haiti that foreigners who visit there construct for themselves."

—*The Huffington Post*

"Savvy, acerbically affectionate and unsparingly probing . . . Each vignette helps readers explore, in a nuanced way, our questions about this perpetually hard-hit place. . . . Particularly enlightening are Wilentz's lucid recaps of Haiti's history."

—*More*

"It's a testament to Wilentz's considerable storytelling skill, and the depth of her passion for this tragic place and its resilient people, that she has crafted such a remarkably fluid read from such anguished and conflicted material."

—*The Miami Herald*

"An extraordinarily frank cultural study/memoir that eschews platitudes of both tragedy and hope."

—*Kirkus Reviews*, starred review

"[A] bracing memoir . . . Readers get a stimulating immersion course in Haiti's culture, history, and political machinations. [Wilentz] introduces a fantastical cast of characters who inhabit the many layers of Haitian society and those individuals who flocked to the island following the earthquake, burdened with motives ranging from the base self-promotion or redemption of sundry celebrities. . . . An unsentimental yet heartfelt journey to a country possessing the power to baffle some, yet beguile others."

—*Publishers Weekly*

"[Wilentz] loves and knows Haiti deeply, and her stories about her old friends and new neighbors . . . show a Haiti different and more complex than the myth created by naive though well-meaning outsiders."

—*The Daily Beast*

"Mixing memoir, history, and current events, Wilentz weaves together a kind of profile writ large of the Haitian people."

—*Foreign Affairs*

"Writing with brandishing intensity, wit, skepticism, and indignation, Wilentz exposes systemic corruption, attends a voodoo ceremony, considers zombies and dictators, and marvels over everyday survival. Zestfully candid . . . her portraits of Haitians instruct and humble us."

—*Booklist*

"The award-winning author guides us through this grindingly poor, politically chaotic, disaster-prone nation's remarkable history and culture, mixing reportage and anecdotes to paint a bright-dark portrait of this magical, tragic place."

—*Elle*

"A journalist penetrates the heart and soul of the confounding country that is the love of her life."

—*O: The Oprah Magazine*

"I can't imagine there's a better book about Haiti—a smarter, more thoughtful, tough-minded, romantic, plainspoken, intimate, well-reported book. Amy Wilentz has paid exceptionally close attention to this dreamy, nightmarish place for a quarter century, and with *Farewell, Fred Voodoo* she turns all that careful watching and thinking into a riveting work of nonfiction literature."

—Kurt Andersen, author of *Heyday* and *True Believers*

"No one has plumbed Haiti more thoroughly, or explored it more passionately, than Amy Wilentz. In *Farewell, Fred Voodoo*, she embraces that obsession and follows it unflinchingly where it leads, deep into the phantasmagoria of Haiti—and into herself. She has written a beautiful, compelling book."

—Mark Danner, author of *Stripping Bare the Body: Politics Violence War*

"Amy Wilentz knows Haiti deeply: its language, its tragic history, the foibles of her fellow Americans who often miss the story there. This makes her a wise, wry, indispensable guide to a country whose fate has long been so interwoven with our own."

—Adam Hochschild, author of *King Leopold's Ghost*

"*Farewell, Fred Voodoo* is written with authority and great affection for Haiti and Haitians and for some of the people who are trying to help them. An informative and wonderful piece of writing, it is a work of considerable artistry, immensely evocative. I read it with pleasure and with mounting gratitude."

—Tracy Kidder, author of *Mountains Beyond Mountains*

"With great storytelling and a wry sense of human comedy, Amy Wilentz explains Haiti—its characters, its romance, and its unique place in world history—and brings it all to life with passion."

—Mark Kurlansky, author of *Cod* and *Salt*

"*Farewell, Fred Voodoo* is engrossing and gorgeous and funny, a meticulously reported story of love for a maddening place. Wilentz's writing is so lyrical it's like hearing a song—in this case, the magical, confounding, sad song of Haiti."

—Susan Orlean, author of *The Orchid Thief*

ALSO BY AMY WILENTZ

The Rainy Season: Haiti Since Duvalier

Martyrs' Crossing

*I Feel Earthquakes More Often Than They Happen:
Coming to California in the Age of Schwarzenegger*

FAREWELL, FRED VOODOO

A LETTER FROM HAITI

AMY WILENTZ

SIMON & SCHUSTER PAPERBACKS

New York   London   Toronto   Sydney   New Delhi

Simon & Schuster Paperbacks
A Division of Simon & Schuster, Inc.
1230 Avenue of the Americas
New York, NY 10020

First Simon & Schuster paperback edition December 2013

SIMON & SCHUSTER PAPERBACKS and colophon are registered trademarks
of Simon & Schuster, Inc.

For information about special discounts for bulk purchases,
please contact Simon & Schuster Special Sales at
1-866-506-1949 or business@simonandschuster.com.

The Simon & Schuster Speakers Bureau can bring authors
to your live event. For more information or to book an event,
contact the Simon & Schuster Speakers Bureau at
1-866-248-3049 or visit our website at www.simonspeakers.com.

Illustrations by Rory Panagotopulos

Designed by Akasha Archer

Manufactured in the United States of America

10 9 8 7 6 5 4 3 2 1

The Library of Congress has cataloged the hardcover edition as follows:
Wilentz, Amy.
   Farewell, Fred Voodoo : A letter from Haiti / Amy Wilentz.
      p. cm.
   1. Haiti—History. 2. Haiti—Description and travel. 3. Haiti—Foreign relations—
United States 4. United States—Foreign relations—Haiti. 5. Haiti Earthquake, Haiti,
2010. 6. Wilentz, Amy—Travel—Haiti. I. Title.
   F1921.W55 2013
   972.94—dc23
                                                                    2012018547

ISBN 978-1-4516-4397-8
ISBN 978-1-4516-4407-4 (pbk)
ISBN 978-1-4516-4400-5 (ebook)

for Nick

Everything was transformed or deformed by an empty stomach: love, pride, willpower, and tenderness.

—Jacques Roumain, *Masters of the Dew*

It is astonishing how much money can be made out of the poorest of the poor with a little ingenuity.

—Doctor Magiot, in Graham Greene's *The Comedians*

Development consists of the removal of various types of unfreedoms that leave people with little choice and little opportunity of exercising their reasoned agency.

—Amartya Sen, *Development as Freedom*

It seems to me curious, not to say obscene and thoroughly terrifying, that it could occur to an association of human beings drawn together through need and chance and for profit into a company, an organ of journalism, to pry intimately into the lives of an undefended and appallingly damaged group of human beings . . . for the purpose of parading the nakedness, disadvantage and humiliation of these lives before another group of human beings, in the name of science, of "honest journalism" (whatever that paradox may mean), of humanity, of social fearlessness, for money, and for a reputation for crusading and for unbias . . . And that these people could be capable of meditating this prospect without the slightest doubt of their qualification to do an "honest" piece of work, and with a conscience better than clear, and in virtual certitude of almost unanimous public approval . . .

All of this, I repeat, seems to me curious, obscene, terrifying, and unfathomably mysterious.

So does the whole course, in all its detail, of the effort of these persons to find, and to defend what they sought: and the nature of their relationship with those with whom during the searching stages they came into contact; and the subtlety, importance, and almost intangibility of the insights or revelations or oblique suggestions which under different circumstances could never have materialized; so does the method of research which was partly evolved by them, partly forced upon them; so does the strange quality of their relationship with those whose lives they so tenderly and sternly respected, and so rashly undertook to investigate and record.

—James Agee, *Let Us Now Praise Famous Men*

CONTENTS

A NOTE ON THE USAGE OF THE WORD "VOODOO"

I have chosen to use the word "voodoo" in its common English orthography throughout the text, rather than the more current and anthropologically acceptable "vodun" or "vaudou." When I write about voodoo in this book, I am examining the historical engagement of outsiders with the religion, and so I wanted to capture—with the very word—all the negativity that's been associated with this ancient form of worship by unschooled visitors and a dismissive outside world.

FAREWELL, FRED VOODOO

SLIDESHOW/PROLOGUE

Apre bal, tanbou lou
After the party, the drums are heavy

Even after an officer from the international police force secured the criss-cross seatbelt around me, I didn't feel safe. We were taking a helicopter to a town in the north of Haiti that I'd managed never to visit, although I'd been coming to Haiti, and sometimes living here, for eight years, and had been almost everywhere that was even remotely accessible. The roads were nearly impassable from Port-au-Prince, Haiti's capital, to where we were going that morning, and, as far as I knew, the little town that was our destination had nothing much to recommend it. It was the stuff in between that I wanted to see.

It was late October 1994. Ray Kelly was my guide on this jaunt to the north. The former New York City Police Commissioner had been deployed to help out with the latest U.S. military intervention in Haiti. Kelly was training a new police force in order to keep the Haitian Army in check and, ostensibly, to prevent them from once again overthrowing the elected president of the country, Jean-Bertrand Aristide, whom the army had already tossed out once, and whom the United States had just returned to the presidential palace after three years in exile. The intervention to reimpose Aristide was called Operation Uphold Democracy. Offhand, I cannot recall another U.S. military deployment that performed regime change by *reinstating* an unseated leader, but Haiti is always singular, and so is America's long, torrid relationship with it.

We took off. As anyone knows who has experienced helicopter flight, it is an organically counterintuitive thing to go straight up when you are used to the more gradual, more natural upward incline of an airplane. An airplane's flight resembles that of a bird. A helicopter's is more like jumping, and the end result of jumping, in practice, is coming back down, almost immediately. Also, I am not at my best in any aircraft. I fear flight, though most of my work requires flying. I didn't want to go on this trip, but a reporter cannot reasonably turn down an offer to fly alongside the American officer in charge of the new police in the country she's been writing about for nearly a decade—even a reporter who is sensitive to the big fact about helicopters: that if there's a problem, these machines are not aerodynamic. They simply drop to the ground. Anyway, I thought the trip would give me the chance to interview Kelly in an informal setting, as journalists like to say. I didn't know about the noise inside a helicopter, the headgear you have to wear to protect your ears from the sound, the headphone intercom system that the pilots use just to be heard above the din.

So there I was, strapped in. Because the men around me were military men, they left the helicopter doors open—not something I knew could be done in flight. Kelly gave me an evil smile from across the aisle. Mine was a window seat. I prepared to be very, very frightened.

Instead, I was dazzled. Down below me lay Port-au-Prince, a glittering, gorgeous warren of tin shacks and the tiny squared-off fretwork of shantytown after shantytown, with the enormous white presidential palace, where Aristide was presumably working right now, at the center, a palace built by the Marines during an earlier U.S. occupation of Haiti. The shantytowns draped themselves over the hillsides around the capital like sequined gowns, and then we were off to the Artibonite Valley, green, lush, and wide below us, with the brown river flowing through it.

The landscape was wonderful to me. Watching Haiti open up below us was like taking in at one gulp the entire place, with all its social complexity and all its history and geography and topography. It was like looking at what the book I had written about Haiti five years earlier ought to have been, all the knowledge about the country concentrated into a single page scrawled with forest, mountain, river, and sand. Caught up in the emotional surge that flight can trigger, I was transfixed, spellbound. The cresting mountains and the flat green valley, and then the desertified wasteland that spills toward the Caribbean—the brown, then green, then blue waters reaching out and away—seemed to explain everything to me, all at once. My love of this place (and no other word will do), an overwhelming emotion that I had thought lost to me with time and too much knowledge, came back with the force of pain and ecstasy. I was within inches of the Haitian skies; I was inside the Haitian clouds; I could see all of Haiti.

Farther north we flew, into cloud and out of cloud, with the sun beating through the mists like a living thing. I kept craning my neck so that I could see what lay below. But now there was only the pink and golden froth and spume of cloud.

"Here we go," said Kelly, leaning toward me, his voice right there in my head. "Want to see the Citadelle?"

I felt he was offering me the most fabulous present I could ever receive. I couldn't speak, but nodded. He turned to the pilot, and I felt the machine falling.

We circled out and then back in toward something, some target, and then, like Leviathan, the Citadelle parted the clouds, half shrouded in a shawl of yellow, gold, and white mist, as if Napoleon himself had thrown his heraldic banner around its shoulders. The fortress's stony battlements sprang upward toward us from the mountaintop where it had been built by former slaves almost two centuries before Ray Kelly and I made this descent on it in our fragile, tiny, unimaginable air machine. As we flew over and around the huge thing, I didn't blink. I didn't want to waste a second of this vision.

This massive redoubt was built by the revolutionary leader Henri

Christophe, I knew. A former slave and mason, waiter, and hotel manager, Christophe had bought his freedom by the time of the Haitian uprising in 1791, in which a huge population of slaves fought for their freedom against an overwhelmingly armed colonial power—and won. It was the first and last successful slave revolution in history. Although France was the final imperial power to fall before the slaves' onslaught, the British and Spanish had also been thrust aside by the revolutionaries.

After the revolution broke out, Christophe fought for independence and was made a general by Toussaint Louverture, the foremost leader of the revolt, in 1802. In 1805, a year after independence from France was declared, Christophe began the construction of this citadel, not far from his palace, Sans-Souci (which means "no worries," and has to have been ironic).

Foundations for the colossal structure were erected on the highest promontory overlooking the northern coast, in order to protect the new nation from invasion—and in order to allow Christophe to survive internal dissension and attack, as well. Six years after work had commenced, Christophe declared himself king of Haiti and ruled the northern half of the country for more than nine years as such. He reimposed a slavery-like system in the half of Haiti that he governed, and was unloved by his people. The title he created for himself was:

> Henri, by the grace of God and the constitution of Haiti, King of Haiti, Sovereign of the islands of Tortuga, La Gonâve, and the other adjacent islands, Destroyer of Tyranny, Regenerator and Benefactor of the Haitian nation, Creator of its moral, political, and military institutions, first crowned monarch of the New World, Defender of the Faith, and Founder of the royal and military order of Saint-Henri.

It's estimated that it required some twenty thousand people to build the Citadelle. As I looked down on the steep mountainside where it stands, I could imagine their almost Sisyphean travails. But somehow, at the cost of hundreds of workers' lives, the stones of the Citadelle were put in place.

Many of those stones and bricks were taken from the revolutionary wreck-age of French plantations along the coast—another example of Christophe's sense of architectural irony.

King Henri had a stroke in 1820 as the murderous work on the Cita-delle was nearing completion. There ensued mutinies among his troops, and soon afterward, at the age of fifty-three, he shot himself rather than be taken in a coup. His loyal retainers covered his body in lime and bur-ied the decomposing remains deep within the fortress walls. I thought of Christophe's dust lying below me as we overflew the courtyards of the monument, some of which, I could see, as I peered carefully through the helicopter's open door, were still piled high with unspent cannonballs from his day. The only other approach to the Citadelle, at the summit of Bishop's Cap mountain, is on foot or on donkey-back.

The Citadelle is the biggest colonial-era fortress in the Western Hemi-sphere and has been appropriated over time as the great national symbol of Haiti. On tourism ministry posters and bank calendars, on postage stamps and on currency, the ship-like fortress looms. Haitian companies are often named after this incredible edifice. Images of it appear in the logos of car rental companies, airlines, insurance firms. It is the physical manifestation of Haiti's declaration of eternal independence from and resistance to foreign intervention. Or so most Haitians would assert.

But the symbol is hollow. For almost a century after its completion, no foreign power seriously attempted to conquer the land the Citadelle protected. And that was not because of the imposing fortress. Precisely because Christophe's revolution had succeeded, the country he and Tous-saint and the rest of Haiti's slaves created had become undesirable and no longer needed such protection. Haiti had been the most profitable colony in the New World, but now its fabulously lucrative economic system, plantation slavery, was ruined. The French, who had died by the tens of thousands trying to keep their sugar plantations and their slaves for France, were through with Haiti, at least for the long historical moment. But not all foreigners had finished their work here. In 1915, the Americans came by ship to distant Port-au-Prince with a plan to control Haiti. Even at its lofty height of three thousand feet, the Citadelle could not monitor that faraway harbor.

Now, foreigners come by air, like me and Ray Kelly. So in the end, the Citadelle, the greatest creation of Christophe's imagination—other than freedom, and Haiti—was unnecessary, even meaningless, a national embarrassment: grandiose, extravagant, cruel, useless.

The conundrum of the Citadelle lies at the heart of this book, because this book is about Haiti and its relation to the rest of the world, about Haiti's relationship with us. But really this tale begins and ends, for me, with three little black plastic boxes, numbered 18252, 18254, 18256. I came across these the other day, as I was finishing work on this book.

Although I hadn't seen them for twenty-five years, I knew almost immediately what they contained: "Quality color slides," as it said on their tops, in raised print camouflaged by age. Treasure.

Inside were pictures from my first trip to Haiti.

So much was contained in these three small boxes. I sat down with them, transported back to the first few days I'd ever spent in Haiti, an amazing time, a terrible time, an exhilarating time, a shocking time, a time of unrest and upheaval. I held the slides up to the light. The crowds were carrying trees; fires were burning in the background; people were massed in such numbers on vehicles that you couldn't see the trucks beneath them. Bodies were lying on the ground. After almost thirty years in power, this was the Duvalier dynasty coming to an end. Jean-Claude "Baby Doc" Duvalier had fallen on this very day.

It was February 7, 1986.

When last I had looked at the slides, the day I picked them up from the developer at the end of that February, everything that was happening in each mini stained glass window was obscure to me, like stations of the cross if you didn't know the whole story and all its dramatis personae from beginning to end. I was so new to Haiti. The slides seemed like formal medieval tableaux filled with messages and import, with mysterious splendor, shadowing forth—as they used to say—the meaning of all the Haitian drama I was yet to witness. The pictures had some significance, I knew, but at that moment, they illuminated almost nothing. I didn't yet possess the Haitian alphabet necessary to read them. I fumbled and groped to understand what they were showing, but I couldn't yet see in the kind of twilight they provided.

I put them aside, and then forgot them.

The place, however, stuck with me. I was not to be the kind of foreign correspondent who goes from hot spot to hot spot, covering the dramatic moment, the revolution, the war—news, in short. No, no. In fact, I was not a foreign correspondent at all. I fell into Haiti from my desk in New York at the very staid *Time* magazine of those days. There was something eternal about Haiti that, to use ideas and terms from the ancients, called to me as I sat in my office on the Nation hallway on the twenty-fifth floor of the *Time* offices at 1271 Avenue of the Americas in deep Manhattan in the mid-1980s, massaging articles on the fate of ephemeral legislation in Washington.

I'd been following the Haiti story from up here already, in a desultory fashion. I'd read Graham Greene's novel about the reign of François Duvalier, known as Papa Doc, who was Jean-Claude's vicious and obsessive father and had preceded him in office. The scenes from *The Comedians* have never faded from my mind: the dark palms; the crumbling gingerbread hotel; the body in the empty pool; the innocent, hilarious, vegetarian Americans; the mercenaries; the guerrillas in the hills; the funeral interrupted by the Tonton Macoutes, Papa Doc's personal secret police.

"Impossible to deepen that night," Greene said of Haiti under Papa Doc, in his introduction to the novel, which was published in 1965. With all its tropical color and romance and danger, *The Comedians* was a novel that would naturally appeal to someone stuck in a twenty-fifth-floor office in Manhattan.

I spoke French, too, and would occasionally pick up the demented

Haitian exile newspapers (of which there were many) at my local newsstand on 115th Street, papers whose columns were so colored by the political longings and machinations of their publishers that they were nearly incomprehensible to the newcomer. Reading them was like turning on a decades-old soap opera for the first time as it was coming to the concluding episode of the season. This, I began to gather, was the season of the end of Duvalier, the concluding episode in a show that had gone on for long enough, already.

I can't really explain how I felt about this at the time: the dictator's imminent departure, how soon it might come, how he would take a whole Haitian world with him as he fled . . . and that I might have missed the Duvalier era—that I would never see it, therefore never understand it, that a part of my essential body of knowledge was rushing to escape me before I'd even begun to acquire it. I felt my heart would break if I missed it; in retrospect, you could say that what I was feeling was destiny.

I know that it wasn't Haiti's incomparable art that drew me, nor the island's green, mountainous landscape—since I didn't know much about either of these until after I'd arrived. Nor was it the country's long western beaches, certainly, nor the drums, sequins, pomp, and rugged, meaty African splendor of voodoo practice and ritual—I didn't know these either. It wasn't even some sense of obligation to the suffering people of the world that pulled me toward the country. I had little sentiment at the time—and have even less now, after my Haitian education.

Above all, back then, I needed to see the Tonton Macoutes. I wanted to have the chance to witness them. I was obsessed with it, with observing them as they really were, unmediated by Greene or any other interpreter. I wanted to capture them in my mind before they faded into history's darkness, seize them for my own as they strode the Haitian streets in broad daylight, in all their arrogance, guns tucked into the waistlines of their jeans, denim hats pulled low over their sunglasses, sniffing down victims.

And so, a week before Jean-Claude Duvalier would end up fleeing from Haiti, I flew down for the first time, on the American Airlines morning flight out of JFK. When we emerged from the plane onto the tarmac of François Duvalier International Airport, a three-man band was playing "Haïti Chérie," a lilting Caribbean melody. There were the Tonton Macoutes, moving in shadows behind immigration. The baggage claim was an insane welter of shouting and shoving, of bodies, bags, soldiers, customs officials, porters, antique trolleys, beggars.

I clutched my camera and squeezed my way out of there, not neglecting to pay a small bribe to customs en route, in order to liberate my bag from that terrible place.

Not that day, but soon after, I began taking the pictures that I had just now rediscovered.

In those intoxicating first days, I roamed the city with Milfort Bruno, a guide attached to the rickety gingerbread Hotel Oloffson, who now runs a struggling trinket shop across the street. Milfort and I went everywhere together; we saw everything. I took pictures of the Tonton Macoutes in the shantytowns; I watched a big macoute force a young girl to dance at a pre-Carnival street party. I saw the sticks and knives of lesser macoutes. After Duvalier fled the country, Milfort and I got in a car accident fleeing from a running crowd. Another passenger managed to bash Milfort's thumb as we were shutting my car trunk, as Milfort enjoys recalling to this day. I have a set of dominoes Milfort helped me pilfer from the ruins of the Tonton Macoute headquarters in a town that was then called Duvalierville, and a notebook recording the whereabouts of guns, from the headquarters in Pétionville. We watched the crowd take apart two of the Duvaliers' houses, in an action that was called *dechoukaj,* or uprooting—in the countryside this was something farmers did in a more literal fashion before planting a new crop. We watched the crowd scale the walls of the CARE warehouse and rush away with bags of food. We saw a man shot outside the walls.

Milfort ran through the crowds who were celebrating Duvalier's departure; he located the bodies of unfortunate Duvalierists and Tonton Macoutes for me. He led me to a crop of presidential hopefuls; there were so many, each one sitting stiffly in a business suit in a living room with formal chairs and artificial flowers on a coffee table and a wife in the background. It was as if there had been a bottleneck of presidential candidates waiting through the long, long years of the Duvaliers' rule (father and son were both "president-for-life"), and now the thing had come uncorked and out the candidates popped by the dozens.

Milfort carried a big plastic bottle around with him, filled with homemade raw rum; that was a perk for him for covering this story. The sunny days were filled with incident and his bottle was filled with *klerin.* Frenzy and ecstasy were the rule of the moment, and we bobbed and drove from one historic scene to the next, working all day and all night. Bottle in hand, on the passenger side, Milfort, silent and wondering, guided me with grave, kingly generosity.

He realized quickly that I would interview anyone who had anything to say. And after Duvalier left and the Tonton Macoutes threw off their denim uniforms and rushed into hiding, everyone had something to say. The whole country had burst out talking (they haven't really stopped since). I put reams of quotes into my notebooks, and when I'd get back to the Oloffson's terrace, my new friend Greg Chamberlain, then a reporter for the *Guardian,* would ask me what I'd gotten (that's how reporters refer to the culling of information). *Whatdja get, whatdja get?*

I'd say that I had talked to this priest and that general, and to some presidential candidate, and to this guy I met in the street, and a market lady, and some man who said he was a tailor.

"Ah," said Greg, "you've been interviewing Fred Voodoo." He said it with a smirk. This was the reporters' joking name back then, I learned, for the Haitian man (or woman) in the street. It's a name that has faded as reporters have gotten younger and more politically correct—although I suspect that there are still retrograde British journalists who use it.

And Greg was right; that's what I had been doing. Fred Voodoo always had a lot to say.

What did Fred Voodoo want to talk about? What did he care about? What were Fred Voodoo's subjects?

I first talked with him—me hobbling through Creole learned on tapes put out by the University of Indiana—near the intersection of Avenue John Brown and Avenue Martin Luther King. Fred wanted to discuss democracy. He was thinking about what it would be like to be free, not to have a stick or a machete or a gun threatening him all the time, to walk around without cringing, not to have to give the local macoute money, women, things—and how it would feel to vote freely for a president who might care about him, who might worry about Fred Voodoo and all his problems.

Fred also wanted to make sure I knew which macoutes were the worst ones. He was focused in an unhealthy way on Jean-Claude Duvalier's wife, the fashionable, beautiful, upper-class Michèle Bennett, and her furs and her refrigerated closet. I should be aware, Fred Voodoo often told me, that the First Lady was a whore. Fred Voodoo often showed me his house. He would guide me around the one room, with the one bed, no kitchen, no lights, no bathroom. A pregnant wife and a bunch of skinny kids. Fred was thinking about food, about having enough of it, for himself and his kids, and about how a real country, a free country, would have enough food and at prices people could pay. He wanted a real house, too. With cement walls. He wanted a television. He did not want to go cut sugarcane in the Dominican Republic for a third season, or to have to emigrate to Guyana.

To me it was like: come on, Fred, think *big*. Because to me, coming from Manhattan in 1986, it didn't seem adequate to dream of voting and eating and personal security. How about learning pure math and classical philosophy and applied engineering? How about jobs and training, and making more than a dollar a day? How about public health care in a land where diphtheria and polio and tuberculosis were rampant, were considered everyday diseases to have, and to live with—to say nothing of AIDS? And did I mention sewers and running water, sanitation, street cleaning, public transportation, and electricity? I forgot to mention these. I didn't even get to them, and neither did Fred Voodoo.

~~

There is barely a moment in all Haitian history that has no relation to the United States. Haiti is like a fifty-first state, a shadow state, one that the United States wants to keep hidden in the attic and that bears all the scars of the two countries' painful twinned narrative. As the historian Laurent Dubois has written, "Haiti and the United States grew up together." It was never a healthy sibling relationship. We can start with the Haitian Revolution, which ensured the freedom of Haiti's slaves by 1804, while the United States still had a slave economy and trembled at the thought of black insurrection only a few hundred miles from our shores. And we can go on from there to the first U.S. occupation of Haiti, from 1915 to 1934.

Papa Doc's black nationalist movement, or *noirisme,* however sincere or insincere it was at the beginning, was a direct reaction to the U.S. occupation, which ended the year François Duvalier turned twenty-seven. During his formative years, Papa Doc had watched while the Marine-controlled administration favored Haiti's lighter-skinned, wealthier class, the mulatto elite, as it is sometimes called, whose power came down to them from slavery days. Papa Doc and his friends and classmates all came from the newly rising black Haitian middle class (also in some ways a product of the available mid-level clerical jobs created by the Marines' presence), and were just marginally tolerated by the elite.

So some twenty-plus years after the Americans left, Duvalier was ensconced in the presidential palace, surrounded by his henchmen. Formerly quiet and unassuming, and seemingly low-key, Papa Doc had by now charged his batteries up to a hundred percent, and *noirisme* had devolved into an odious code now called Duvalierism. All lit up and glowing with fury, then, Papa Doc turned on the elite with a wrath that could only have come from profound resentment combined with the reasonable fear that this class would do anything to unseat him and recover its hegemony. During his rule, hundreds if not thousands of members of Haiti's elite, its best-educated and most sophisticated people (many of whom were also leaders in the Haitian Army), were assassinated. For perceived threats or insults, entire families were sometimes executed; thousands of others fled, in a terrible brain drain from which Haiti has yet to recover. The elite were not the only victims of Duvalier's total domination of Haiti's political sphere, however. People from all walks of life died because he or his minions ordered it.

Papa Doc liked to believe that he was the political descendant of the fieriest figure of the revolution, Jean-Jacques Dessalines, who was Christophe's comrade at arms and was bloody-minded, intransigent, wily. Dessalines was the revolutionary leader who is said to have cried, "*Koupe tet, boule kay,*" as the slaves continued their insurrection against Napoleon and France and the plantation masters. "Cut off the head, burn down the house," it means. And that's what Dessalines's followers did. From the leisure of old age, a French officer and witness of those revolutionary battles recalled Dessalines's troops:

> You had to have seen their cold bravery to form an idea of it. Their chants, sung out into the air by two thousand voices, with cannons providing the bass, produced a frightening effect . . . These black masses marching in ranks to their death, singing under a magnificent sun, are still present in my memory, and today even, after more than forty years, this imposing and grandiose tableau is as vivid to me as it was in those first seconds.

According to legend, Dessalines also said, "*Blan bon lè li san tet.*" Or, a white man's only good without his head.

In 1804, having defeated the French at the Battle of Vertières, Dessalines declared the new country's independence, named it Haiti (from the indigenous word for mountains), and took over the reins of power in the southwest half of the country. He gave himself the title "emperor-for-life" and ruled with great pomp and glory until he was assassinated two years later. It is said that Christophe, in the north, knew of the plot against Dessalines but decided not to warn his former ally. To Haitians today, it all sounds like politics as usual, but on a grander scale.

Papa Doc identified with Dessalines both because the emperor was visibly the man who had created Haiti and had therefore become a symbol of Haitian nationalism, and because Dessalines was the one who, with enormous military aplomb and cruel violence, defeated the French plantation system. In Duvalier's mind Dessalines was a great symbol of black power. Dessalines's treatment of the enemy was to be emulated, and Papa Doc went on to cut off the heads of his rivals and foes, and to burn down their houses as well. Like many a nationalist leader, Papa Doc thought of himself as the state, and so anyone who was his enemy was Haiti's enemy, was Dessalines's enemy—and deserved the most brutal punishment.

When Papa Doc came to power in 1957, Haiti's best hope was only a toddler, four years old. When Papa Doc died and Baby Doc took over, Haiti's best hope was eighteen years old. Baby Doc was only a year older.

I met Haiti's best hope almost by accident one evening. Milfort Bruno took me to him. Baby Doc had fled the country just the day before. Milfort guided me down to the shantytown near the end of Grand Rue, called La Saline. I worried that we were on a fool's mission, as I often had been already in Haiti, after only a few days, and as I have been so many times since. (And who's the fool? Me.) It was dangerous to be in the streets at night while Haiti had no real leadership, although it had also been dangerous to be in the streets when it *did.*

Milfort and I parked in front of a small white church. It was sunset. People were heading home for the day, iridescent-winged roosters under the men's arms for cockfights, and plastic buckets of water on the women's heads, translucent with the setting sun. *Brouette* men, or cart haulers, pulled their wares down the broad central avenue. Market ladies brave enough to have opened their stalls during the unrest were closing them up now. From his seat on the passenger side, Milfort shooed me out of the car with a backward-pushing flick of his fingers. He would remain inside, listening to music and protecting the vehicle. He had his trusty plastic bottle with him. Ask for Father Aristide, he told me. Haiti's best hope.

And I did. I met this slight, bespectacled, skinny little man in the interior courtyard of the vocational school that was attached to his church, St. Jean Bosco. Then still a parish priest, Aristide was surrounded by his orphan boys and some young men and women, and everyone was happy and smiling because Duvalier was gone. I would come to know those orphan boys well, and one especially: Filibert Waldeck, the wild one. To many reporters, Filibert would have been Fred Voodoo, a kind of speaking cipher. But in the end he turned out to be, for me, Filibert Waldeck, a real, particular, single human being with plenty of his own foibles and problems, and his own sad fate.

There's a reason that that awful and potent name has stuck with me: Fred Voodoo. It sums it all up, in a way. First of all, how Haitians have been reduced to a very few things in the outsider's mind, and even those things not understood. When I watched television news in my kitchen in L.A. during the days that followed the 2010 earthquake, before I went back down again, I kept thinking of Fred Voodoo; that's how the television reporters were talking as they stood in their khakis and work boots amid the rubble. That's how the camera crews were shooting. You didn't need to say Fred's name in order to summon the sentiment, which is a kind of condescension filled with pity. Look at this! the footage shouted. Yo, the morgue is just a scene of *damnation*! it went on. Look how bad this is over here! it said. Can you buh-*lieve* people are living like this? (that was always an aspect of Haiti coverage, but especially after the earthquake). The objectification of the Haitians' victimization—that's one aspect of the Fred Voodoo syndrome. How beautiful the Haitians look in their misery; they always do. You can count on them.

You can count on them to give the camera a huge, photogenic smile upon emerging from the rubble more than a week after the earthquake. You can count on them to be bathing in a thin crystalline shower of sparkling water at sunset, half naked, with smoke from a garbage fire burning nearby and the thin sheets of the tents they're living in transfused with late sunlight: gorgeous. You can count, also, on guns, on uniforms. You can count on a dark, angry sky over a colorful crowd as the sun goes down, or comes up. In Haiti photojournalists are active at sunrise and sunset, because the light is beautiful and people's features more readable in the slanting sun. All of this makes the person known as Fred Voodoo alluring and mysterious to the outside world, strange and impenetrable, and lovely as a visual object. If I've learned one thing in Haiti, it's how to deconstruct a photograph of suffering, of poverty, of the pain of others. The fact that he or she is also voluble and highly quotable, and very articulate, makes Fred Voodoo excellent *material* for video and excellent *copy* for the page. Indeed, for pages not unlike these pages.

But that was something I always wanted *not* to participate in: the uses of Fred, the abuses of Fred.

And let's just mention his last name, which of course is most important: voodoo, Voodoo. This was the label, the only label, that outsiders knew they could paste onto every single last existing Haitian. No one in Haiti was not Fred Voodoo, to a foreign correspondent, to a wide-eyed missionary, to an exhausted development worker. Outsiders were always looking for something easy to define. The cliché about the country is that 90 percent of Haitians are Catholics, and 100 percent are *vodouisant,* or voodoo worshippers. So you could call a distinguished academician Fred Voodoo; you could pin this nametag on a provincial bishop. You could even think of the country's president that way. Certainly every shantytown dweller was Fred Voodoo, to an imperceptive, uninitiated eye.

Voodoo was something that could be understood as—most important—*not us.* It was other, and both seductive and alien. It was everything the white Westerner was not: exotic, African, pagan, exciting, dangerous, deep. The people who called Haitians Fred Voodoo—or who thought of them that way—often had very little idea of what the traditional religion encompassed, and even less of all the other factors that went into making Haitians Haitian, such as French colonialism, the period of slavery, the loss of Africa, French blood and tradition, the relationship with America.

~

While he was still a priest and not internationally known, I used to say to Aristide—after a season of terrible unrest, or after a season of assassination attempts against him—that it would be pleasant one day for us to sit in facing rocking chairs in front of a little house somewhere when I would come down for a visit to Haiti, and to remember all he'd been through. We'll have gray hair, I would say. He would laugh, humoring me. I used to tell him, because I was a romantic who believed in all sorts of outmoded nineteenth-century things like honor, sacrifice, and martyrdom, that I would rather visit him in the national penitentiary than in the presidential palace. I literally and word for word told him that, several times. He would smile, tolerant of my girlish, romantic, American ideas.

But he had other plans.

In 1990, about a month after he told me he would never participate in elections in Haiti because they were run and controlled by the U.S. government, he announced that he was running for president, and then—upsetting the plans of everyone who'd been participating, including the U.S. government—he won. He was ousted in 1991, less than a year after taking office, during the administration of the American president whom Haitians like to call Papa Bush.

Three years later, with Bill Clinton in the White House, Aristide was flown back to Haiti on Air Force One. Ray Kelly was down in Haiti already, preparing the way.

I got a tour of the private palace rooms from President Aristide; we looked at Michèle Bennett Duvalier's disco closet and her fur refrigerator. Her closet was the kind of thing you thought must absolutely be an urban legend, invented by Fred Voodoo, but there it was. It reminded me of the gold plates that an American friend of mine had heard about from the shanty dwellers she was working with. These plates, the people told her, were used on the table of a Haitian doctor, a member of Haiti's Syrio-Lebanese clan who ran the big health clinic in the slum. Now, how could such people, living in one-room shacks with dirt floors, know that this doctor had golden dishware? My friend laughed about the plates and thought of the story as a metaphor for money and plenty. But later, when she was invited to dinner at the doctor's house up on the hill, it turned out that his family really did have gold-plated service chargers beneath the regular dishware on the table. "The story," my friend pointed out, "must have come from his servants up there, all the way down into the shantytown."

Just before Aristide ran again for president (a Haitian politician can hold the office twice, but not in consecutive terms; no more presidents-for-life, that is—we shall see), I came down in 2000 to interview him for the *New York Times Magazine*. We'd had our ups and downs by then. I'd written a piece for the *Los Angeles Times* that he thought was unfair to him—in retrospect, perhaps it was. In any case, we hadn't spoken in four years before this meeting. I was disappointed in what he'd been able to achieve in his sporadic moments in the presidency, although he had been working against very harsh odds. Because I'd written about these disappointments, he no longer trusted me.

At our meeting, Aristide was stiff, formal, and correct, as if with a stranger. I had broken trust. We sat in his big white office in his big white house. He showed me that a friend had re-bound for him all the books in his library that had been damaged by looters after he was ousted in 1991. One of the books was the one I had written and published in 1989, in which he figured largely. He showed it to me as if to say: this is a reminder of how you once thought of me.

But I could not think of him in any simple way anymore, in any pure way. Between him and me lay not only many wasted political opportunities, I felt, but also, figuratively, the body of our old friend Jean Dominique. Dominique was one of the most famous men in Haiti, and the country's best-known and best-loved journalist, who had been a great and valiant foe of the Duvaliers and had survived, largely by fleeing into exile. Now, even though Dominique's old friend René Préval was in office as president, this courageous democrat had been assassinated, along with a security guard, in front of his radio station—just a few months before I came down to visit. Until a few weeks before he was killed, Dominique, too, hadn't seen Aristide in years. When I met with Aristide that summer after the assassination, no one had been arrested or prosecuted for the killings. This was typical of Haitian justice, but I had believed that things were going to be different under Aristide, and under Préval. I could see that Préval was trying to depart from the norm, and trying to bolster the investigation. But he wasn't having much luck.

A few months later, Aristide was reelected president. He didn't have much more success in the Dominique case. He and I have never spoken again, although I have repeatedly tried to renew the conversation. He's told mutual friends that "there will come a time" for us to talk again—I doubt it. He finally had three people arrested in the Dominique case, but they were never brought to trial. Six more were later arrested and also never tried. After three years in office, Aristide was overthrown again, this time under Baby Bush, and ended up in exile for seven years in South Africa. The three men his government had had arrested in the Dominique case escaped after that coup.

Let's go back to those slides now. But let me say right away that these were very bad pictures, many of them taken in the midst of demonstrations and mob attacks and army actions, and also poorly taken by someone who did not know what she was seeing—who was not a foreign correspondent and who was certainly no photographer. A naïve person, and a romantic. That was me back then, before my Haitian education. I knew at the time that I was seeing history in the making, and even history itself, but I wasn't sure who was who or what was what. Some of the slides are utterly black, taken at night by a person who did not know how to take a picture at night. And in the others, I didn't know enough about what I was seeing to place the important action at the center of my pictures.

But now I know.

Here, first of all, was the great white mausoleum of the Famille Duvalier, in a prominent corner of the national cemetery in Port-au-Prince. Here were the Haitian people crowded around it, on the day Baby Doc

Duvalier left Haiti. They were taking the tomb apart tile by tile and brick by brick, with their bare hands, ripping away stucco and cement. Next slide: bones pulled from a coffin that the crowd found in the mausoleum. Next slide: the fire that was set to burn the bones. Next slide: a blackened femur, smoke, flame, bits of a hand. Was this Papa Doc? The crowd wanted to think so. I want to think so.

They were ridding the country of Duvalierism. That's what the picture said to me then. That's what I faithfully believed, for years. But at the beginning of 2011, twenty-five years later, Baby Doc came back! To only mild protesting. He set up house back on the hill where he had formerly lived, and went about the normal life of a rich Haitian businessman—dining out, going to dinner parties, appearing at public events. So, needless to say, the pictures have a different meaning for me now, a deeper meaning, less easily interpreted but truer.

Here are the people, in another slide, pulling one of the Tonton Macoutes from his headquarters. This guy was a well-known leader, and also happened to be the mayor of his town. The people surrounded his headquarters, and they grabbed him . . . Next slide: they've got him . . . Next slide: he's sitting, pretty comfortably, in the back of an army pickup truck, surrounded by soldiers. Innocent that I was then, I thought that the army was arresting him, taking him downtown for booking, as if this were a state functioning—suddenly—under the rule of law. But now I know: the army had been summoned *by him,* to save his skin from the immediate danger. The soldiers were protecting him from the crowd. A few days later he was interviewed at his nice suburban house. He was wearing a beige suit and a diamond ring. He didn't seem too worried.

Not, of course, that he should have been lynched, but it showed you, if you understood it, where the army stood in Haitian affairs in 1986. This was one of the reasons why, when Aristide disbanded the army eight years later, it was considered a great victory for human rights in Haiti.

Soon after Baby Doc returned, and a few weeks before the 2011 presidential elections, Aristide came back from his long exile in South Africa. He was greeted by a large crowd. Chantal Regnault, a Frenchwoman who has spent many decades in Haiti, was there at the airport. She was unimpressed (the French often are): "Yeah, he came out of the plane and spoke in Zulu for two minutes; then he pointed out that it was his eighth language. Then, he talked about the chambers of his heart. Well, the kids who came to see him had no idea what he was talking about and were bored out of their minds." Still, the crowd accompanied Aristide and his wife and two daughters and the rest of the convoy all the way from the airport to his suburban home, where he had to be hustled inside.

Today, Haiti's new president, Michel Martelly, a pop singer, wants to reinstate the army Aristide disbanded. Martelly also approved the dismissal of human-rights-violations charges against Baby Doc. He went to kiss Baby Doc on New Year's Day. (Afterthought: he went to kiss Aristide, too, but the embrace was not as hearty.) In speaking of a pardon for Duvalier, Martelly didn't mention justice—only reconciliation. Martelly and Duvalier also observed the second earthquake anniversary together, at a burial ground north of Port-au-Prince formerly known as Titanyen, meaning "Little Nothing"—a depressing site, a seaside paupers' grave-yard, where bodies are thrown and then covered with dirt.

Hundreds and perhaps even thousands of the earthquake's victims were brought here in municipal dump trucks in the weeks following the catastrophe, and quickly buried. But, as everyone in attendance must have known, Titanyen was also where the victims of Papa Doc and Baby Doc ended up. Bill Clinton arrived at the ceremony, too, and shook Duvalier's hand.

So much for Operation Uphold Democracy.

This book in your hands, then, is my attempt to put Haiti back together again for myself, to understand why all the simplest hopes and dreams of the men and women they call Fred Voodoo have been abandoned, and to stack the pieces flung apart by the earthquake back up into some semblance of the real country. I wanted to figure out, after so many attempts by so many to uphold democracy, why Fred and all his brothers and sisters have become, in our eyes at least, mere victims, to be counted up on one ledger or another as interesting statistics, casualties of dictatorship, of poverty, of disaster, of outside interference, of neglect, of history—of whatever you want to point a finger at—rather than as active commanders of their own destiny. I wanted to examine the so-called "Afro-pessimism" that outsiders often feel concerning Haiti, because the country is seen as a chunk of that easily misunderstood continent, floating in the wrong seas. Why, in outsiders' minds, are Haitians still slaves, or worse, zombies?

I also wanted to explain the perception that the average Haitian is sitting around, after the earthquake, being once again "resilient"—a favorite word of outsiders when they note the Haitians' special ability to put up with the ignorance and downright humiliation that others often dish out to them, as well as the series of unfortunate events that their history has comprised. Most of all I wanted to understand and explain why the outside world keeps sticking its fingers in the messy Haitian pie. Did we imagine we would pull out a plum? Was our compassion actually a form of contempt, as some analysts have suggested? I wanted, in short, to explain myself—and others who are like me, and not so like me.

I needed to go over it all again, for myself.

Because the thing about Haiti, for me and for everyone else who has come to know it well, is that it is not like anywhere else, not like anything else. It defies categorization. It's an original (see under: *revolution*). It's eccentric and unexpected. At every corner, in every conversation, with every new event, Haiti makes you think, it challenges you. Here in this stray corner of the Caribbean, many worlds and many times collide with one another: Europe and Africa, North America and Latin America, the colonial period and the age of technology, the era of slavery and the era of globalization.

After the earthquake, I tried to stay away. I thought to myself, why see Haiti in this situation, when it might suddenly be like any other place. I feared that with the capital and outer towns destroyed and the people homeless and wandering, Haiti might seem just like Aceh or

Managua after their awful cataclysms—an epicenter of chaos and ruin, indistinguishable from the rest. Catastrophes tend to equalize.

So I waited, and waited, until I couldn't stand it any longer. I used clever means of persuasion on myself, to keep me at home. I recalled Haitian politicians' grandiloquence, which I assumed would be exacerbated by the disaster. I considered the sheer awfulness of so many of the outside groups who'd been angling for a piece of the Haitian action for so long; now they'd be slavering and ravening at the airport, at the wharves, in the camps and hospitals. I thought about resilience: Could I stand to see it in action again? I wondered, too, if I could bear to watch the difficult lives of most Haitians rendered even more unbearable by this dreadful event—I wasn't sure about my own resilience. I worried, conversely, that I might experience "sympathy fatigue," and then I'd have to hate myself.

I brooded about voodoo. Surely its adherents (which is to say, Haitians) would come up with an explanation for the catastrophe that worked within their system of belief. Oh, God; I didn't want to hear it. I imagined, too, the celebrities and celebrated nonentities who would no doubt take this opportunity to cleanse themselves in the stream of Haiti's misfortune. Already, they were making plans, making media noises. So I almost had myself convinced. While they went down from Hollywood and Minneapolis and Boston and Chicago and New York to Haiti, I would take the moral high ground—I tried to tell myself—and stay at home in Los Angeles.

I was trying to outrun the earthquake, not to let it enter my deeper consciousness. More foolish, I was trying to outrun Haiti, to evade it before it took me over once again. In vain. After so many years—after three children, three books, and thousands of pages of articles on dozens of topics—Haiti was still my great love. So down I went. I couldn't even put it off for two weeks.

I flew to Boston and took a bus to a small airport outside of town. My plane was full of young doctors. As I gazed out the window at the light dusting of snow that had fallen over New England the night before, the woman next to me began talking about the child she'd been trying to adopt in Haiti for two years. She was going over a list of required documentation. She was talking about the obstacles. I thought of Filibert Waldeck when he was seven or so: a friend of mine had once contemplated adopting *him*—incredible if you knew Filibert, even at that age. I wondered if I would see him; had he survived? And I thought back to that long-ago helicopter ride over the Citadelle. I thought about planes flying and planes crashing, about buildings rising up and buildings falling down. I thought about the view from above, the overview—and about all I had learned in my many years down on Haitian ground. I was sorry about the earthquake, blankly sorry, the way you feel when something is too big and too terrible to imagine. But even in such conditions, even for such reasons, I was so happy to be going back.

1

TOUSSAINT CAMP

Ti pay ti pay, zwazo fe nich li
Straw by straw, the bird builds his nest

Back when I first went down to live in Haiti, six months after the fall of
Baby Doc, Aristide, then still a parish priest, became one of my usual
sources and a subject of the book I was writing at the time about Haiti
after the fall of Duvalier. His sermons were fiery, explosive, eloquent
things that heaped irony, invective, and metaphor in stunning blows
upon the reputations and personalities of the ruling junta and the thugs,
soldiers, and gangsters who continued to wield power in the months and
years after Duvalier fled. Aristide's personal courage was also astounding.
He would simply walk into places where he knew his life was threatened;
he would give his regular sermon at Sunday mass even on days when he
knew the regime was sending its killers out into the church. I sat in the
hot, overflowing church for so many of those sermons, squeezed between
proper church ladies in their Sunday satins and taffetas, or between men
in thin suits, their backs rigid with attention.

I used to talk with Aristide in his dark, mosquito-infested office, in
the shadow of an effigy of a Tonton Macoute that stood in a corner, and
I got to know all of the orphan boys who made up his coterie: Filibert

Waldeck (the wild man), Ayiti (the beautiful), Ti Bernard (the smart one), Ti Sonny (the suck-up), Johnny (the corner boy). Those were just a few. They would hang around outside the office door; they'd play soccer in the courtyard with a deflated ball—like playing soccer with a pancake. They'd wash my car with rags and water so dirty that the car was even less presentable afterward than it had been before their ministrations. Nonetheless, I still owed them five dollars—they were clear on this point. Some of these orphans were not orphans at all but had run away from desperately impoverished homes or had simply been abandoned. The boys ranged from about six to about ten or twelve years old, and they were my second set of Creole teachers (after the Indiana tapes); they wanted me to learn the language fast so that the importuning and begging for which they summoned a surprising amount of rhetorical brilliance would be more efficient and effective with me. *Chich, rasè*: these were among the first words the boys taught me. *Chich* means cheap. *Rasè* means broke. I could immediately understand the meaning of the words "Amy gimme fie dolla."

I still know these kids: that is, the ones who have survived since 1986—about 50 percent of them, at best. The ones who haven't already died of AIDS and tuberculosis, of drugs and murder.

Filibert Waldeck continues to be a touchstone in my Haitian life, turning up here and there—not easy to find until he presents himself. He lives hand to mouth, has no job and two sons. He's among the poorest of the capital's poor, among the most destitute in every way. I always look for him when I go down to Haiti, and I was looking for him after the earthquake, too. Eventually I found him, but not where I thought I would. Instead I found substitutes, but no one could duplicate the intensity of Filibert, his schiziness, his high-energy quotient, his need, his boulevardier fizz.

I cruised the early earthquake camps, asking after Filibert, but no one had heard of him. The fact that I wasn't finding Filibert bothered me—or, rather, the fact that he wasn't finding me. I was worried because I knew that if he could, Filibert would turn up somewhere he thought I'd be:

at Toussaint Camp or the other downtown camps, say, or at the hotel where I had stayed on and off during my visits to the country. I hoped he had survived. (This was at a time when Haitians would answer their cell phones with these words: "*Alo*. Yes, I'm alive.") He would know, even better than I had known, that the earthquake would bring me down, along with dozens of rookie reporters who were easier touches. Filibert was a savvy student of the habits of journalists. No doubt he'd be frequenting reporters' haunts in hopes of some friendly contributions. So where was he?

In my vain attempts to find Filibert, I'd found a bunch of other former Aristide orphans living—only for the moment, everyone hoped—in tents in Toussaint Camp, across the way from the Plaza Hotel. They were in their thirties now. They were unemployed. Some of them were fathers. In any case, they were no longer ragamuffins and baby street-toughs. One morning, when it was already too hot and getting hotter, I went out to visit two of them, Jerry and Samuel. This was my third trip down after the disaster (and I can't say for sure, but possibly my thirtieth and maybe my fortieth trip to Haiti). Mangoes were coming to the end of their season.

Toussaint Camp was not a new place for me, but it was a changed place now, after the earthquake. The camp was in the center of Port-au-Prince. Before it became a tent camp, it had been the Champs de Mars park, the beating governmental heart of town, with the presidential palace on one side and, farther away, the Justice Ministry and also army headquarters—back when there still was a Haitian Army. The improvised camp had sprouted up fast here in the center of the square, where, every morning, promptly at eight (possibly the only thing that has ever consistently happened on time in Haiti), the Haitian flag was raised and all traffic stopped in acknowledgment as a tinny national anthem sounded from the palace.

What was left of the fruit on the few mango trees in town hung precariously above our heads like depressed decorations; yellow pulp and chewed pits littered the streets. I had on my crap camp shoes, for trekking through mud and whatever. The rainy season had just begun; the storms would come toward evening. A tap-tap jitney passed by in front of me, spraying me with filthy curb water from yesterday's rains. This morning, Samuel and Jerry and Black Rouge and a few of the others had promised to play some more of their post-earthquake hip-hop stuff for me on the camp's one computer (no Internet hookup, but a pair of human-size speakers). I'd heard bits and pieces on an earlier visit to the camp on a secondhand, outdated ghetto blaster.

When Jerry and Samuel and Filibert and the rest were his boys, long before the earthquake, most of Aristide's orphans lived in shacks in one of Port-au-Prince's worst shantytowns, or on the streets, or in the abandoned voodoo temple he'd found for them in a neighborhood called Tokyo. The temple was like a big warehouse: one vast room. Later, after Aristide became president, a few lucky boys migrated to the palace with him, where, from the grand French windows, they could look out on the statue of Toussaint Louverture in the middle of the square, Toussaint, the slave general and hero of the Haitian Revolution and the most famous of the founding fathers of Haiti.

Today, walking toward the camp, I could see, rising from among the tents, the very top of that bronze Toussaint, head and shoulders only, hatless in his revolutionary pigtail and broad black cape as he presided over the earthquake's refugees, the hero's camp a camp like all the others that had sprung up wherever there was open ground, wherever tent poles could be planted: backyards, courtyards, parks, unpaved parking lots, highway medians. The rest of Toussaint was lost among the tent tops and tarp peaks.

Just a few months after the earthquake, it was astonishing how the camps had morphed. What Toussaint Camp (and others like it) most resembled by now was a more than ordinarily ramshackle Haitian shantytown, not so different from the one where the boys once lived years ago in shacks and in Aristide's voodoo temple. Like a shantytown, the camp had alleys and streets and was strung with frail, unauthorized electric wiring. Its paths were dotted with barbershops, cell-phone-charging stations, lottery shacks (also called "banks"), tailors' stalls—each run by a single tailor with a pedal-operated Singer sewing machine—tiny restaurants, and private, one-woman day-care tents. At the edge of the camp was an ad hoc youth center, where Samuel and his friends tended to congregate. This is where I was heading, but first I had to meet up with the guys.

So I'm walking in this heat, and I am thinking about Aristide's boys, who are no longer boys but some of whom I knew when they were little and cute and not so miserable—not so miserable in part because they were little and didn't get it. A *papadap* man is walking just ahead of me, wearing his bright red *papadap* sign. He's selling digital minutes for Digicel cell phones. You can buy twenty minutes, or you can buy one minute. This morning, I've come out of air-conditioning at a friend's house up where the rich people live near the top of the hill above Port-au-Prince. One of the servants there made me a cheese omelet for breakfast while I sat on the terrace and dealt with my email over the WiFi connection. On my cell phone, I called Bony, a freelance taxi man, on *his* cell phone and hired him and his motorbike taxi to take me down the hill. That was fun, although perilous. Things are pretty easy for me now in Haiti. I know where I want to go, whom I want to see. I can find people, and I know how to make arrangements. My living conditions are pretty good, post-quake; sometimes I live with friends, other times, I get paid to come down and write, and so I can stay in hotels if I choose.

And here, now, I'm walking across the street to see these kids. They will not be emerging from air-conditioning (it's called *friz* in Creole). Jerry, I know for a fact, is living with some other young men and a few steady girlfriends in a squalid tent as hot as a charcoal pit. The boys when I meet them today won't have had breakfast—they have one meal a day, normally, when in funds. Also some of them are sick with fever, so they're not really hungry. They don't go to the doctor. They simply languish all day instead. They don't rent mototaxis. (One of them has two brothers who share control of a mototaxi, so he's the lucky one; his brothers also sell weed in the camp, I've been told.)

Jerry and Samuel and Black Rouge don't have special shoes to put on for walking around where they live. They wear knockoff sneakers (kept a dazzling white, somehow) or black plastic flip-flops. The only parallel between their lives and mine is the cell phone, but even in the world of mobile communications, their lives are more constricted than mine. They don't have credit; they don't have a phone plan; they don't have data. Their phones are not smart. With cash, in small amounts, they buy *papadap* minutes on the street that are downloaded onto their phone numbers. Often, they share phones: I call Jerry, I get Black. Or Samuel. I have no idea whose phone it is. Often, they will call me and then really quickly tell me to call them back, hanging up almost instantaneously. Callers pay for calls here. Receivers do not.

Strung along the curb facing the Plaza Hotel are stalls selling wooden statuettes and fried chicken and bandanas, poor-quality bead and shell jewelry, carvings of non-Haitian animals like giraffes, goat horn boxes, and some ritual voodoo items, charms and rattles, beads and satin kerchiefs, and the like. The target consumers for these things are the journalists, humanitarians, and consultants who stay at the Plaza. CNN was a big client of the hotel; sometimes the television crews would take up whole hallways with their cables, cameras, communications, techies, producers, and assistants. When CNN was on-site, Christiane Amanpour and her entourage occupied the terrace that overlooks Toussaint Camp, which provided an excellent backdrop for interviews. Cameramen and photojournalists would also descend from their rooms and come across the street to shoot pictures and video in Toussaint Camp and in the adjacent Constitution and Christophe camps. Wyclef Jean, the Haitian hip-hop musician who ran for president a year after the earthquake, did his preelection interviews at the Plaza. It was a useful setup, camps across from the hotel, and I suppose that the Plaza's guests would buy trinkets out front as souvenirs or for family and friends. Then there were petty merchants selling things to the camp dwellers: one skinny man in a hat was pushing a shaved-ice cart, with a ring of translucent syrups in many colors. Another was selling *mabi,* a drink made from soaking the bark of a Haitian tree; it's said to cure a bad stomach.

From their rickety wooden stalls, the vendors call out to me, "*Gade, gade.*" Look at what we have to sell. I couldn't be less interested: I don't

drink *mabi* and I don't eat ices in the street in Port-au-Prince anymore—
having seen so many times how the ice sellers drag their blocks of ice
through the streets on dirty blankets to the cart men—and I already
own my share of giraffes and voodoo rattles and kerchiefs. I have given
away more Haitian things in my life than my friends at home can stand
to receive, more things than I can bear to recall. I ignore the calls of the
vendors. The boys and their music, I am thinking of.

When Samuel and Jerry and the others were his, Aristide supported a
flock of such boys, kids who would flutter and fight around his legs in
the sacristy or the courtyard, and whom he took care of by offering them
straw sleeping mats and some food, sometimes a little spending money,
some vocational classes from time to time, and, occasionally, electric light
at night, for a couple of bucks a month paid to the guy who was stealing
it from Électricité d'Haïti's wires. That's how shantytown dwellers get
their power. Leaving the boys behind in the sacristy each Sunday morning, Aristide would emerge before the congregation and, from his pulpit,
fire off his stormy sermons against the Duvaliers and their dictatorship.
Afterward, his best lines would be repeated in the street, dying away only
when overshadowed by a new round of clever, harsh, punning phrases
from his next sermon the following Sunday.

Just before the earthquake, his former boys, now grown up and no
longer in Aristide's keep, lived in Cité Soleil or La Saline, the waterfront
shantytowns, or in the St. Martin or Fort Nationale neighborhoods, two
quartiers populaires. Before that, when they were adolescents and younger,
Aristide had set the boys up first in that abandoned temple and then—
after the Church kicked him out of that parish for his political activi-
ties—in a house in Turgeau, a nice middle-class neighborhood, much to
the neighbors' disgust.

Aristide was always being got rid of: not only was he eventually overthrown twice as president (a record even in Haitian history), but earlier,
he'd also been kicked out of his parish and his church. Today, his boys

were living in the camps in Port-au-Prince and he was ensconced in Pretoria, married now, with two daughters and a teaching position at the Centre for African Renaissance Studies at the University of South Africa. He had received a PhD from the university for a thesis comparing Zulu to Haitian Creole. According to news reports, his chief hobby in Pretoria was Ping-Pong. Others said his chief hobby was phoning Haiti.

Jerry says he remembers me from the old days when Aristide was still a shantytown priest. Samuel says he does, too. I wonder. It's possible and even likely that they're confusing me with any number of white women who were in and around Aristide's church at the time, in the years after Duvalier fled. When I first ran into Samuel after the earthquake, I rattled off names of other Aristide boys: Ti Sonny, Ti Bernard, Ti Claude, Johnny, Ayiti, and, of course, Filibert. Jerry and Samuel knew all of them, and each name was like a segment of a long password between us that signaled—over the giant gaping hideous crevasse that lies between our worlds—that once we frequented the same byways; that we'd come out of a shared historical passage into very different lives.

Well, maybe Samuel, the more clearly opportunistic of the two, doesn't see it that way: probably he feels that our paths' crossing twice is a fortunate coincidence for him that may bring in some extra dollars. Or maybe he's never seen me before in his life: Aristide's is a name anyone can invoke. To be honest, I don't remember Samuel exactly, and his is not a face you'd forget; his upper lip is deformed by a thick keloid from an infection, his eyes are huge and sad, his lopsided grin is a combination of drugged and disarming. Perhaps, indeed, he and I have never met before, and he is simply playing on my desire for connection and what he surely believes to be my innate white person's stupidity, in order to reestablish a relationship where formerly there was none.

I'm happy to oblige: I need Samuel to fit into my story. Samuel's into it, too: he needs me to give him money, which is what he no doubt believes white people are for; he'd like me to buy him food, or cigarettes—not to smoke but to sell. Between us, Samuel and I have a willing suspension of disbelief that suits us both. A Haitian journalist recently wrote a funny piece about post-quake race relations entitled "Every Haitian Has His Own White Man." I was Samuel's white man—at least for now, until another, better white man (which is to say richer, or stupider, or preferably both) came along.

And that was okay because the converse is also true: every white man has his own Haitian.

Now that there were so many of us white men and women down here in the earthquake's aftermath, I had added white men to my list of things to think about in Haiti. I was continuing my study of *us*: What did we think we were doing here? It wasn't the first time I'd asked myself the question, but the earthquake seemed to make it more pressing, more urgent. What could we do for Haiti, if anything, and conversely, what did Haiti do for us? What kept us here? Why did some of us come back, and back again, and again? Like me.

I'd been wondering about all this months earlier, on my first trip down to post-quake Haiti, two weeks after the disaster. I'd thought about it as I toured the broken city, as I walked past the crumbled cathedral and down through what had once been the business and banking center, passing the ruins of the office where, years ago, I'd once rented a car; the ruins of another office where I'd once picked up an express package from New York; the ruins of the intersection where I'd once—no, scores of times—changed money on the black market, with my habitual money changer. His corner was collapsed. I hoped he hadn't been there at 4:53 PM on January 12, 2010. Downtown was a mountain range of devastation, leading to the sea. I was writing in my notebook as I went on, stumbling over a variety of detritus: shards of stained glass, decapitated busts of Haitian revolutionary heroes, dented satellite dishes, fenders, school notebooks, abandoned luggage, bits of doll.

Around a corner, bulldozers from the United States, manned by the 82nd Airborne Division, were pushing rubble and refuse across the broad avenues. American soldiers hopped in and out of their vehicles. From behind a hillock of crushed cement, a boy emerged, wearing a T-shirt that said "Rest Assured—No One Cares." I blinked—this cannot be. But it was—even as the world community was pouring out charitable donations to international organizations, hoping to help Haitians like that boy survive. A block away, Haitians stood guard before what remained of the merchandise in destroyed stores and warehouses. Every Haitian has his own white man, and every white man his own Haitian—but what currency are we trading in? I wanted to know.

As I stand here now, hoping that Jerry will turn up—or Samuel; I'll take Samuel, if necessary—I try to imagine myself away from this corner of vendors and the Plaza Hotel and take my mind back around the rest of the city. I've been all over town, and beyond, in the earthquake's long aftermath. I've driven the streets of this city, everywhere that's drivable, and it's a new place, remapped by the earthquake and changed profoundly from the city I had known for years. I've walked through all the old neighborhoods where I once lived, where my friends lived: Pacot and Turgeau, Belair and St. Martin, and Cité Soleil and La Saline, too. The city's a wreck, a wrecked place.

It was a wrecked place before the earthquake, by the way. Before the earthquake, the city was punctuated by half-built houses and half-built walls; sidewalks were falling apart, gates swung at crazy angles, there were gaping, dangerous holes in streets and paths. In the old days Port-au-Prince was wrecked from being built up, but now it's all fallen down, even the half-built homes where people used to live on the first floor in expectation of future money to build the second.

Now, ridges and crests of cement block rise and fall underfoot, as well as garbage, refuse, junk, and sucking mud. Nothing is recognizable. Landmark buildings, so important for orienting oneself in this crowded and complicated city, have come down, leaving all of us lost and disoriented. In one neighborhood, I came across the remains of a little Haitian bank. They are really numbers places, lottery shacks, called banks or *borlettes* in Creole. This one, with its yellow and blue sign, was called Solution Borlette. It was lying in the dust, flattened in such a way that it seemed as if—were you to pull it up from the side—it would stand right up again, like a child's paper construction. The name seemed resonant.

When I arrived from Boston just after the earthquake, people were turning in circles amid the rubble, trying to figure out where they were. What was still standing was like a marker, and then you tried to remember that one little house you knew so well on this block, and you'd count the countable ruins away from what was still standing, or from the sign for Solution Borlette, in an attempt to determine where your aunt's house once was, a house where she made you supper once a week on Sundays, including the Sunday right before, and now it's gone and she's gone.

The only ones who are oriented and undisturbed by the ravages of the earthquake are the Port-au-Prince pigs, who, a few short days after the earthquake, gathered again at their accustomed corner to chow down on the usual garbage—and more garbage, now—that had collected there. Incredible to me that of all the regular rituals of Port-au-Prince from before the earthquake, this one, seemingly among very few in the immediate aftermath, should remain. Hi, pigs.

They're like old family friends. I've been driving past this same family of pigs for a quarter of a century. The cathedral's gone; the presidential palace is a ruin; the ministry of finance, the bureau of taxes, St. Trinité church, the two major art museums—all destroyed. These, then, are the unstunned, unaffected remnant of old Port-au-Prince, physically and traditionally: pigs surviving, pigs gathering, pigs en famille, dining in piggy splendor. They are not thin pigs, either, who have collected here, cheerily snuffling through orange peel, plastic bags, and a largely unrecognizable compost of what's been cast off, thrown away, or tumbled down in the quake. Thanks, pigs—a heartfelt thanks, for being here, still. For knowing the right street corner at the top of Rue Trois.

More things that continued in the aftermath: your heart stopped to witness the children walking through this detritus with their perfect, shiny backpacks, their exquisite braids (tied with barrettes or ribbons), as they tiptoed through the wreckage of their *patrimoine* in crisply ironed shirts, their bright school uniforms painfully clean—a cliché, but . . . The girls' delicate white patent leather school shoes tripped lightly over miniature mountains of former homes, former schools, former stores, former lives. Above them hung danger, ready to descend. Over the city's main roads, ruins lurched like menacing malefactors.

That was then. There are cobwebs in the rubble now. I had seen one, stretched between two pancaked floors, as I walked down toward Toussaint Camp. And Haitians—who in the first days were asking for an American governor to rule Haiti and put it back up, who were hoping Bill Clinton, already (before the earthquake) the UN's special envoy to Haiti, would come in and set everything straight—are now disgusted, not just with the outsiders who've failed to rescue them, but also with the whole Haitian scene.

Here's a list of things Samuel and Jerry have told me they are sick of: First, President Clinton, whose multi-vehicle convoy often holds up traffic and brings the city to a standstill; and then, elections of any kind; also the UN, in all its forms; the former Haitian presidents Jean-Bertrand Aristide and René Préval; the Red Cross; the soon-to-be-former presidential candidate Wyclef Jean; the future president Michel Martelly; the Haitian police, whom Jerry and Samuel laugh off with special disdain; and, most of all, spaghetti, which for a long time after the earthquake was the only food available. The lack of power after the earthquake meant that refrigeration, always scarce, was gone, and meat and vegetables rotted, while markets were disrupted and nothing fresh was arriving in Port-au-Prince. Which equaled spaghetti, cooked in bottled humanitarian-relief water, over coals.

～

But here I am, thinking about pigs and spaghetti, and standing on the sidewalk across from the Plaza Hotel, waiting for Jerry to show up. He's late but not by much, at this point. It's only fifteen minutes after rendez-vous time.

Jerry's going to guide me into Toussaint; I like to go in with some-one from the camp. It's more comfortable—but, just to be clear, I have never been frightened for a minute or even a second in the camps, and I've gone in alone, I've gone in with my own Haitians, I've gone in at night, in the evening, in the morning, and at noon, in the rain and in the sun. I haven't been frightened, and it's not because I'm brave. I am not brave. I would even say I am decidedly not brave. But in the camps and shantytowns, no one has threatened me, ever, or stolen from me, or even pestered me. I've never seen a weapon, unless you count machetes being used to skin sugarcane or cut open a coconut. It just doesn't happen, even though it could, of course.

I'm not a very stupid white person, and I know that there really is no force of order in Haiti except for the twelve thousand or so troops of the United Nations Stabilization Mission in Haiti, or MINUSTAH, who are not always on the alert for simple street or camp crime. Organized kid-nappings, which have plagued Port-au-Prince on and off in recent years, were coming back into fashion now, to a degree. And I knew that. The Domino's pizza delivery box I'd seen at a party at a house in the Bourdon suburb was a small part of the evidence. On it, the delivery man could check little boxes to show what problems he encountered en route that might explain a pie's late arrival: the BAD WEATHER box has a storm-cloud symbol over it. The TRANSIT PROBLEM box shows a red bus. And the box marked KIDNAPPING has, above it, a blue UFO.

Right after the quake, though, kidnapping all but disappeared. There was speculation about this. The optimists thought it was possible that many kidnappers had been killed in the quake. Or maybe their bosses had fled the destroyed country. Or was it just that, with the streets strewn with rubble, getaways were impossible? All routines and relationships, which are so useful to kidnappers, were disrupted, and there was no ready cash. A kidnapping is not a simple matter, unlike rape, the incidence of which rose spectacularly after the earthquake. Kidnappings in Port-au-Prince can be baroque in their complexity, with multiple drops, multiple cell phone numbers, multiple hideouts, often in the shantytowns or *quartiers populaires,* and rapidly rising or falling ransom demands, depending on the circumstances and how negotiations are proceeding. Such clever-clever to-and-fros don't thrive in the midst of natural disasters, with cell phone towers down, banks closed, roads impassable.

Or was it that the kidnappers were themselves caught up in the rescue of friends and family, an ironic but plausible theory? And just possibly, one hoped, they might have lost the heart for it, in the midst of all the tragedy. Another speculation Haitians put stock in was that Brazilian members of the UN forces, who were commonly thought to have imported the habit and the practice of kidnapping to Haiti, were too busy patrolling the wreckage to keep the rings going.

So I do think about kidnapping whenever I am standing alone on a sidewalk in Port-au-Prince. I'm wary, but not frightened. Even now that there are so many white people in Port-au-Prince who have come down to lend a hand in the rescue and reconstruction or to do other work, I am often enough the only white person around, and this can make someone self-conscious. You stick out as an easy target for anything: begging, selling, awkward conversation; the proffering of random email addresses and cell phone numbers; pleas to finance relatives' funerals or to purchase prescriptions (scripts that have the appearance of Napoleonic documents, faded, torn, and dry, aged and stamped and signed with a flourish, recycled scripts for which—over and over—many kindly, well-meaning white people have handed out cash).

I'm waiting for Jerry and listening to the peripheral chatter directed at me. The streets around me are cleared of debris. In front of me is the Plaza Hotel, visibly untouched by the tremor. Behind me life is carrying on in the camps. Things are weirdly normal.

And then coming at me, like some kind of demented homeless vision of a zombie, is a man with dust-colored debris and pieces of cement adhering to his face and a ragged blue T-shirt wrapped around his head. He looks as if he's just walked out of the earthquake, or just emerged from a burial ground. He seems disoriented and dangerous. I feel that I recognize him.

And I do, I do. I remember: he is the man whose close-up portrait, taken by Shaul Schwarz, appeared in *Time* magazine a few days after the earthquake. In the photograph, the man's face is plastered with crackling cement and dust and his head is wrapped in a blue T-shirt. This picture also appeared on the back cover of a photo book published by *Time* that was called *Haiti: Tragedy and Hope.* So I remember the man and his portrait; it's a pretty stunning photograph that seemed at the time to encapsulate the horror of the quake and also the endurance of Haitians. (In the Schwarz picture, the guy is alert and almost smiling, in spite of his dusty condition. Now, a year later, he's alert but not smiling—he's looking for business.)

And I notice right away that this apparition from history has singled me out as, for the moment, the only stupid white person available who might want to take his picture for money. With the unwitting help of Schwarz and *Time,* he has turned himself into a living tourist attraction, for the few tourists and many development workers and humanitarians who are visiting Haiti now. He is a fragment of the past more vivid than the statue of Toussaint, and he has joined the many—Haitians and outsiders, too—who are capitalizing on the Haitian earthquake. He just happens to be the most literal embodiment of this phenomenon. He is Rubble Man.

I can see this; I absorb all of this as he is coming toward me. I absorb the full absurdity and instrumental aspect of his getup. Even as I see him coming down the street, coming nearer, I'm also beginning to wonder about the original photo—was the rubble on this man's face real back then, or had he already understood the earthquake's value, had he applied the earthquake to his face like a Carnival mask, and was he already using the white journalists' gullibility for his own future benefit? I don't like to contemplate the possibility that such a degree of artifice could have been wielded to create a seeming authenticity, but then, as a friend of mine says about Haiti: *Tou sa ou we, se pa sa.* Roughly translated, this means "Nothing you see is what it seems," although the original Creole phrasing has an aggressive, dismissive kick to it that is almost an attack on any naïve interpretation. And still, the man is approaching inexorably, and I can see that I am a target in the crosshairs of his financial hopes. The thought does occur to me: Maybe he's for real—can rubble stay in your skin like that? Anyway, he's getting nearer, and I'm thinking, shit, what do I say? I'm having what I've come to call charity anxiety. But just as he's about to cross the street and reach me, Jerry arrives, with Samuel behind him, and takes my arm.

"Let's go," he says, and we all duck into the camp.

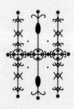

2

WHITE FLIGHT

Pa jire kayman avan w pase rivye-a
Don't curse the crocodile before you cross the river

Samuel kept looking over his shoulder at me, to make sure I was following. Jerry was half skipping, half loping next to him. We wound around the corridors of the camp. We seemed to proceed in concentric circles, the camp even in broad daylight growing darker and more crowded as we moved closer to the center. Finally we arrived at a tree or shrub; a shred of tree, one of very few in this camp, with a tent tucked under it, a tent the worse for wear, ripped by the wind, blowsy-looking. This was Samuel's tent, and we picked up a collaborator of his here, Véus Mathurin, who really was more like a boy, although he claimed he was in his early twenties. Véus had beseeching, bovine eyes, and a head too big for his slender body, like a bobblehead doll. He wore a floppy, droopy hat of some kind. Véus was the composer of the music we were to hear. Having picked him up, and with him the CD, we cruised back toward the outer rings of the camp, Samuel, Jerry, and Véus circling around me like a posse.

People were watching us as we passed by, but not with much energy. A few kids were playing soccer, but it was hot, and what little activity there was seemed lethargic. A group of women gossiped as they cut up a cabbage and boiled water for . . . spaghetti. The chatter stopped when they looked up to watch our procession go by, and then began again, behind us. I heard some uncomplimentary comment on my footwear. The joke was passed up the alley by mouth and I could hear people repeating it, a wave of whispering and laughter as we continued on. Véus carried the precious CD under his shirt. A smattering of small boys and girls followed behind us, flittering and scattering every time Samuel shooed them away, then quickly reassembling. Eventually, we got to the youth center, a little house that had been there by the side of the road before the earthquake. It was cheerfully painted. Most of the kids and young adults who were sitting and standing around this gathering place were stoned. The youth center is a weed sales point, too.

The owner or manager of the computer and speakers was a bluff guy in his early twenties, very into the equipment, self-important, very not stoned. He was, after all, in charge of what seemed to be the only computer in the camp. There was a lot of security around the computer, men and boys watching it every minute. Samuel, Jerry, and Véus gathered around; we were all hunching over the computer. A crowd developed behind us—it's not my favorite thing in Haiti, the way a crowd forms and presses whenever anything of the slightest interest is going on. A cloud of sweet smoke enveloped us.

The first song was about politicians and their dirty lies. It came on, and immediately the formerly boisterous crowd became silent. The song was called "Manigèt." Loosely translated from the Creole, the word *manigèt* means manipulation, hypocrisy, lying, or *magouy*, which in turn means dirt, graft, falsehood, or *blòf*, which means just what it sounds like. There are many words in Haitian Creole for fraud and deception. The song is post-quake hip-hop. To say that Véus and his friends wrote it is to say that they made it up and memorized it: the lyrics were never written down on paper, because almost all of these musicians and lyricists are functionally illiterate, especially in the Creole that they speak, which had no formal orthography until 1979 and is not taught in Haitian schools. An illiterate Haitian may be able to scrawl a few words in French, but he cannot speak French; in Creole, which he speaks, he can't really write. A few kids and men in the crowd nodded in stern agreement with the song's words, which excoriated corruption and mourned poverty.

The second song opened with cries, screams, sobbing, and praying recorded during the earthquake. It was a hip-hop dirge called "I'll Never Know (the Day I Will Fall)." It's in a minor key, and the lyrics consist of descriptions of blood in the streets and concrete falling, and everyone, rich and poor, suffering, trying to cope, helping one another, dying, surviving. It's a beautiful song, full of the pain of the recent tragedy yet buoyed by a surging belief in the world's strange mysteries.

Jerry bounced his head to the music. Samuel picked at his lip and mouthed the words. Weed was being passed around, furtively—pressed forward against the house by a crowd of about thirty young men now, we were nonetheless visible from the street. The computer owner had some kind of a DJ pad attached to the machine and he scratched the music and skipped it and replayed bits, much to the irritation of Véus, who seemed to like his own composition pure. Once he had convinced the DJ to stop tinkering with the sound, Véus tranced out, his peculiar little boy's face relaxing. He pulled his hat down over his big eyes and leaned up against the yellow wall of the house, listening to his own lyrics, moved by them.

I thought about Véus after that day. A dreamy, lovely man with so much damage and death swirling in his head. Someone who makes music in the midst of all the chaos, blood, and misery. An artist in a floppy hat living in the middle of a destitute camp. The name, too, Véus Mathurin—so beautiful.

It got me thinking of other Haitian names. Haitian names are like poetry, like an echo from another, more seemingly whimsical age—actually, they are from the profoundly unwhimsical days when French slave masters often gave plantation kids first names of classical figures from the Roman era, followed by the last name of the master's family. (Cassius Marcellus Clay was in this tradition, in the United States.)

Haitian names are rarely useful or plain. Here, for example, are some of the names of the people in the 2011 Haitian Chamber of Deputies, a worldly bunch whose names nonetheless transport you back to the salons and minuets of eighteenth-century France, and—with their occasional -*us* endings, back to Rome, also: Levaillant Louis-Jeune, Sadrac Dieudonné, Cholzer Chancy, Vikens Dérilus, Sorel Jacinthe, Worms Périlus (a personal favorite), Jobes Jolicaire Michel.

Here are some more, who were founders and presidents of Haiti (it helps to get the feel of it if you just say them out loud with your best French pronunciation): Toussaint Louverture, Faustin Soulouque, Pierre Théoma Boisrond-Canal, Lysius Salomon, Fabre Geffrard, Nissage Saget, Cincinnatus Leconte, Tancrède Auguste, Sudré Dartiguenave, Sylvain Salnave, Florvil Hyppolite, Boniface Alexandre . . . And here's a miscellany of friends and notables, honest men and criminals, heroines and militants, writers, artists, and businessmen, living and dead: Charlemagne Péralte, Levoy Exil, Myriam Merlet, Magalie Marcelin, Odile Latortue, Aubelin Jolicoeur, Prosper Avril, Rockefeller Guerre, Himmler Rébu, Krushchev Clermont, Roosevelt Jean-François, Willy Romélus, McKenly Gidéon. And Filibert Waldeck, Aristide's boy. History and literature and foreign relations are neatly packaged up in so many of these.

I worried about a lot of things after the earthquake: about all the proper things, like loss of life and limb, destruction of landmarks and artworks. But I also worried about the shrinking of culture. Would the food always be spaghetti? Would there never be a landmark again that exposed the corruption and beauty of Haitian history like the U.S.-Marine-built, French-inspired presidential palace? I feared, too, that soon all Haitian names might be thin and straightforward, like André Pierre or René Préval or Alice Blanchet, like names from a French primer.

I should have worried less. Or, perhaps, I should have worried more, because, like rebellion and revolution, an earthquake of such awful magnitude changes everything at the beginning, but in the end, perhaps nothing . . . or not very much. In situations of breakdown and unrest, change often appears to be right around the corner, only to flee in its ephemeral way when you approach it too closely and when the dominant, overarching class reasserts itself. That was my initial experience in Haiti, and it has been my continuing experience.

When I first started going down to Haiti, just before the fall of the Duvalier dynasty, the American Airlines 8:00 AM flight out of JFK was itself an education in Haitian culture and sociology. Up front in first class were Haitian Army officers, Haitian clergymen (there was even a bishop on that first ride, in a business suit), Haitian government ministers and assistant ministers, Haitian businessmen who worked both in Haiti and in the United States, a few American businessmen with interests in Haiti, and a French diplomat. The dominant class.

In the back of the plane were grandmothers and grandfathers who spoke no English; mothers and aunts and market ladies bringing on board huge hauls of disposable diapers, as well as giant radio cassette players and other hardware; men wearing old-fashioned formal hats; boys in ill-fitting, super-starched suits; girls in satiny ruffled Sunday dresses with uncountable numbers of bows and doodads in their hair; scores of illiterate adults who did not know how to put on a seat belt. The people that the British journalists would call Fred Voodoo, in other words—and me.

For many of the passengers, it was clearly only the second time they'd ever flown. There was a lot of praying that went on when the plane bounced, and there were many complaints about the food, because this meal was such a special meal, a free meal up in the air—back when airlines offered free, full meals. On one of the flights I took on this route at the time—this one from Port-au-Prince back to New York—the "kitchen" ran out of its beef dinner, and a Haitian woman just went crazy when they could give her only the chicken, because beef was such a rare event in her life, and she had been counting on this special pleasure. Normally on these flights I would be the only white person, or one of maybe three or four. The others, when there were any, would invariably be in first class.

Then Duvalier fled. Along with the rest of the international media, I saw him go, driving his BMW up onto a U.S. cargo plane in the middle of the night, with his wife in the passenger seat, wearing something silvery, or so it seemed in that fleeting view, smoking a cigarette and looking out the window at us all with remarkable cool. For me, a newcomer to the practice of foreign media coverage, it was shocking and exhilarating to be allowed to see history unfold, to find myself suddenly permitted to *be there* when Papa Doc's son was forced to flee Haiti, to see it all in detail, from the red ants biting us in the dirt near the tarmac to the cool cigarette of the about-to-be-former First Lady, as if I had been whisked into Haiti's history book. The big car, the now former president-for-life at the wheel, disappearing into the cargo bay of the black plane. This was the moment when I began to belong to Haiti. (As might be expected, the favor has never been returned.)

What followed was a bloody period when the people expected change and democracy and a hastily patched-together military-civilian junta pretended it was arranging free and fair elections. I was living then in Haiti. This phase was called Duvalierism without Duvalier. Warning: there is a lot of back-and-forth to come here. Haitian politics can seem like a soap opera, in which the writers leave you every damn day with a cliffhanger, and every day the dénouement is expected and never comes, and the story repeats and repeats and repeats—and you're absolutely addicted. Or, suffering from overload, you turn away cold turkey and pay attention instead to the long view—I've done both daily dosing and cold turkey.

Anyway, Duvalier fled, and, as I said earlier, eventually Aristide was elected, and then he was ousted, and then he returned, and then he was elected again, and then he was ousted again. Get the picture? There you have it in a nutshell.

There went change.

Aristide was overthrown that second time even though he had learned the lessons of his first ouster, and had sacrificed almost all of the commitments to the popular agenda that he had sworn to uphold during his priesthood and first presidency. Aristide, who had once recorded an album of preachings and songs called "Capitalism Is a Mortal Sin" (in Creole: "*Kapitalis Se Peche Mòtel*," or, as the jokey international press corps translated it: "Capitalism Is a Peach Motel"), was now, in his second term, meeting regularly with the International Monetary Fund and the World Bank to open Haiti up for business. He appointed several known Duvalierist figures to his cabinet, hoping to appease his opponents. His administration was accused of human rights abuses, as well.

In the end, no matter how he struggled or what compromises he was willing to make, he was trapped by the huge disparity between Haiti's millions of impoverished peasants and slum dwellers, and the tiny elite that was accustomed to running the country for its own enrichment and profit. Broadly speaking, he could not reconcile the irreconcilable, and, pushed to the very edge by the forces arrayed against him, he fell that second time—and again, change did not happen.

But this is all viewed with hindsight.

This was during the years when the flights between Haiti and the United States were still filled with Haitians and me, and some diplomats and foreign businessmen. This was when I was still hoping, as were many others—perhaps naïvely—that change might emerge, as change had emerged before in Haiti, from the bottom up, from the grassroots. Instead what came from beneath—after I'd known Haiti for so many years—was the earthquake, and after that, all the help and change that was supposed to matter came from above, from the air: from outsiders flying down to Haiti with their money, their development résumés, and their hopes and dreams.

The flight I took down for my visit with Jerry and Samuel boarded in Miami. Sitting near me at the gate was a group of Americans who were involved in the Hands & Feet Project, according to their T-shirts. Hands & Feet seemed to be a missionary group, a small nongovernmental organization, or NGO. Many of these kids were reading the Bible. All of the missionaries sitting at my gate were wearing the Hands & Feet T-shirt, like kids on a school trip. On the back of their shirts was this quote: "Religion that our Father accepts as pure and faultless is this: To look after orphans and widows in distress." That was on a *T-shirt.* I Googled the organization from my phone: "An Awesome Adventure," the homepage for their mission sign-up proclaimed. On the website, palm trees waved behind the motto as if post-quake Haiti were a tourist destination. And maybe it is. Yeah, that's what it is now: a feel-good tourist destination.

There at the gate, one girl from the group was wearing a teddy bear backpack; another was knitting. They were all eating sandwiches. Many were carrying little stuffed animals down into earthquakeland. Paul Farmer, the Harvard professor and physician who is the founder and head of the venerable Partners In Health, deplaned from Port-au-Prince and walked past us incognito toward a connecting flight. Farmer had recently signed up as Bill Clinton's deputy envoy to Haiti. No one here among the newbie missionaries and NGOers recognized this man who is arguably the most effective deliverer of aid that Haiti has ever known.

Foreigners such the Hands and Feet kids are now supposed to be what are called, in the development industry, "change agents" for Haiti. The journalist Linda Polman has called them, more accurately, perhaps, "the crisis caravan." Missionaries, engineers, health care workers, development specialists, architects, sanitation experts, water delivery specialists, housing producers, adoption agencies, and disaster professionals of all kinds, and the huge bureaucracies of development and security and construction that now thunder in in the wake of massive disaster in impoverished countries—these were to be Haiti's salvation post-earthquake.

So there we all were, some for the first time, others, like me, *not*— outsiders and Haitians alike, standing on the teetering edge of change, looking down into the social, cultural, and physical craters and wreckage created by the quake, and hoping. Many of the people who were flying down in those days—and some of the Haitians whom they were coming to rescue—believed that the earthquake would provide an unparalleled opportunity for Haiti. They were subject to what Deborah Scroggins, author of *Emma's War,* about an Englishwoman in the midst of the Sudanese civil war, calls the "clichés of mercy."

To save this country, you first had to destroy it. That might have been how one could have summed up prevailing outsider attitudes toward the earthquake situation and what it seemed to promise. (In a way, those who didn't value him thought Aristide had that same plan. That had also been the agenda of the revolutionaries in the era of slavery.)

Most of the people on those white flights were excited and energized by what they thought might be the new possibilities offered in disaster conditions, what Scroggins would label a "salvation fantasy." If everything had fallen down, the theory was, isn't this a great time to build everything back up, better? These were not really long-standing members of the crisis caravan, who know enough to know that crises, including an inconceivable natural disaster, have problems that are not exciting or fun to fix. Rather, these were the eventual thousands of newbies attached to the caravan, who believed that their presence and work in Haiti—by the very virtue of their newness and the fact that they were unsullied and untouched by cynicism, world-weariness, and resignation—could generate real solutions to Haiti's problems, problems that had been intractable for at least a century and that had strong roots in Haitian history and the country's foreign relations that were not easily *dechouké.* The newbies mistook themselves for part of a grand solution when, actually, they and the caravan itself were obviously and immediately identifiable as part of Haiti's ongoing problem. As Scroggins wrote about a different country (Sudan): "There it was again: the noble cause, the great saving illusion . . . I didn't say anything. I thought . . . of all that vainglorious rhetoric about pasting nations back together with a few bags of food."

But there were others on those white flights, perhaps gentler souls, possibly more experienced hands, people who were more concerned with matters of fact than with theories of development and relief, not bright-eyed but clear-eyed, who didn't prejudge and who were willing to wait to see how such a catastrophe would play out in this specific place at this specific time given these specific political conditions and actors. And there were also those who came in and did what they really knew how to do well—fixing, curing, mending, healing, patching, soothing, attending—and who did it in Haiti the way they'd always done it everywhere, anywhere, whether in Minneapolis or San Francisco, in London or Tel Aviv, in Darfur or Taipei, in Boston or Port-au-Prince. These were the doctors.

3

TRAUMATIC AMPUTATION

Depi tet pa koupe, gen lespwa mete chapo
Until your head's cut off,
there's hope that you can put on your hat

Without question, doctors and health care workers have it best in regions of deprivation and emergency. They can offer something to the people around them that may well have an immediate, life-saving, and life-changing effect. They can really fix something. This accounts in part for the often optimistic attitude of physicians in the developing world. They can give you an AIDS cocktail, cure your TB, provide a prosthetic leg.

For months, Dr. Megan Coffee did not take a day off work after she began tending to people at the university hospital in Port-au-Prince in the days following the earthquake. Why was that? Even the most dedicated doctors need a break. Dr. Coffee wanted a break, but she couldn't take one—for many, many reasons, but really, secretly, it was because Pierre, one of her tuberculosis patients (her favorite), needed to be on constant oxygen, and she could trust no one to ensure this but herself. He was her favorite because he was funny and because he was a "geek," as she says. He was always reading. Like Pierre, most of Dr. Coffee's patients come out of the camps and the shantytowns in Port-au-Prince, but many also come down from villages all over the country. Dr. Coffee's a funny geek, too, well-read, intense, perfectly talkative but not much of a socializer.

She is a white woman from the United States, even though her last name can mean, in Haitian Creole, the tan color of a light-skinned black person, just as *wouj,* or in French, *rouge,* is a coloring in Haiti of African-American mixed skin—a light color with freckles, and almost reddish hair to go with it. (Black Americans have been known to use this same term: red.) In Haiti the word *blan,* which literally means white, really means foreigner, and *neg,* or black, means just a person. So you can hear a Haitian discussing someone who is a *neg blan,* or a foreign guy, which literally translated means "a white black." Conversely, a *blan neg* is a black foreigner, or literally "a black white." Megan Coffee, from Maplewood, New Jersey, though, is a plain old *blan,* and at the time I met her, she was the last foreign doctor remaining at Haiti's State University Hospital (HUEH) in Port-au-Prince.

But in the weeks just following the earthquake, there were hundreds of these doctors around rushing to and fro in scrubs they'd brought with them, establishing triage tents, separating the doomed from the badly injured, with orthopedists especially in demand. Doktè Kafe, as her patients call her, is neither an orthopedist nor a trauma specialist. She's in infectious diseases, which turned out to be a very useful specialty in Haiti. There were many doctors of different kinds in Haiti at that time, from all over the world, and each had his or her own specialty and assistance to give, and each had his or her own reaction to Haiti in its moment of need.

While Dr. Coffee was working at the hospital in late January 2010, Dr. Mark Hyman, one of the first foreign doctors to arrive, was already leaving. A Massachusetts family physician and guru of something he calls "functional medicine," Hyman, too, is neither an orthopedist nor a trauma doc. He, too, ended up at HUEH. He'd gotten into the country almost immediately after the earthquake struck, in a private plane organized by Partners In Health.

I met Hyman in the middle of the night at Toussaint Louverture airport a little less than two weeks after he'd arrived. I had just gotten in; he was trying to get out. Several planes full of fresh young doctors came in while we were there on the tarmac. Hyman was in a state of high agitation, unsure whether he'd be able to find a U.S. military plane flying out that would let him have a seat. Getting in and out of Haiti was a complicated affair in the early weeks after the earthquake; commercial flights were canceled, so if you didn't have a specific charter to get on, you had to spend a lot of time at the airport, waiting and bargaining and begging.

So Hyman was rushing around on the nighttime tarmac from one military officer to the next in a near frenzy. They seemed to look upon his frantic importuning with an assessing but tolerant regard. When the new doctors arrived, Hyman took a break from his pleading and jumped in among them as they stood clustered with big scared eyes and with backpacks and sturdy walking shoes, waiting for their organization's people on the ground to get them out of the airport and into the operating theater.

At the center of a circle, illuminated only by his headlamp, Hyman began an ad hoc lecture, arms flailing and gesturing to accompany a dramatic account of what he'd seen so far. He told the Haiti newbies that they were about to practice medicine as it had last been practiced during the Civil War. They were transfixed. I was transfixed. He mentioned doctors pissing into bags because the work was so unrelenting that you didn't have time to find a toilet. He mentioned dehydration, reminding these inexperienced innocents that water was as necessary for overworked doctors as it was for patients who had lost limbs and blood. He mentioned exhaustion.

And then, in the middle of a sentence ("Sorry, sorry . . ."), he whipped away back to an air force guy he'd been dealing with and whom he'd just spotted again in the near distance. I sat down again in the backseat of a car, waiting to be released from airport custody into Port-au-Prince. Here, I chatted with an old friend from Partners In Health and with a military officer who'd flown in on our plane. Hyman was PIH's responsibility, and I was traveling in a PIH car, so we had to wait for him to be securely on his way out of the country and out of PIH's care before our driver could leave the airport. The military officer in the backseat next to me was growing restive.

Suddenly Hyman came rushing back toward our car, where he had parked his luggage, emerging from the darkness into the airstrip lights like a gawky giraffe rushing over the veld. He whipped open the back door of the car, where we were sitting, and, arms windmilling, spent the next ten minutes muttering expletives and scattering the contents of his one piece of luggage over the tarmac—underwear, books, rehydration salts, dirty T-shirts, energy bars, flashlights, water—as he searched for his missing passport, without which there was no chance of departure. (Eventually he located the missing document in his backpack.) "Thank you, Lord," said the military officer I'd been talking to, as Hyman rushed away.

When Hyman was working in Haiti, although apparently he and his colleagues couldn't manage to get to the bathroom, he did manage to blog for the *Huffington Post* and to appear on *60 Minutes*, both of which were arguably important to getting the word out on the enormity of the catastrophe, and links to which can be found now on Hyman's website, drhyman.com. Here's one thing he wrote in his first *HuffPost* blog: "Tomorrow we will start the first surgery here after the earthquake: the first amputation with nothing but a hacksaw and headlamps and a bottle of vodka to sterilize the equipment and a few rusty instruments to start. But we will do it because it has to be done and there is no one or nowhere else to do it." In the *60 Minutes* section, you can see the actual hacksaw being used on a child, and hear Hyman lament the lack of sterilizing alcohol and laud the appearance of the vodka bottle. It is a comment on the weirdness of our world that a doctor flying down into an earthquake could blog for the *Huffington Post*—via satellite phone or iPhone or whatever—but have nothing better on hand for amputations than a hacksaw.

Afterward, on his website, Hyman wrote: "Through it all I had the privilege of experiencing the indomitable Haitian spirit." That is to say, while he was amputating limbs without anesthesia? Or while he was blogging? Or what? One can only speculate what the scar from that hacksaw must look like compared with that of an amputation done at Summit Orthopedics in the Twin Cities, say.

Summit sent down a handful of doctors in January 2010. I know this because one day I ended up needing them.

I was driving around with a friend to inspect the damage outside of town, and we stopped at the clinic of Doctors Without Borders in Léogâne, a town near the epicenter of the earthquakes. Supplies were coming in on trucks, and tents were set up, but there was a long line of patients waiting to see the doctors, among them McKenly Gédéon, a two-and-a-half-year-old boy the size of a child a year younger. McKenly was sitting silently on his mother's knee, on the shady side of the clinic's drive, waiting to see a doctor. His seven-year-old sister, McKenzie, had been killed in the quake by a falling roof, which had, at the same time, cut off both of McKenly's hands. Except for the bandages on the stumps of his wrist and elbow, and his utter silence, you wouldn't have known anything extraordinary had happened to him. He wasn't crying, although his mother told us that the reason they were there was that they'd run out of painkillers for him and needed more. There was a lot of this blankness among injured Haitians, I noticed. Was this, I wondered, the resilience and the indomitable Haitian spirit of which Hyman and so many others were always speaking? Medical friends told me it was shock and post-traumatic stress.

We left and drove on. People were living on the highway median; an old woman and another dozen people had relocated into a municipal ga-zebo made of iron, from whose eaves they'd hung sheets for privacy and to ward off the sun. The big cemetery in Léogâne was all but destroyed; it looked as though a cosmic cannonball had been rolled through it. "Bientôt: Université," read a sign on a great big white school that had pancaked next to the main road—"A university will be coming soon." As the Haitians were saying about so many projects, "*Poko fini, deja tonbe.*" Not yet finished, already collapsed.

On our way back to town, I decided we should look in again and see how McKenly had progressed. His small, solemn face and his terrible future had disturbed my usual journalistic crypto-distance. And there he was, still—this time on the other side of the clinic's driveway, again out of the sun but otherwise no farther down the line of waiting patients. A European doctor took several minutes away from his work to give me a long, animated talk about the difficult job. Like Dr. Hyman, he seemed inexorably drawn to the media. I was blogging for *Time* magazine, which made him effusive.

While he talked, a young Haitian man jumped out of an ambulance and ran up to him, saying, "*Cas d'urgence, cas d'urgence.*" Emergency, emergency. When the doctor barely turned and showed no interest, I said to him (I couldn't help myself), "You'd better see what it is." But he waved the Haitian away twice, with visible irritation. The young man stood to the side, crestfallen and worried.

"When I do this," the doctor was telling me, with a wide Romance-language gesture that encompassed the ignored man, the ambulance, the clinic tents, the long line of waiting patients, "it's for me a kind of paradise. It's a passion and an engagement. That's why I'm with Doctors Without Borders." By the time he and I were finished talking, the ambulance and the young man had driven off again.

I was sure I knew of a better place for McKenly, but it meant taking him out of Léogâne and into Port-au-Prince. We consulted with his mother and sent word to his aunt, who was watching his surviving siblings. They were all living outside in a neighbor's yard—more than two weeks after the earthquake, no one dared to sleep under a roof. So we opened our car door and McKenly and his mother got in. In an hour we were back in Port-au-Prince at the Saint Damien Hospital, run by the Swiss foundation Nos Petits Frères et Soeurs, near the airport. I sat down in the waiting area with McKenly and his mother. The hospital was full of earthquake victims, some of whom were just being brought in by family members on stretchers made from broken doors.

In the mad jumble of the injured, no one came to see why we were there. I was freaking out as I sat there in a row of yellow plastic seats under high windows and bright lights. No one took notice of the little boy with no hands and old, bloody bandages that were fraying around the edges. We were presented with no waiting list, no sign-in sheet. I felt I had abducted McKenly and his mother from their home for no reason. To them, I must have seemed like a disaster vision, a maddened white kidnapper. After a few minutes it became clear that we were in a scrimmage situation, where the person who was most vocal and most irritating and most visible would get the fastest attention. Especially if that person was white. In any case, no Haitian among the waiting patients seemed ready to plunge into the maelstrom of the medical rush. They all sat there quietly. Who knew if they would ever be seen? Was this the indomitable spirit? So I pushed myself into action, and not too much later we were being "admitted" by Mary Aschenbrenner, a certified physician's assistant with the Summit Orthopedics group from the Twin Cities.

She seemed like a saint to me as she asked McKenly's mother questions and I interpreted. I think she seemed like a saint to McKenly's mother, too. Everything that had happened to the mother in the past weeks was so unimaginable: earthquake, her daughter's death, her son's cruel disability, living in a tent, the ride to Port-au-Prince with a nutty white lady, and now this attentive saint, bent over her boy's bandages, looking, cooing, examining, writing things down. Aschenbrenner told me that what had happened to the boy was called "traumatic amputation," in the lexicon. She gently let go of McKenly's stumps, which had been sewn up by Doctors Without Borders, and said she thought he needed what orthopedists call, with medical euphemism, a "refinement operation" to fix the earlier job.

They took him for X-rays. I waited with the silent mother. Yes, he needed the operation; they would perform it tomorrow. No, his father was not in the picture; on the trip up from Léogâne, McKenly's mother told me that he'd left after New Year's to cut sugarcane in the Dominican Republic, and even after the earthquake, he hadn't called her to find out about how they had fared in the catastrophe. Maybe, McKenly's mother speculated, he was dead. I slipped money to her and then consulted with a Haitian friend's cousin who was working at the hospital and who took McKenly and his mother under her wing.

McKenly had the operation, and although there was talk of another aunt in Miami, and of getting prostheses for him from the United States, he and his mother disappeared back to Léogâne a few days later, where his family would try to take care of him. I imagined his status in the family: in the thirty-five seconds it took for the earthquake to wreak its damage, McKenly had been transformed from a possible future provider for his people into another mouth to feed for a lifetime. In Haiti, where resources are so short, this could easily prove a death sentence. With three other children to feed, his mother might feel compelled to make the choice to give him only leavings and scraps. It was possible; I'd seen such things. And so my sporadic attempt to find McKenly a new set of hands continues. Next time I go to Haiti I'll search for him in Léogâne and see how he is doing. Doctors have told me that by now, a child of that age will be compensating amazingly for the loss, and be able to do surprising things with the remaining stumps. Somehow this doesn't comfort me.

In Dr. Mark Hyman's real life (every doctor who came to Haiti after the earthquake has a real life, but perhaps hardly any so public as Dr. Hyman's), he is the founder of the UltraWellness Center in the quaint colonial town of Lenox, Massachusetts. He testifies before the Senate on matters of detoxification and alternative medicine. His specialty is a new field, invented by him, called "functional medicine," which he describes in his personal biographical blurb as "a revolution in 21st century medicine that provides a new road map for navigating the territory of health and illness." Before he came to Haiti, Hyman was already the author of "multiple *New York Times* best-sellers," according to his blurb in the new-agey health section of the *Huffington Post,* "including *The UltraMind Solution, The UltraSimple Diet, UltraMetabolism,* and the weekly *UltraWellness Newsletter,* in which he provides insight into how you can integrate functional medicine into your life and achieve the state of UltraWellness."

On the website for the UltraWellness Center, we see the yellow Victorian house where its offices are located; we see a picture of the staff (eight white people); we see a picture of a woman client speaking to Hyman with his computer between them, in front of a window that shows a pretty Lenox neighborhood (caption: "How to Become a Patient"), and we see a final picture of Hyman, in Port-au-Prince, surrounded by Haitian kids giving the thumbs-up gesture, with the caption "My Commitment to Haiti." (Some of this online material was later replaced by Hyman's Haiti photo journal from January 2010, and Haiti is no longer featured on his website's home page.) The essay accompanying the picture of Hyman and the Haitian kids includes most of Hyman's original writing for the *Huffington Post.* Haiti must have been a shock for someone whose website opens with this claim: "Lifelong health and vitality is our birthright."

Hyman is nurturing his commitment to Haiti from home, with occasional visits back, a normal pattern for outside doctors trying to help out while also maintaining a family and professional life. One cannot deny that he came down and made himself useful, but his motivation seems sketchy. He appears to have been an early adopter of the Haiti earthquake backdrop. He was in Haiti for a brief term as a celebrity and a doctor, a celebrity doctor, much as Anderson Cooper was there as a celebrity journalist.

Megan Coffee, on the other hand, has remained "in country," as development people call it, since her arrival—with just a few breaks back to the United States. She's a different breed. These two doctors represent the two opposite extremes of outsider involvement in Haiti, one with a sporadic but continuing interest that is in part self-motivated, and the other with what will probably become a lifelong commitment. Naturally, I empathize more with the one who has been more profoundly sucked in.

~~

Even on a normal day, the general hospital where Dr. Coffee cannot cope with the health needs of the Port-au-Prince population—not enough beds, not enough doctors, not enough medicine, a limited nursing staff, and a besieged administration. The city morgue is also located in the hospital. Never efficient, it was easily overwhelmed by quake victims, and when Dr. Coffee and Dr. Hyman and other foreign doctors first arrived in the earthquake's aftermath, the entire courtyard was still stacked with cadavers. Victims of the disaster came to the hospital and expired on the grounds before being seen by any medical staff. Families dragged the injured there. Women gave birth among the dead and dying. Doctors in white coats had to step around the bodies. Dump trucks came to the hospital gates to pick up the bodies en masse for burial. It was a Boschian scene. The facilities were exhausted, doctors taxed beyond the utmost of their capacities.

In the wake of the catastrophe (*katastwof*, in Creole), Dr. Coffee started out, like Dr. Hyman and all the other foreign doctors and medical staff who rushed down into the earthquake, doing triage and assisting with amputations, stopping bleeding, treating septic infections and gangrene, and hunting for antibiotics, for oxygen tanks, for catheters, stents, crutches, and for the files and rasps and mallets, the drills and burrs, the reamers and special saws, and the knobs, screws, and wirings of orthopedics.

Dr. Coffee came down to Haiti because one of her best friends is Haitian-American. She'd spent the New Year's before the earthquake with that friend, and she had saved up all her vacation days for a trip to Haiti. She was planning to come down for the first time ever in May 2010, just to visit a place she'd heard so much about, but the earthquake intervened, and that changed everything, Dr. Coffee says. After the quake, she took a free JetBlue flight out to the Dominican Republic, the flight donated for people coming in to do humanitarian work, and she crossed the border into Haiti. On her way she met someone who told her that the general hospital in Port-au-Prince really needed an infectious diseases doctor. So that's where she went.

Megan Coffee graduated from Harvard in 1998 and then received her PhD from Oxford for work in mathematical models of epidemiology, concentrating on HIV. She turned thirty-six in 2012. Her mother is a mathematics professor at the City University of New York, and her father is a law professor at Columbia; he's also director of the Center on Corporate Governance there. Dr. Coffee is an only child; her father is one of three brothers born in the space of three years, so he wanted only one child. "I'm his son," she says, smiling.

She finished Harvard Medical School in 2005; her residency was at Massachusetts General Hospital. In 2008, she left Massachusetts and went on to further graduate study at UCSF and Berkeley. Her work in San Francisco was a good preamble for what she has ended up doing in Haiti. San Francisco, she has said, "was excellent training . . . It's probably the only place in the U.S. with a higher HIV infection rate, among men anyway, than here." Dr. Coffee says she chose the Bay Area because "they have a lot of HIV, TB, and syphilis there."

Although there was a connection between the infectious diseases work she was doing in San Francisco and the work she ended up doing at HUEH, Haiti after the earthquake was a different medical scene from either San Francisco or Haiti before the earthquake. It was altogether on a different scale, and it demanded an entirely other set of skills. Port-au-Prince post-quake was as new an experience for Dr. Coffee as it was for most of the other foreign doctors who came down to help with the emergency situation. It was a new experience for Haitian doctors, too.

For instance, at first she was living in a tent, like most of the other doctors who arrived, which was a little better situation than most of the capital's residents, who were sleeping under sticks and sheets or simply under the stars in the first weeks, because the quake and the condition of its victims had put them in mortal fear of roofs—and they did not yet have tents. Nor was Dr. Coffee's infectious diseases specialty in very great demand—yet. In the first days that follow them, earthquakes are almost exclusively about trauma and orthopedics.

"I lost so many patients in those first days just because I couldn't find oxygen," Dr. Coffee says, peering into her ward from under the trademark white bucket hat she wears against the sun, which makes her look like a hippie who somehow got involved in big game hunting. Her long auburn hair, which is graying at the temples, streams down her back from under the hat, more often than not in a ponytail. Her skin is creamy white and no match for the Haitian sun after seven thirty in the morning.

Oxygen and oxygen tanks have been a constant preoccupation for Dr. Coffee since she arrived. Proper oxygen flow is a lifesaver in advanced cases of tuberculosis and, administered early enough, can help control the disease. Her work in Haiti quickly evolved from trauma assistance into treatment of TB, a particularly important field here, where tuberculosis is rampant even among the non–HIV infected population. TB is a disease that loves squalor and close quarters, and Haiti has what the United States Agency for International Development has called "the highest tuberculosis burden in the Latin American and Caribbean region." The disease is the second leading cause of death among youths and adults in the country, after HIV/AIDS.

Its varied tropical aspects, however, were often unfamiliar to non-specializing doctors. In the earthquake's aftermath, Dr. Coffee's foreign colleagues saw a lot of children with intense abdominal pain. "They kept telling me kids had appendicitis," Dr. Coffee says, "when it was pediatric abdominal TB."

Dr. Coffee is on the small side, and blue-eyed, and more than a year after the earthquake, she trucks around the hospital in her orange sneakers and white trousers as if it were the courtyard of a comfortable country palace, and she were among the proprietors. She's at home on the expansive grounds, among the tents and the wards, the petitioners. She knows everyone there, and everyone knows her. Doktè Kafe's reputation has also spread outside Port-au-Prince, and people come scores of kilometers to seek her counsel, many on foot, down from the mountains above the capital. She is known to be generous with medicine and food. "I do what I can," she says. The humility isn't false—it's just an honest assessment of one person's abilities in the face of the health situation's enormity.

Dr. Coffee's first waiting room at the hospital was the broad, sun-struck alley outside the small nursing tent. There, prospective patients and outpatients would gather to seek treatment, hospitalization, prescriptions, refills, or just a kind word. They were starving and skinny, or sturdy and cheerful if they'd been on meds for some time. They were at death's door or recovering; they'd walked for miles or they lived in the Marché Salomon nearby. They were grandmothers and children, and babies in their aunties' arms. Some were formerly strong young men, now wasted to stickman dimensions. Some were twenty- or twenty-five-year-olds who had reached only the height of middle-school children because their disease had gone untreated for so long. And many, many of Dr. Coffee's patients were HIV-positive.

I'm sitting on a folding chair in the sun near the waiting area. Two healthy-looking Haitian-American girls are walking by like tourists, wearing teeny shorts, halter tops, and sunglasses, on a post-quake tour of the homeland. Noticing the crowd gathered in front of Dr. Coffee's tent, seemingly ready to receive something, they stop. They're interested in anything that might be handed out. Dr. Coffee is looking at prescriptions and X-rays and giving out some refills.

"What's this?" they ask Dr. Coffee in English over the heads of the waiting patients.

Dr. Coffee, looking up briefly from an X-ray, taking in the girls with a measuring glance: "TB."

Girls: "Is it free?"

Dr. Coffee, looking back down at a chart: "If you have TB."

Girls: "We don't have it. Okay, thanks. Have a nice day."

They move on.

Dr. Coffee shakes her head as she continues working.

Most who come to see her are more serious, and very sick. They all want to be in her care. But not all have tuberculosis.

"I break people's hearts all the time by telling them they don't have TB," Dr. Coffee says. Those patients get sent elsewhere.

She turns this way and that as she proceeds down the center aisle of the ward, between rows of old-fashioned metal cots. Things in this provisional ward are better than they used to be in the hospital before the earthquake: now there is just one patient per bed. The heat is stifling, though, and the air doesn't move. Like all visitors to the tent, Dr. Coffee wears a protective mask while she's inside because TB is so contagious. But the mask makes the heat just that much more unbearable—in Haiti there are levels of unbearableness.

Before the earthquake, there was only one sanatorium in Port-au-Prince for TB patients. But it fell down in the shaking, killing many of them. "After the earthquake, we had two or three tents," says Dr. Alix Lassègue, who was then the director of HUEH, "and Dr. Coffee was there specializing in infectious diseases, and she stayed. And so in March, she began to take over care of patients in the tuberculosis tent. This was the only place for them." A Haitian nurse at the hospital had been following a handful of TB outpatients before the earthquake.

Dr. Lassègue doesn't mean that Dr. Coffee's tent was the only place in the hospital. He means the only place in the region. Then suddenly, one day, the hospital began taking down earthquake tent wards and removing patients to the old, repaired wards of the hospital. "You naturally don't want tents in the middle of a hospital's courtyard," says Dr. Lassègue, "and there were places in the hospital for those patients to go to other than the tents: ICU, orthopedics, et cetera—all the kinds of patients who formerly had space in a building. But the TB patients did not have another space to go to, so they remained under the tents."

Until Hurricane Tomas threatened, in late October and early November 2010. That was when it became clear that the tuberculosis patients needed something stable, something permanent. While Tomas lurked over the Caribbean, Dr. Coffee says she was being told that the TB ward had to get out of the tents and that it was going to be downsized in future. She was forced to disperse her patients and to discharge the least sick in advance of the storm. And she was worried that the storm was being used as a means to get rid of the TB ward altogether; the politics inside the general hospital in Haiti are as harsh as the politics outside the hospital, and almost as harsh as the politics in American hospitals.

While she was worrying about the entire venture, Dr. Coffee was also hunting for somewhere to lodge her favorite patient, Pierre, as the storm blew toward Haiti. He needed to have an oxygen concentrator on electricity or a tank of oxygen every day. She tweeted serially at the time:

> I wanted to say a bit about the patient who has always been secretly my favorite. Other young patients ask for candy or sneakers or money./ This patient would ask for a pencil. And he would write with the stub of a pencil he had. He would copy dictionaries/Or anything he could get his hands on, learning English. He says that all his life he could not run as fast as other children/And by age 21 he was constantly breathless. He's articulate with a sardonic sense of humor./When I used to have no one else at the hospital at night, I would call him to check on things for me, or to do something I forgot./I used to have to roll one of those 200 lb. O2 tanks for him every day./So in the midst of hurricane preparations I am afraid he is going to get lost.

In the midst of impending catastrophe, Dr. Coffee kept tweeting about Pierre—using Twitter as a means to find her patient a bed with oxygen available, somewhere, anywhere, a place where he could be assured of power during the storm so that he could use his oxygen machine. She kept her patients strictly anonymous in her tweets, but everyone knew she was talking about Pierre. To keep him safe during an outage, she needed to find a place that had emergency generators.

More tweets, from an increasingly desperate Dr. Coffee, written while she waited for a lift home in the days before the storm:

> Any thoughts on where to find a decent room w good power for an outpatient needing an oxygen machine in Port-au-Prince?/His lungs

look like huge pockets of air. He has two huge cysts taking up the upper 2/3s of both lungs./I need a safe place for him to be with his machine . . . if the power goes out./And that's where I'm getting stymied. In any other city, I could just rent a room for the storm./It reminds me how difficult the real estate market is in a city where buildings are gone and a lot of [nongovernmental organizations] have come in./The [real estate] market is skewed toward NGOs. Will have to find out about more affordable prices./I will call to see if the [Hotel] Oloffson really is 69 bucks a night for my patient./And I think I will be a little jealous of my patient shacking up at the Oloffson.

And then, the next day, with Tomas about to blow in: "You can really feel the low pressure system in Port-au-Prince. I now have a room in a building for my patient. So all good." At the last minute the hospital administration decided to accommodate Dr. Coffee's remaining patients, including Pierre, in a room on the first floor of surgery during the storm, at least. There, Pierre would have access to oxygen tanks.

Not long after Tomas, a semipermanent structure was built for the tuberculosis ward. No one told Dr. Coffee or any of the other staff that that's what it was as it was going up. They were watching the construction, imagining enviously who might be destined to occupy it, she says. And then suddenly, there they all were, with a nice, apparently sturdy new building all for themselves, paid for by the hospital.

Pierre, though, could only be stabilized, time and again, but never cured. His hold on life was temporary—the disease had ruined too much of his lungs. Dr. Coffee repeatedly took huge, detailed, personal trouble over him, as she did with many of her patients. She was vigilant, but sometimes vigilance is not enough.

As Dr. Coffee walks down the aisle between the two rows of patient beds, each patient extends a finger to her so she can fit it with her oxygen meter. She knows each patient by name, or nickname, and chats and jokes with everyone who's well enough to engage in conversation. The first time I made rounds with her, she had forty-five hospitalized patients and about a hundred outpatients for whom she was providing food and medication, and sometimes clothing. People often come to her with nothing but their illness. She finds things for them. She's an all-purpose medical phenomenon. Although she doesn't speak French and at first had learned only bits and pieces of Creole, she communicates seamlessly with her Haitian staff and patients.

In fact, her Creole pronunciation is atrocious, but it's enthusiastic and unhesitating; she's not embarrassed.

"I find that the way I speak the language means that everyone jumps in and gets involved," she says. "It means that everyone knows what's going on, and as they talk and help me make myself understood, their illness and even HIV become something that's discussed and open." Haitians around her are always smiling inwardly as she makes medical pronouncements in Creole to staff and murmurs sweet little things to babies and grannies—all in her broad American accent.

To her patients, Dr. Coffee is at first an apparition, a savior, as Mary Aschenbrenner was to McKenly and his mother. She's miraculous, a kindly, heavenly phenomenon, even though she never puts on airs and is always matter-of-fact and responsive, rather than grand or godly. As they get to know her, she becomes more like a tremendously useful and successful older sister who is constantly getting them out of a jam.

Dr. Coffee takes a fifteen-minute lunch break every day in the hospital courtyard under a raggedy tree with a colleague who buys lunch from the market stalls outside the hospital gates—a lunch that invariably consists of a Haitian peanut butter sandwich on deadly tasteless Haitian bread (I've shared this meal, and I know this bread well), a banana, and a bottle of Coke or Ragaman. Dr. Coffee is vegan, in Haiti; her patients find this unimaginable, meat being the most desired and most unaffordable food they know. The Ragaman soda, a Haitian ginseng drink, is supposed to give you *fòs*, or strength. Ragaman seems to work for Dr. Coffee. She never talks about exhaustion or even fatigue. She never mentions being afraid or worrying about her health or security or about the dangers in Haiti. She's averse to such subjects. She's a person who simply rises to a situation, with no pretensions.

In the aftermath of the earthquake, she walked into a perfect vacuum of need that she was uniquely able to fill. A person like Dr. Coffee will call this luck. Especially since not all health care work in disaster zones is so clear-cut. Dr. Coffee, for example, has never been the person who has had to shepherd her medicines and supplies through Haitian customs—a Herculean task that often involves bribery and political gymnastics that even Haitian politicians who are used to the game sometimes find baroque and twisted. Someone else does the dirty work for her. She didn't have to build her ward; she didn't have to beg for jets to fly in emergency crews and medical matériel. The earthquake proved to be an apt medical assistant, a provider. All Dr. Coffee had to do in the beginning was arrive on the scene and then be there, roll up her sleeves, see what the need was, organize everything, make sure everything was in working order, and get down to work herself. That's all. And that's what she did.

Later, it got harder.

4

BLACK ROUGE'S TOUR: I

Pousyè pa leve san van
Dust doesn't rise without the wind

Jerry and Samuel's friend and cell phone sharer is Black Rouge (not his real name—but his real nickname). Black has been living in a slapdash shack in the Marché Salomon since the earthquake destroyed his house and his Internet café. He is old enough to remember Jean-Claude (Baby Doc) Duvalier, and he's sick of Duvalier, who—at the time when I was hanging out with Black—was poised to return to Haiti. When I ask Black Rouge what's worst about life in Haiti now, he adds Baby Doc to the list of what's to be despised, and also the UN's International Organization for Migration, which has had a very visible presence in Haiti since the earthquake.

Black Rouge's neighborhood in Marché Salomon was totally destroyed in the catastrophe, although you wouldn't know it if this was the first time you were seeing it. Black tours me around the area. He's an effusive, even ebullient guide, for one who lost so much. He points out that the new shacks, which were built by the people of the neighborhood, look pretty good. They line the streets and have real doors with locks. But when it rains, he says, "we're all in the mud." *Nou tout nan labou.*

So many of Black Rouge's friends and family were killed or injured in the earthquake, he hasn't even counted them. "But that's why these little shacks are big enough," Black Rouge says. "You don't have to have rooms for the dead." He's thirty-five and living with a younger cousin who lost his wife and kids (the cousin keeps a wallet-size studio photo of them in his backpack—all that remains). The shack also houses Black Rouge's girlfriend and another relative. "None of us can really sleep in here, so we just wait for morning, when we can go back into the streets," Black says. He has a diamond earring and the buckle on his belt is a bull's head made of brass. He's got some heft to him, unlike most Haitians. He'd be building something new now, but it's too expensive to clear away so much rubble, he says. When the earthquake struck, Black was adding a new floor to the building where his business was, across the street, but the guy whom Black had paid for the material was killed with his wife, next door, and all the material lost. Black gestures at the spot.

On the afternoon of the quake, Black went out to buy a snack. That was when the house that his father had built for his very extended family, which included thirty-six children, collapsed. Black Rouge's Internet café was a part of the complex that he and his father had kept adding on to over the years as the family expanded, so when the house fell, the business was also destroyed. One reason the house and houses like it in the neighborhood were so easily brought down by the quake was that they were not ever *designed.* They did not have what one might call architectural integrity or anti-seismic rebolting. Sometimes they did not even have four walls under a roof, but only three or so walls; the buildings were always in a state of construction, which made them look, like so many neighborhoods long before the quake, as if they had never really gone up, or were *always* falling down or about to fall down. *Poko fini, deja tonbe.*

Black Rouge doesn't think about how things might have turned out if his house had been built to some code or standard. This is not because he is irresponsible or unthinking, but because he lives inside

Haitian reality. Since here there is no state as one thinks of it elsewhere, no long arm, no reach into the daily life of people (except as a vacuum or omission, a negative force, a blank space), the idea of norms, standards, and regulatory control is not part of the common language. When such concepts are introduced, mostly just in theory, they are often batted away as just too expensive or difficult or as unacceptable intrusions on personal freedom. In this way, Haiti can be seen as a libertarian's dream. The lack of responsive government has understandably generated a civic tendency toward rejection of regulation. In many ways, Haiti feels like a country still in the throes of self-creation— something like the Wild West in the United States, little more than a century ago. That's also why the country attracts so many rogues and speculators from the outside.

Black Rouge takes me around the ruins of his old place. Schoolbooks lie in the rubble; a ruined computer sits in the dust, next to a headless, naked, one-legged doll. It is a cliché of photojournalists' pictures of wreckage and war around the world that there is always a half-naked doll, foreground. But there always *is* a half-naked doll. No one photographs, or even mentions, human shit, but that, too, is always there in the wake of disaster. Here, among scattered cement blocks, is the customary discreet pile, as well as empty bottles of beer and *klerin,* the raw Haitian rum that Milfort Bruno used to enjoy. People have been drinking here recently, sleeping here, possibly living here.

We leave one room and come into another: the wall between the two rooms has fallen down, but the door frame is still up, and Black Rouge opens the door formally, ushering me before him, rather than simply passing through the emptiness where the wall once was. This next room is more like a terrace now. It's all floor and has no walls whatsoever, and no roof. I can see the Caribbean from here. Nice: it looks very blue and free. I look directly down once, but not twice, because the view from what must have been the fourth floor of this building is vertiginous now, and I'm standing on a thin floor that extends beyond the rubble of other floors like it. It's not clear what's supporting this ledge I'm standing on.

Over in the other direction, within Black's ruined compound, a woman in a yellow and orange shift is sitting on a metal folding chair, almost as if she were in a room floating in air—her chair resting on a promontory that sticks out from a warren of half-destroyed walls and roofs. Her graying hair is straightened and pulled back in a bun, and she's sewing something blue. Behind her a curtain waves in a slight evening breeze. Behind the curtain must be the remains of a room. The seamstress is at least 150 yards away from me, but I can see her because, between the floor I'm standing on and her ledge, all the other rooms and houses and stairways and walls have fallen away. She's serious. She's older. She has a job to do and she's doing it, miraculously. It's as if, seeing her there floating over the gray rubble in her yellow dress, preoccupied, her hands busy, her head bent toward the blue project on her lap, I am looking back through time and the earthquake and those vanished walls at old Haiti.

Black Rouge assures me that there are many people like the seamstress living and working in the condemned housing in the neighborhood and all over the city. In this one block of destruction, people are building all kinds of new housing. Fresh walls are going up in the distance, their mortar whitish and clean, and some new roofs stretch out below my perch, none of the construction seeming to code, to any code whatsoever. To be honest, I don't like being up here—it's a little too obvious what might happen if there were an aftershock.

It was true that the Ministry of Public Works—the Ministère des Travaux Publics, Transports & Communications—had gone around town assessing buildings that had been shaken as the earthquake passed. Its personnel branded thousands of buildings with MTPTC's stenciled initials spray-painted in red (condemned), yellow (must be reinforced), or green (fine as is). But afterward, MTPTC normally did not have the resources or documentation that would have allowed it to inspect new construction, so the recent work at Black's was free-form and DIY. Anyway, I happened to know that there were people from Public Works who, for a price, had allowed homeowners to stencil shaky houses with whatever color they chose. So even those painstaking MTPTC stencils—a surprising sign of municipal responsibility in a place where normally there was none—could not be trusted.

5

ZOMBIES OF THE WORLD

Bokò ba w pwen, men li pa di al dòmi gran chmen
The priest gives you protection, but he doesn't say
now go lie down on the highway

I'm sitting at the gate at Miami International Airport. This is my third flight down to Haiti after the earthquake, the flight on which I first noticed the buildup of white passengers. I'm listening in on the conversations not just of rookie missionaries and sinewy contractors from Arkansas, and Swiss medical teams, but also of Haitians who live abroad and are returning to help rebuild the country. These are a handful of men and women in their thirties and forties; most are dressed in business clothes. They are flying down for meetings. As with the outsiders, you can feel their résumés growing against the background of the earthquake's destruction. Nonetheless, here they are. Two of the women are going down for an educational nongovernmental organization they helped start up in Carrefour, near Port-au-Prince, after the earthquake. Some of the men are going to be working with construction-aid groups (or did they mean rubble-removal?); one of these sounds as if he'll be working in security. And there are three who are going back home to participate in the latest round of elections. There's a joke in Haiti that if you get three Haitian men together, you'll have three presidential candidates. These three are talking politics and I gravitate toward them.

They are doing the usual star turns, speaking the usual *bla-bla-bla,* as empty political talk is known in Creole. First, one of the men gives a peroration on corruption and responsibility. The next speaks about justice and the Constitution (a new constitution was written in 1987, after Jean-Claude Duvalier fled; it is a liberal, utopian document that is today more honored in the breach . . .), and about the earthquake and change. And then, inevitable among the politically minded in Haiti, the conversation turns to the Haitian Revolution, a true bottom-up rebellion if ever there was one, the real change agent in Haitian history. The heroes and events of this revolution show up in Haitian political talk with the constancy of morning. It is as though every time an American talked about a presidential election, he were to launch into an analysis of Jefferson and Washington and Adams. The revolutionary forefathers are present in Haitians' minds, at least in the minds of the political class, as virtual contemporaries.

The average person, too, can give you some pretty good details about the battles and the uprisings of the slaves' revolution against France that transformed Haiti from a golden sugar colony, the most profitable of all France's domains at the time, into the world's first black republic. Even charming, illiterate ragamuffins in the shantytowns will launch into Dessalines discussions when talking about "*sitiasyon-nan,*" or the situation. They know something of the record, from the days of the Jamaican-born slave leader Boukman in the embryonic stages of the revolution, to the retaking of power by the mulatto elite, a fraught and complicated period of about three decades that began with the 1791 slave attacks on the sugar plantations of the north. The attacks were organized and coordinated by the slaves at a series of legendary voodoo ceremonies in the forests that the white masters believed were Sunday "dances" where the slaves let off steam.

Indeed.

Toussaint, Dessalines, and Christophe—first slaves and then revolutionary generals, all—walk beside modern political figures like Baby Doc, Aristide, and Préval in Haitian minds. This is a country whose political class constantly refers—as if seeking advice and counsel—to eighteenth-and nineteenth-century decisions made by former slaves in the face of an intransigent and brutal colonial power. In analyzing the country's problems today, they see exact parallels to the problems the slaves faced in the late 1700s. Perhaps because that history is so remarkable, and singular.

The most important of all prerevolutionary voodoo ceremonies was at Bois Caïman (or Crocodile Woods), where, according to legend and oral tradition in the area, Boukman presided over the sacrifice of a pig and swore the congregation to revolution. Boukman, according to some accounts, had been sold from Jamaica to a slave master in Haiti and could read (hence his name); his Jamaican owners sold him, it was said, because he had a tendency to run away and had also tried to teach other slaves to read. With astounding organization for the era (no Twitter or Facebook, no telephones, no short-wave, and, indeed, not much posting of tracts on poles or reading of pamphlets by mostly illiterate slaves, but only drums and word of mouth), the slaves on the plantations of the north rose up within a week of the Bois Caïman ceremony and began to burn down the masters' houses and sugarworks. Soon, all of the northern plantations were held by the revolutionaries, and the surviving masters found themselves holed up with their families (and often with their loyal retainers) in the northern capital, Le Cap. Not long afterward, Boukman was killed by the French, and his severed head displayed on a pole. In spite of its leader's fate, the success of the inciting ceremony and voodoo's historic connection to revolution and liberty have left an indelible mark in Haitians' minds.

By the way, controversy still rages around Bois Caïman itself, with some historians arguing that it is myth and others citing French contemporary information, gathered through torture of slaves, seeming to prove the ceremony was very real indeed. In any case, a Haitian meeting today where any kind of radical development or action is contemplated might be called, by its participants, the Bois Caïman of post-quake Haiti, say, or the Bois Caïman of education reform.

~

I'd seen my own mini Bois Caïmans, voodoo ceremonies with politics and without. Here is the one without politics, years ago, in the countryside in the southwest:

I'm lying on a mat under the stars. It must be at least one in the morning but I'm not wearing a watch. The place is so crowded that my mat isn't even under the peristyle's roof, a weaving of fronds. I'm looking straight up at black night, bright stars, Milky Way. Toddlers careen in drunken sleepiness around me; they stumble over me. One small girl has tucked herself under my arm. The wailing is still going on inside the temple, and Miss has just come to me with a topless thermos of hot coffee that tastes as if it has cinnamon or maybe chicory in it, and so much sugar. I was staying with Miss, on the floor of her two-room house. So grateful for the coffee. I'd been about to fall asleep: with a little distance, the drums lethargize you, while they're energizing the inner circle. But now, the three drummers under the palm frond roof are going double time, it seems, and the ground beneath me is shaking.

Possibly Ogoun, the warrior god, has come down, but I can't see through the bodies as I sit up and turn to look. I can't tell one kind of drumming from another, the rhythm for the arrival of one kind of god from the rhythm for another. Haitians can. Over in a corner where I can see them, a couple is locked in an enthusiastic embrace. Miss sits upright next to me on my mat. All day today, she was picking beans and working in the little family field, and worrying, as usual, about her sister-in-law Lucy's cough and fever. So tonight, the ceremony feels particularly welcome to her. A crowd of men is standing on one side of the temple. When the coffee takes hold, I rouse myself and stand and push through the crowd to watch what's happening.

An older woman I've met several times is reeling around a circle of worshippers at the peristyle's center. The crowd concentrates so hard; no one will answer my question: Who is this? Which god, or *lwa* in Creole, is in possession here? These are all people who know this woman, have known her since they were small. She's got a stall in the regional market at Fond des Nègres. But right now they don't treat her as the person she is in daily life. They make way for her, they bow slightly when she approaches. She's smoking a cigar, I see now. Whatever, whatever. I don't get it.

A young boy is sick with a fever and he is pushed toward her. She puts her hand on his head and looks down into his eyes fiercely. She slaps at him with the flat of her machete. She's clearly not a woman right now, but a man, a male god. She is, I later learn, Ogoun, warrior god. The boy stands totally still under her grasp. She turns, takes something, and washes the boy, his hands and his face and his hair, in *klerin*. She puts both hands back on his head. He's immobile. And then, roughly, she pushes him away. I see the boy later, sleeping with his mother and sister under a tree. The ceremony continues almost until sunrise. And Miss gets up from her mat to go to the fields again.

Here is the voodoo ceremony with politics, a two-hour drive from Port-au-Prince, and probably the most formal service I've ever seen:

This is Souvenance, a traditional Easter-time festival in the Artibonite Valley, a weeklong *bamboche,* or party, that welcomes politicians. Here, voodoo worship openly combines with electoral politics. Voodoo networks in the Artibonite are especially well organized, and Souvenance always feels more like a national convention than a service. On my first visit to the festival, a little more than a year after Duvalier fled the country, men in suits stood here and there all day, conniving, gossiping, and planning in the shade of a giant *mapou* tree, which was impressive and antediluvial, with roots that reached out from the sides of the temple all the way to the cars in the parking area. (The *mapou* belongs to Legba, the master of the crossroads, one of the most important gods in the pantheon, Apollo to Ogoun's Ares.)

At the time of this festival, in 1987, the priest at Souvenance was Bien-Aimé, and all the senatorial candidates and presidential candidates were coming to seek his approval, virtually his endorsement, since in a sense Bien-Aimé was like a local machine boss and could get out the vote, when finally there was a real vote in the wake of the overthrow of the Duvalier dynasty.

As night fell, the generator kicked in, lights went on around the temple, and the drums began. Chickens and goats were sacrificed, and the men continued doing what they do, arriving and departing in jeeps, standing in the peristyle or under the *mapou,* their heads together, making alliances or splitting into factions, bargaining, lobbying, exchanging favors, doing deals. At the same time, the gods who came down into the service were making arrangements and exacting promises from the worshippers about illness, disease, love—and politics. Bien-Aimé, emaciated and gray, walked among men and gods like Gandhi, seemingly apart, in his thin trousers and loose shirt of poverty (though he was not poor), an ancient—and holy in his demeanor, but very much a factor in all the machinations around him. Bien-Aimé died in 1990 and his son, Fernand, whose day job was in business in Port-au-Prince, took the reins.

The thread of this ancient religion touches everyone in Haiti, in the country and in the city, among the elite and among the poor, in business and in farming, in politics and in daily life, day and night, in every season. Even visitors, often without their knowing, are affected by it, because voodoo often influences Haitian behavior, as any central cultural orientation will affect a people's behavior.

History itself comes alive through the gods' appearances in ceremony, and during a service, certain characteristic behaviors of historical figures are sometimes imitated. Voodoo carries in it the thread of Haitian history because it was there at the beginning. It's a back-and-forth relationship. The behavior, attitudes, and even the physicality of revolutionary leaders like Boukman, Toussaint, and especially Dessalines, who was the only one of these three still standing at the moment of independence from France in 1804, have been incorporated over the years into voodoo, which helps make these figures from two hundred years ago familiar and seemingly contemporary to all.

When it is the fierce and powerful warrior god, Ogoun, who comes down into a service, this is particularly evident. In voodoo ceremonies, when Ogoun possesses a worshipper, he regularly behaves very much as if he were one of the early generals, as oral legend and a few depictions have portrayed them to later generations. Like Dessalines: Ogoun of the straight back, the rigid posture, the superhuman grip, the three-cornered hat, the sword, the fire. It bears mentioning here that no historically verifiable image of Dessalines has come down to us from his day. This makes his physical presence, so instantly recognizable, even more resonant: a myth, an idea, made flesh. Only two facts are known with some certainty about Dessalines's physical being: He was strong. He was stout.

It goes without saying that Ogoun came before the heroes of independence. He is probably at least as ancient as Jehovah and, in one form or another, perhaps far older. He carries the same kind of weight in voodoo that Ares did in early Greek religion, and he is also affiliated with iron-working, like Hephaestos. But as a figure in voodoo ceremony, the *lwa* Ogoun has also incorporated an eighteenth-century revolutionary's aspect. During a service, this god strides, and sometimes wields a whip as if he were a foreman or slave driver on a plantation (in the French colony, slave drivers were usually prominent slaves themselves, and as chattel were at least twice as valuable as the average field hand). Sometimes—in a more elaborate, well-funded ceremony— Ogoun may even appear on horseback, as a slave driver might have done. During a service, Ogoun makes important, even self-important, pronouncements. He decrees. He's like a general, but also like an arrogant political leader.

You can be at a ceremony under a tree in the Haitian mountains or in a seaside shantytown or in the rubble of the earthquake or in a living room in Brooklyn, but when Ogoun enters the service, with his red kerchief (the color of war and blood), and his terrible, awesome toughness and inescapable control, you are not just in the presence of an ancient African god and ruler, you're in the thrall of a mythic Dessalines. From 1915 to 1934, during the U.S. occupation of Haiti, Haitian rebel guerrillas also evoked Dessalines and Ogoun, often wearing the god's red scarf as they descended on the Marines.

And yet I still feel, after attending a voodoo service, that it's just possible that everyone's pretending, or at least wittingly accepting. One says to oneself: Can they possibly believe all this? It's stunningly theatrical and participatory. It's as if, instead of hearing about Jesus being the embodiment of God as man, you yourself have the privilege of embodying that contradiction yourself, when the god arrives to possess you. The people who attend voodoo ceremonies—even the poorest of the country people and shantytown dwellers—may have sometimes seen television. They have, possibly, come into contact with and even eaten frozen foods; they sometimes make use of the combustion engine. Many use cell phones. They are not eighteenth-century enslaved people. And yet they worship the gods of old Africa who come down poles or up out of the earth to possess worshippers, who then spit and swing machetes at the congregation. It's very hard to see and understand all this without the hypersecularism of modern Western attitudes affecting one's ability to accept.

One wonders sometimes—often—if the *houngan* is simply acting the role of the god, and whether the congregation is well aware of this, and whether, possibly, everyone is just staging a ritual they all know has little, or nothing, to do with higher powers. Perhaps, as Jews will sometimes say about their own religion, some of these Haitians are doing what they do because they've always done it, and they've been doing some form of it for two thousand years or longer. And of course in juxtaposition to my sophisticated, secular, postmodern desire not to believe in the ritual and rigmarole of any religion is many Haitians' fierce and even desperate desire and need to believe.

If the possessions by the gods are not wholly experienced as real, but can sometimes be improvised theatricals played according to strict rules, what does that mean for the religion's practitioners, and even for Haiti? You are not supposed to ask this question, in part because it could be interpreted as demeaning to believers. It is wholly an outsider's question, and not one that is easily put to congregants, or even easily put down on paper. For most Haitians at a ceremony, this is community, escape, entertainment, and as much transcendence as is allowed to them. For others, the ceremony represents Haitian patrimony and inheritance, and they take pride in it even when they have little or no religious belief. Still, the foundational and pervasive religion of the country is considered even by its practitioners to be performance, a show of sorts, prepared like theater, with props, costumes, and some degree of planning, and rehearsed in part, like theater. There is more narrative and plot and drama in a voodoo service than I've seen in any Western religion, including those that are inflected by African custom. Stories are not told by priest to congregation but rather acted out by all. This is a culture that values theater and a certain degree of artifice, even a great degree.

Artifice and duplicity were natural and necessary survival methods during slavery, when whole areas of slave life were kept hidden from masters, and when one slave might pretend to be his own brother or cousin in order to avoid punishment—or worse. (Slaves often had one name in the fields—their slave name—and another more traditionally African name when they were in the quarters among themselves, a *nom de guerre* from birth, in a sense.). The Haitian language itself, with the words *li,* as the all-purpose pronoun that stands in for "he," "she," "it," "him," and "her," and *nou,* the all-purpose pronoun that can mean either "we" or "us" or "you" plural, effectively hides identity and agency, and can—sometimes purposefully—mislead those who do not fully understand the whole context of a narrative. Nonnative speakers often confuse the use of these slippery pronouns with simplicity of grammar, but it is not that, or not only.

Complicated forms of "hiding" exist in Haitian history, and in behavior today, as well. During slave days, slaves hid voodoo practice behind a façade of Catholic worship, and even today, every voodoo god has a syncretic saint. Ogoun himself is often addressed as Saint Jacques. There was literal hiding, too. Slaves who were facing corporal punishment or who were just sick of the viciousness and submission of plantation life not

infrequently fled the slave shacks to run into hiding, and relative freedom, in the mountains. This was known as *marronage,* which basically
means taking to the hills, from the Spanish *cimarrón,* or dweller in the
hills. In English, such runaways were called maroons. From their mountainside villages, hidden from the planters, the fugitive slaves would now
and then sneak back to the plantation to steal necessities or bring family
members away into hiding. Often, great bands of slaves lived in hidden
mountain colonies. These hidden slaves were much feared.

In common parlance today, *marronage* has come to mean hiding in
full view: a Haitian who works for the State Department in an aid program, or—now—an earthquake relief program, might very well think of
himself or herself as doing some interim work but also (in private and
in private conversation) as being a militant leftist fighter for the Haitian
people. He might tell his close friends that he's involved in a kind of *marronage.* This word was used frequently by Aristide's supporters and friends
to refer to his status when he returned from his first exile—under the
aegis of the U.S. Marines and the Clinton administration. He was seen
as pretending to side with the planters, while he was—metaphysically at
least—still in the mountains with the rebels.

The flip side of this metaphorical *marronage* is what's known in Haiti
as *la politique de doublure,* or "the politics of the stand-in." Both *marronage* and *doublure* involve duplicity or falseness where Haitians' political
and personal dealings with a light-skinned ruling class or a foreign interloper are concerned. The term *doublure,* which means understudy in
French, comes from the habit, during the second half-century of independent Haitian history, of installing a dark-skinned president while the
entire administration was actually run by light-skinned members of the
mercantile elite; so that a malleable, complaisant black man would keep
the population happy and provide a public face for the Haitian government while behind him, the elite operated as usual, with all its corruption, its machinations, its deals, and its exploitation of the state. (One
could argue that this was what the Clinton people hoped to do with
Aristide in 1994.) This habit, however, was quickly abandoned by the

Marines during the U.S. occupation, whose officers, often hailing from the Southern states, did not take to black administrations; possibly *doublure*'s use was not fully understood by American officers so soon, only a half-century, after the end of the Civil War. In any case, the occupation featured four light-skinned Haitian presidents.

In other words, the habits of masquerade acquired during two centuries of intense slave conditions have continued to play out in Haitian governance and society. The British writer Graham Greene called the Haitians "comedians," in the French sense, meaning actors or players, as well as humor-mongers. This is still true (obviously, only to a degree), especially when Haitians are dealing with outsiders. (Greene, a particularly acute but short-term visitor to Haiti, would have counted himself among these.) Haitians may do what we expect of them, but they don't necessarily mean it. A false and often charming aspect can serve them as a protective shield.

Equally, Haitians often suspect that the outsider is not as he presents himself. They certainly don't believe in our innocence and the purity of our motivation, even when we ourselves do. The American movie director Jonathan Demme, for example, once phoned his friend Jean Dominique, the seasoned Haitian journalist who was later assassinated, to wish him a happy New Year.

"Happy New Year, Jean," said Demme, a man who is notoriously wide-eyed and sweet.

According to Demme, Dominique's acid and immediate reply, in French-accented English, was "Jonathan, what is your *agenda*?"

Many Haitians will approach outsiders with suspicion and dread, as well as, sometimes, opportunistic expectancy. These behaviors are based on history—the self-defense of the slave in plantation economies—but also on the habitual watchfulness of voodoo, which may be the same thing. A new outsider coming into a village, or a voodoo ceremony, or a shantytown courtyard, will be hard-pressed to discover who is the person in command of the situation. It's rarely the person you're guided to, or the person who seems to be running the show. More often, it's the little old man, like Bien-Aimé, or an unprepossessing woman sitting off to the side, almost invisible under her broad-brimmed straw hat.

One morning a few years ago, Wyclef Jean came to the palace with his entourage for an interview with President Préval. Jean himself would soon be running for president of Haiti, but he had lived outside Haiti for his entire adult life and had some of the outlook of a foreigner. He was wearing a pinstripe suit. He's a big, tall, imposing man, and he was primed for this personal meeting with the supreme Haitian authority. So he was quite peremptory when a slight, soft-spoken man in a guayabera, trousers, and sandals began chatting with him and did not seem likely to stop.

"I'm here to speak to President Préval," Jean said, barely hiding his impatience.

"Well, that's good, because I am President Préval," the man replied.

Préval told me this story, with relish.

As all the new outsiders coming in from Miami and LaGuardia and elsewhere landed on the tarmac at Toussaint Louverture airport in Port-au-Prince and met up with their new Haitian friends and contacts, everything was bonhomie and jokes and laughter—light banter and joking being a *specialité* of the country. But over time, those relationships would come under siege, and some would turn false and bitter as people were pushed and pulled in the cruel machinery of politics and development. This is what happened to many small-time, first-time, would-be American missionaries when they arrived here to rebuild Haiti at the community level, after the earthquake, and were simultaneously welcomed and rebuffed, treated with respect and lied to, deferred to like dignitaries and mocked as fools. Defensiveness is often a default mode here.

Even in a good situation, it takes a very long time for the wall to come down between Haitians and their foreign friends. What makes it odd and difficult is the seeming closeness, the apparent intimacy, the jocular delight. With a new English or French friend, one rarely feels an immediate bond, but many Haitians, when one first meets them, seem utterly available and transparent. It's no surprise that they're not, but it's hard for many outsiders to understand, especially if they don't have much time to spend in the country. With most of my Haitian friends, I've gotten beyond this barrier, but with a few, I've simply stopped trying to get past the ramparts of the citadelle. We remain at one level. Even with Samuel and Jerry, who claim they've known me virtually since they were born, I'm still not beyond the barricade. I'm a white object, not quite a person, certainly not a Haitian. Sometimes I think they don't exactly believe I'm real. I appear in their lives and then disappear, like a spirit.

Ogoun's costume and speech may exhibit small regional and temporal tweaks, but like the other gods of the pantheon who visit voodoo ceremonies, Ogoun is always essentially the same no matter whom he possesses, no matter where the ceremony takes place. It's the eerie, inescapable truth of voodoo. And who can say which came first, the traits of the god, or the traits of the human hero? Ogoun as he appears today may have taken on revolutionary traits, but it is just as likely that Dessalines and Christophe adopted familiar traits of Ogoun, knowing that this would resonate with their followers. So today, Ogoun and the heroes have become nearly interchangeable, and each resonates with the identity of the other.

The gods can be useful in this way. François Duvalier adopted one himself. Because of his long love affair with death, and his desire to instill fear, Papa Doc chose Baron Samedi, god of the cemetery. This was an effective ploy. Baron is the gravedigger of voodoo. A dead person cannot cross to the other side, cannot truly rest in death, without Baron's good offices, like Charon, who pilots the ferry across the river Styx in Greek mythology. When you hear the voice of Duvalier on tape, it's the same reedy, soft, nasal, and physically creepy voice that you hear from Baron when he enters a ceremony, and Papa Doc and the god look alike, with their aura of darkness, formally dressed in a dark business suit (or—for the god—just a frayed business jacket, if the ceremony is poor), wearing dark glasses and a dark old-fashioned hat.

Papa Doc used voodoo symbolism broadly. He dressed the Tonton Macoute death squads (more formally known as the National Security Volunteers) in a uniform of denim clothing and a slouchy denim hat like that of the peasant god of the fields, Kouzin Zaka. In Haitian folklore, the actual Tonton Macoute (which translates as "Uncle Bag," and for whom the secret police was nicknamed) is an offspring of Zaka. Uncle Bag is a menacing fairy-tale figure from the voodoo tradition, a nighttime, countryside bogeyman who carries a straw bag known in Creole as a *makout,* into which he disappears naughty children—a sort of anti–Santa Claus.

Duvalier's son, Jean-Claude, who followed his father to power, never found a god with whom he could be identified, and this contributed to his lack of popularity. But then, with his large head and bulky body and his physical awkwardness and personal diffidence, he resembled nothing so much as a Teletubby, supremely ungodlike even in the voodoo pantheon, which includes many idiosyncratic and flawed gods.

With outsize historical figures such as Dessalines and Christophe marching around in their psyches, Haitians—again, especially the political class—appear sometimes to be following a script as they make decisions. When Haitians think about powerful outsiders in terms of politics (for example, the United States, the French, the UN, the Canadians, the World Bank, the Organization of American States), they see the racist, imperial face of Napoleon at the turn of the nineteenth century. (As if, again to put it in American terms, we were to imagine George III every time we thought about our diplomatic relations with the Court of St. James.)

When Haitians think about do-gooders like the ones rushing down to Haiti since the earthquake, they remember the on-again, off-again relationship between the rebel slave leaders and the friendly-seeming directorate of the French Republic (this is after the French Revolution and during the Haitian Revolution). This early history created a profoundly mistrustful political climate for Haiti, especially in terms of international relations, that still exists today. And if for a moment a Haitian politician allows himself to let down that guard and tries to do twenty-first-century business and deal with the outside world, invariably at some point he will be taken to be collaborating with forces that are bent on destroying the slave descendants' hard-won sovereignty and liberty. He'll be seen in eighteenth-century terms: as a monarchist, a loyalist, a traitor to the revolution. As a quisling, to speak anachronistically.

A description of a recent meeting among Haitian and American doctors trying to organize a new health care group gives a flavor of this kind of thing. This is an American doctor writing:

> What I didn't know about this Haitian doctor was that after a few beers he turns into a regular Che Guevara, oscillating from denunciations of Paul Farmer: "He is my friend . . . (shaking his head Creole style), but I don't concur with his methods"; to denunciations of Martelly: "He comes from nowhere and suddenly (headshake again) he has power and installs all his friends in positions of power"; to denunciations of [former prime minister] Garry Conille: "Come on, what does he know? He was with Bill Clinton . . . not even a Haitian . . ."
>
> Finally this guy tells me that we "must look not to the government or other NGOs but to the *communauté*." By this he means going to the peasants and asking them to run the [new health care organization]. Very romantic. I think Pol Pot tried this and heads did roll. Luckily this guy isn't president.

And so, abetted by its presence in voodoo ritual and ceremony, Haitian history and its habits march directly into the thoughts of everyday people as well as professionals and officials as they brood about relief and reconstruction after the earthquake and deal with the situation. Back at the gate at Miami International Airport, here is one of the politically minded Haitians, waiting in the business-class line now, and explaining to his friends why seductive U.S. plans for Haiti since the earthquake must be resisted: "*Si nou aksepte* French overtures in 1803, *nou* been destroyed, you know." If we had accepted French overtures in 1803, we would have been destroyed.

Toussaint Louverture *did* accept French offers in 1803; the French— at that moment in a position of military strength—promised him his freedom if he would hand over the command of his rebel troops to them. He agreed, securing also an amnesty for his top deputies, but instead of keeping their part of the bargain, the French arrested Toussaint at his country home, along with his sons, and sent him off to the Fort de Joux, a remote prison in the Jura mountains in France, where he died soon afterward, of neglect and exposure.

This is the best-known of the white man's gross betrayals of Haitian trust, and it resonates in Haiti. Their smartest leader trusted the white man, was betrayed, and therefore died. What lesson does that teach you in history class? Especially since it was Dessalines, the intransigent, the survivor, the refuser, the *resilient,* who turned his back on further French proposals and led the country to independence within a year.

This hopeful politician's interpretation of history, at the airport in Miami in 2010, may not have been exactly right, but in its broader contours it was apt. In 1804, Dessalines is said to have ripped the white stripe from the French *tricolore* in order to create the new red and blue Haitian flag. The message: the white man will have nothing to do with our destiny. Without Dessalines's absolute refusal to engage in Napoleonic dreams for Haiti, there might well have been no independence and probably no true liberty for the Haitian slaves for another half-century or more. For whatever "true liberty" has been worth.

As it was, the U.S. government refused to recognize Haiti until 1862—during the Civil War, when the Union saw no further need to protect the interests of the slaveholding Southern states. In her book *Haiti and the United States: The Psychological Moment,* Brenda Gayle Plummer provides the details of the back-and-forth over recognition in the U.S. legislature.

One argument made in the U.S. Congress against recognition was that if Haiti were recognized, the United States would send an ambassador to Port-au-Prince, and Haiti would similarly present its own ambassador in Washington. Representative Samuel Cox of Ohio, no Southerner, described to his fellow congressmen the difficulty he foresaw with this situation, proclaiming:

> How fine it will look . . . to welcome here at the White House an African, full-blooded, all gilded and belaced, dressed in court style, with wig and sword and tights and shoe buckles and ribbons and spangles and many other adornments which African vanity will suggest! . . . With what admiring awe will [slaves fleeing the South] approach this ebony demigod while all decent and sensible white people will laugh the silly and ridiculous ceremony to scorn!

But Cox failed to win over the highly practical Abraham Lincoln, who valued Haitian trade and the symbolic idea of purely black nations (the idea suggesting to Lincoln, then, that the United States might eventually be a purely white one, if black Americans had places like Haiti or Liberia to emigrate to). In the event, Haiti got recognition, and Frederick Douglass became one of our first emissaries to the island. In Jackson Park, Chicago, at the world's fair in 1893, near the end of his life and more than a century after the Haitian Revolution began, Douglass gave a stirring lecture on Haiti at the dedication of the fair's Haitian Pavilion.

"Until Haiti spoke," Douglass told a crowd of 1,500 respectful Chicagoans gathered in a local African-American church, "the slave ship, followed by hungry sharks, greedy to devour the dead and dying slaves flung overboard to feed them, ploughed in peace the South Atlantic, painting the sea with the Negro's blood." Douglass's familiar mane was gray by now, and his coattails long and formal. But the fire was still in him. Standing there before the altar in the recently built church, he unloosed a blistering cannonade against American mercenaries who were busy fomenting internecine battles in Haiti, and told his receptive audience that the United States had "not yet forgiven Haiti for being black." His words ring out from Chicago to this day.

It always surprises me how Haitians are viewed in the media and by people I meet. I hear described to me, and I read about, a people who are destitute, pathetic, uneducated, and probably irredeemable, and who are, as Douglass said, not yet forgiven for being black. But I know the Haitians as the sons and daughters of a history even more brilliant and amazing than our own, and—even in the face of scarcity and disease— proud, able, and useful. It's the inheritance of their history that has provided a bulwark of strength to Haitians over the centuries, and that has developed *resilience* in the national character (if there is such a thing as national character), although Haitian revolutionary history has proven a double-edged legacy.

The Haitian Revolution was one of the three defining revolutions of the 1700s, and as much as the American and French Revolutions, it has shaped the world we all live in. It destroyed the era's economy of slave capitalism; it wrecked the global ruling powers' dreams of eternal colonialism. The Haitian Revolution, outcome of the fervor and intelligence of so many unlettered and enslaved Fred Voodoos, anonymous but valiant warriors, also extended the ideas of the Rights of Man to *all* men and women; and it suggested the concept of labor rights that was later expanded on in Europe and, eventually, the whole world. It distracted Napoleon and forced him to sell the Louisiana Territory to the Americans, thereby turning the United States into a continental power. In addition, the slaves' triumph in Haiti limited France's future economic power and ironically made an opening in the global economy for the rising United States, which was still the beneficiary of its own unpaid slave labor force.

All of this has gone largely unacknowledged, for the Haitian Revolution sought to destroy something very ugly, but at the same time something upon which the greatest fortunes in France as well as in the rest of the European world and in the United States had been based. Simply put, empire was based on slavery. Haiti, during the height of its wealth, was the giant work camp of the world.

The entire colony functioned as a concentration camp. Slaves were worked to death and then replaced by fresh imports from Africa. Instead of valuing the children of slaves as future workers, masters saw them as a resource waster, because it took at least ten years to grow them into useful slaves, and meanwhile, they were eating up calories better spent on working adults. It was smarter business to neglect these children and allow them to perish while replacing their worn-out parents with fresh chattel from Africa. This was not a written policy; rather, it was a plantation owner's economic imperative. In any case, the birthrate on the plantations was unnaturally low, because the ratio of work performed to calories consumed did not allow for normal levels of reproduction. High suicide rates—among slaves, who were adept with poison—also fueled the plantation masters' need for new African flesh.

This slave-replenishment policy backfired on the French masters, however. The low birthrate on Haiti's plantations, along with the failure of many slave children to reach maturity, meant that the slave population had to be replaced and increased not by slaves' babies and toddlers, all of whom would have grown up within the confines of plantation culture and norms, but with new, adult Africans, kidnapped and dispatched by slave dealers, and very angry. The new African slaves, or *congos,* as they were called, were capable of cutting cane, and it followed that they were also good at wielding weapons, since the machete could serve both purposes. By the time of the revolt, slaves outnumbered the master class ten to one. (By contrast, in the United States in 1860, on the eve of emancipation, slaves represented only about 13 percent of the country's population. If they had represented more than 50 percent of the population, there would have been no emancipation.)

This overwhelmingly and overwhelming African population in pre-revolutionary Haiti has led to the most repeated metaphors concerning the French colonial slave masters: that they were sitting on a tinderbox, or living on top of a powder keg. It speaks to the masters' profound misunderstanding of their slaves' humanity that they thought a demographic disparity like this one—combined with the repugnant economic disparity that created and defined it—could be contained.

Haiti has always been the most modern of nations—in a historical sense (I don't mean having lots of air conditioners and escalators and new cars). Its revolution of Africans and African-Americans against the European superpower France was by far the earliest of Third World liberation movements. In fact, Haitian history has been a harbinger of the modern world since the landing there of the white man in the 1400s. First came the initial and signature act of globalization: the genocide of a population, in Haiti's case, the indigenous Arawak or Taíno Indians, who were eradicated (unto the last man, woman, and child, it is thought) through enslavement, disease, and overwork within two generations of the white man's appearance on the island's shores.

The colonial economy that followed the destruction of the indigenous islanders was one of the first entirely globalized economies in human history, at every level a model for the modern global economy. Its globalization was much more complete than that of other slave colonies, in part because of the complete wiping out of the Indians. Another reason Haiti was such a productive and lucrative slave-capitalist economy was precisely the extreme extent of the sugar producers' exploitation of continental—or global—disparities. As in today's globalized world, the workers for these New World plantations were from a continent other than that of their masters. No one resisted the settlers' land-grabbing, because Haiti's original inhabitants no longer existed. Like the heads of multinational employers today, plantation owners sometimes lived a world away, in their French chateaux. The product the slave workers made was, as is so often the case today, almost exclusively for export. Today's globalized worker is grossly underpaid; the Africans who were imported to Haiti to produce were absolutely unpaid.

Eventually, modern ideas of human rights that had had to travel three thousand miles by ship from France added intellectual fuel to the slaves' disorientation, their desperation, and their fury at being uprooted from

home and tradition. At Bois Caïman, these combustible global ingredients—French enlightenment stirred into the volatile mixture of African
belief and slavery's enormous discontents—erupted in revolution in
Haiti: the Haitian Spring, if you like. In the ensuing chaos, most of the
remaining whites fled the island or were killed.

After the 2010 earthquake, the racial demographics of Port-au-Prince
sometimes seemed to be tilting back in the other direction. The White
Man Returns. Whites were descending en masse; it was at times as if the
earthquake had weirdly jump-started Haiti's formerly minuscule tourist
industry. But these whites were not tourists: they were development and
relief workers and missionaries—the people from my white flight. While
in the shantytowns a white face is still almost never seen, in the earthquake camps, and in the restaurants, supermarkets, nightclubs, casinos,
bars, health clubs, banks, and boutiques of Haiti's elite, you can't go for a
minute without seeing a foreigner.

Just standing for a few minutes on a corner near the Place Boyer in
Pétionville, at the heart of one of the best neighborhoods in the capital
area, I saw a white woman and a white man go into a music school; I
saw a big white SUV carrying at least five white people head over to
the offices of Doctors Without Borders; I saw a white guy running out
to a fancy bakery; I saw a white man walking with a backpack and cell
phone; I saw a group of white women buying paintings; and I saw, stuck
in traffic, at least three cars filled with white men (driven by Haitians).
When I went to the Giant supermarket a few streets away (one of a few
that survived the quake), I found young white people pushing carts
down air-conditioned aisles and buying things that you used not to
be able to get in Haiti: Cheetos, Doritos, imported meats, and French
cheeses.

When I first came to Haiti, just one such white sighting in a week
would be a cause for curiosity and conversation. Now, there's nothing
strange about it. We know who these people are and why they're here:
they are helping Haiti recover from the earthquake. Misery in Haiti
today is a job creator for the white man. It may sound harsh, but a white

person can make his or her reputation in Haiti now, or at least pad the curriculum vitae, and feel good about "giving back" at the same time. It's a little like the old days, when a young man without prospects might head off across the sea to the colonies to seek his fortune, because plenty of fortune was to be found there. The earthquake has proven to be the biggest attraction in Haitian history, a more potent draw by far than the island's voodoo ceremonies ever were, than its long white beaches, its hot, pre-AIDS sex trade, or its revolutionary forts.

Like Haitian history, voodoo has many lessons to teach outsiders. Take the zombie, probably voodoo's best-known figure. The first time I ever learned anything true about Haitian zombies, which are a small sideshow in voodoo, I was sitting on a terrace of a Catholic retreat up on a hill overlooking the capital back in the 1980s. (This calm and beautiful place, like so many landmarks of the Catholic Church in Haiti, was completely destroyed—razed into pebbles—by the earthquake.) Here, a young priest in a cassock came to me with a mimeographed booklet, a literacy primer he'd been working on with other members of the liberation theological movement in Haiti. The primer, intended for illiterate adults, was called *Goute Sel,* which means *A Taste of Salt.*

I thought it was a strange name, and I asked the priest about it. In Haitian tradition, he told me, a zombie can never be freed from his eternal enslavement unless, by accident, his *bòs* or master allows salt into the zombie's food. Salt gives food taste, and, fortified by the life-giving deliciousness it adds to his rice, the zombie will rise up, his consciousness restored, and throw off the oppression of his master's control.

I managed later to get an interview with a former zombie—hard to believe, I know. He had one of the great Haitian names: Clairvius Narcisse. But zombies, it turned out, were not really the walking dead. They were people who had been drugged or, more often, were mentally challenged or suggestible enough to believe in their own zombification. Clairvius was odd, as I recall—off in some way, like a person with a mental disability who was not on the right meds. And this was a *former* zombie, one who had, at least figuratively, tasted salt and escaped.

Now, as I sit writing in Los Angeles, not far from Hollywood, I feel that zombies are all around me. They're in the movies, on television, on billboards, skull-like and dripping excreta and something that looks like moss. Often they're portrayed as, somehow, phosphorescent. They come to my door at Halloween. They're trendy. There is something about a zombie, I realize, that speaks to us at the beginning of the twenty-first century. They are inherently "dank," a word that now, in the age of zombies, means cool or good.

The zombie is something we all fear becoming, if we think about it. He's frightening in a primordial way, and in a modern way, too. He's dead but he's walking; he has to work even after death. He's the living dead, an ancient figure, but he's also the inanimate animated, like the robot of industrial dystopias. Baron will not take the zombie across to the other side, to the rest that death promises. The other side, among slaves in the New World colonies, was Africa—idealized from memory as the land of freedom. In Haiti, still, when a person dies, it is understood that he or she returns to *lan guinée,* or Africa, and freedom. Roughly translated, *lan guinée* means heaven. (The rest of the world, to Haitians, is known as *lòt bò dlo,* literally "the other side of the water.") For the zombie, this final rest in *lan guinée,* or paradise, is unavailable. Clever Papa Doc! So smart to identify himself with Baron, the gatekeeper to this precious place.

With his perfect obedience and lack of any future, the zombie, who cannot escape from servitude even in death, is the echt citizen in a dictatorship. He's great for fascism (one recent zombie movie was called *The Fourth Reich*). The zombie is willing. He works for free. You feed him very little. He makes no demands. He's like Apple's Chinese factory workers; or like the refugees in Haiti's earthquake camps; or like guest workers in European countries; or like employees at call centers in India or the

Philippines—except he is not desperate, he simply *is;* as such, he's devoid of hope and consciousness, and therefore unable to come up with a critique of the system he's trapped in, or a plan to rise up from his servitude.

There are too many plausible zombies in the world today, and that's why this old African-American figure from slave days has penetrated the global consciousness. We don't want to be turned into *that.* In Haiti, the zombie is the very purest form of the slave, deadened, soulless, egoless, empty-eyed. Becoming a zombie would make a mockery of a slave's one certain free action: suicide.

One reason Papa Doc had his Tonton Macoute death squads wear sunglasses, along with their denims, was to hide their eyes. This, he hoped, would frighten the population. Those hidden eyes might be flat, blank zombie eyes, and therefore the people would imagine the macoutes (their eyes hidden) to be conscienceless zombies, ready and willing to do Duvalier's bidding—no matter what it might be. And they were, and they did.

The zombie is not just the perfect employee; he would make a good grunt in the Gestapo. I once heard a Haitian radio announcer refer to Klaus Barbie, the Nazi known as the Butcher of Lyon, as *"youn ansyen Tonton Makout Hitler,"* one of Hitler's former Tonton Macoutes. Papa Doc identified himself with Dessalines, with an army of zombies, and with Baron, *lwa* of the cemetery and the crossing to death. Amid tensions with the Dominican Republic in the spring of 1963, when the OAS seemed to teeter on the brink of a Haitian intervention, Papa Doc appeared on the steps of the presidential palace in his usual black suit, his arms dangling unmoving by his sides, his face eerily calm, his smile slow to spread, quick to disappear. He was surrounded by Tonton Macoutes. During the crisis that week, his death squads had already killed an estimated hundred or so of his perceived enemies.

A large crowd of costumed carousers had been fed *klerin* by Duvalier supporters and were celebrating now on the palace grounds while the rest of the city cowered and hid from the terror.

". . . [B]ullets and machine guns cannot touch me because Duvalier is firm and unshakeable," Duvalier told the ecstatic crowd. "[R]aise your

souls to the height of your ancestors, and . . . prove that you are men . . .
[A]llow the blood of Dessalines to flow through your veins . . .

"I am already an immaterial being," he told them. He was a god, or
a zombie, or a madman, was the implication—in any case, fruitless to
resist. "No foreigner is going to tell me what to do."

There are Haitians who take zombies seriously to this day, although
often with a micrograin of salt, so to speak. A while ago, I received this
email from Jacques-Richard, a Haitian friend who lives in a hobbit-style
house tucked into the side of a hill in Port-au-Prince. Except for his
house and a few others, the whole neighborhood was destroyed by the
earthquake. He wrote to me in English:

Hi Amy,

The baby is due Christmas week and hopefully will be fine. Air
conditioning in the car may be fixed in the next month . . .

Smith had some "Zombies" sent on him and had to go to Jérémie
to have them removed and almost died. I don't understand these
things but I guess *sa ou pa konnin pi gran pase ou.* [What you don't
know is bigger than you are.]

He's back now, but I will keep an eye out for any signs of Zombie
presence . . .

See you soon and hope you keep in touch.

6

BUILDING BACK BETTER

Bourik chaje pa ka kanpe
The loaded-down donkey cannot stop

Although many of the camps that were set up after Haiti's earthquake have been emptied and taken down, many remain, housing about half a million people. While some of these camps will eventually be depopulated, others are in the process of *permanentization*. This is not an exclusively Haitian phenomenon. Quick-built refugee camps, often run by international humanitarian organizations, were one of the great shelter innovations of the human species in the twentieth century, and are likely to remain the most important form of human urbanization well into the twenty-first—aside from country people's migration to urban centers, which has also changed the face of Haiti in profound ways.

The permanent refugee camp is not entirely new. If one looks at Israel and Palestine, one can easily see how the international aid and development community and the refugee population may work in tandem to keep refugee camps at status quo long after they are initially set up. The Palestinians have been living in camps for more than half a century; most visitors wouldn't even know that they were in a refugee camp in Jabaliya, in Gaza, say. The buildings there are made of concrete and stucco, and there are streets with names, and numbers on the houses, and there are shops, and all the appurtenances of structured—if impoverished—urban life. And yet Jabaliya is a refugee camp, mean, crowded, offering no historical permanence to its residents. The Palestinians live there to make a political point, not necessarily of their own choosing, and because no one else will have them. They are descendants of refugees forced out of their homes during the Israeli war for independence in 1948. The UN has supported the permanentization of the Palestinian camps: the United Nations Relief and Works Agency for Palestine Refugees in the Near East, established in 1949 and with a mandate now through 2014, is the main provider of education, health, and social services for the Palestinian camps; the refugee population is in its fourth generation.

The refugees in Jabaliya don't have a lot of choices. Israel will not permit them to return to the houses from which their parents or, more often, their grandparents or great-grandparents fled. Other Arab countries didn't and don't want them. So the Palestinian refugee camps created in 1948 have been institutionalized by the international community; services are provided, to some extent, and there is a semblance of stability, though they lack a real economy. Let's put it this way: life in Jabaliya shows more signs of care by a central authority than any place in Haiti, even though the Palestinians, unlike the Haitians, are virtually stateless.

To become permanent, a refugee camp needs political reasons for the population to remain, and it needs services that hold them. Without reasons to remain in camps, and services to keep them alive, refugees will continue on their flight to stability and safety. Refugees from war or natural catastrophe or insoluble domestic unrest, they will become immigrants in another country. But with assistance from the outside and ongoing support for the camps, this is no longer the usual situation. Like the Palestinians, the Haitians still living in earthquake camps have both political and economic reasons to remain. Sometimes they have services, as well, but that's increasingly rare.

Because many of the camps were in such prominent spots, like Place Boyer in Pétionville or Toussaint Camp on the central plaza downtown, they could not be completely ignored by the Haitian government or by the international helping community. Toussaint Camp was right under the nose of the government that was supposed to deal with it, facing the much photographed ruins of the presidential palace, and it was also right in the face of any international media that happened to be in town staying at the Plaza Hotel. To remain in those camps or in the easily seen and accessed megacamps that had sprouted in the fields on the way to the airport meant continued attention for their plight. These most visible camps were the ones targeted for services and also for the initial depopulation campaigns.

The refugee camps that remained, though, had begun to feel permanent. Housing that was originally composed of temporary strings of tarps and sheets and poles and sticks and cardboard, as well as tents, tents in which earthquake victims formerly tried to sleep and from which they emerged every day to receive food and medical aid from international donors, has been abandoned for more solid stuff—wood, cement, even steel—that is more firmly embedded in the ground. The tents themselves now serve as a patch for a leaky roof or a tarp for keeping the TV dry during the rains, or they've been fiddled into a canopy to add a sun-protected outdoor space or used to enhance bedding or flooring—since nothing that can possibly be used is ever thrown away. New outsiders may look at these camps and think that they are squalid, temporary places devoid of life.

Others, like me, look at them with Haiti eyes and see embryonic neighborhoods. One reason I feel no fear in the camps is that they are so familiar to me.

It's not unreasonable to find fault with the international community for its behavior in Haiti, but let me just point out that that community, to one degree or another, has been in Haiti as long as Haiti has been Haiti. It's not making some sudden appearance in the Haitian universe, for all of Haiti's ostensible remoteness and supposed desire to be left alone behind its postcolonial ramparts. The international community is a part of the fabric of Haitian history, not always (and even not usually) for the good.

Just to cite the biggies, let's go:

Without France and the international slave trade, there would have been no slaves, no revolution, and hence, no Haiti. No *bicolore* Haitian flag without the French *tricolore*. After independence: without France, to which Haiti was forced to pay a century-spanning "reparations" debt, there would have been far less poverty during the first days of the black republic, and less of a restraint on the country's early growth. Without the slaveholding United States to boycott the infant nation and shun it, there could have been reasonable integration into the world economy. Without the U.S. occupation of 1915–1934, Haiti could have, perhaps, grown into a mature nation. (Then again, perhaps not.)

How Haiti works in general has historically had more to do with foreigners than is the case in most other countries, and this has never been so obvious as in the post-earthquake era. With so many coming down to assist in relief and reconstruction, so much of it concentrated in the capital, it has sometimes felt as though the country is being taken over by a new occupation, by a different kind of army, an army of the innocent. (This, while the UN continues to provide the only serious force of order. MINUSTAH, with its twelve thousand troops on the ground, claims to be simply a do-gooding humanitarian force but is in many ways an unacknowledged Great Power occupation.) Often as I watch the posses of young, well-meaning American and European missionaries and development people roaming through camps or driving from meeting to meeting, I think about the idea of the innocent army, and am reminded—I can't help it—of *Village of the Damned*, a 1960 horror movie that depicted invasions by huge-eyed innocent-seeming children who left destruction and death in their wake.

The relief and reconstruction era in Haiti has had a strange history. In the first days after the quake, the focus was on relief. As Janet Reitman wrote in late 2011 in *Rolling Stone,*

President Obama, calling the tragedy "cruel and incomprehensible," pledged "every element of our national capacity" to the response. Former Presidents George W. Bush and Bill Clinton created a special fund for Haiti; the American Red Cross launched a wildly successful appeal, raising close to $500 million in one year. In total, an estimated one in two American households donated more than $1.4 billion to Haiti relief, with close to $11 billion more for reconstruction pledged by donor countries and financial institutions. "We will be here today, tomorrow and for the time ahead," Secretary of State Hillary Clinton promised during a post-quake visit to Port-au-Prince.

Of course the State Department is always here in Haiti "today, tomorrow and for the time ahead," and has been here since the U.S. occupation began back in the early days of the 1900s (and before), so that was nothing new. My first book about Haiti was in part about the "American Plan," which began under the first Bush administration and included penetrating Haiti's economy, making it a cash economy rather than an agricultural economy, and dumping subsidized American rice into the Haitian market—all of which came to pass, further impoverishing the country. The rice dumping continued with the support of President Clinton, who also backed austerity measures for Haiti in the late 1990s. Because they undersold Haitian-grown rice, the dumps of subsidized U.S. rice destroyed domestic cultivation and forced people to abandon their small provincial farms to seek their fortunes in the cities, especially in the alluring cash-economy capital of Port-au-Prince. There, on January 12, 2010, thousands of those internal urban immigrants were crushed to death in their overcrowded, slapdash neighborhoods. Clinton has since apologized for what is known in Haiti as "Miami Rice."

Now Bill Clinton was the UN envoy to Haiti, and in the aftermath of the earthquake he promised Haiti that the reconstruction phase, which was to follow the relief effort, would build the country "back better," a phrase that caused many longtime Haiti experts to hoot with bitter laughter. First of all, the United States, in all its meddling in Haitian affairs for the past century, seemed, on the face of it, to have achieved precisely nothing. And then, "build back better" was such a simplistic catchphrase to use in such a rococo situation. It seemed to have a touch of Orwell's totalitarian euphemism about it.

"It would be funny, if it weren't tragic," said Ira Lowenthal, an anthropologist and a former official of the U.S. Agency for International Development. Lowenthal is one of the most cynical longtime Haiti watchers; his own life has been a bit battered in the process of watching. "Build Back Better," Lowenthal repeats, shaking his head and taking another long, feline draw on his cigarette. "It almost hurts."

It was never easy to see where all this help was going when you were in the camps. Most of the hundreds of camps seemed to be functioning autonomously. But in Port-au-Prince and the worst-hit outlying towns, some of the larger and more tumultuous ad hoc camps initially received important, urgent, absolutely necessary sanitation and health support from the international relief community. Relief, we were to learn, is very different from reconstruction, and much less complicated.

There was clean water from giant bladders provided by the Red Cross and UNICEF; these rectangular potato-colored balloons sat at the edges of the camps like the waterbeds of giants. In fact, just after the earthquake the people in the camps had cleaner, better water than most shantytown dwellers had ever had in Haiti. And it was free. As one might imagine, many people whose old housing was still standing after the earthquake flocked to the camps anyway, because of services that were being provided: in some cases, free meals, clean water, health care, tents, and even schools.

As things progressed and the relief effort faded, however, the camp dwellers went back to buying their water from privately owned and operated water trucks, as per usual in the Haitian slums, or to walking long distances to wait for the municipal water pipes to come on, crowding around as if they were waiting at a well in the African desert, with white plastic buckets and empty yellow vegetable oil containers on their heads.

At first, in the early days after the earthquake, the camps were surrounded by porta-potties donated by outside groups, who also provided employees in rubberized uniforms and water trucks and hoses for cleaning them out, on a schedule, a beautiful thing to see in Haiti, where normally the latrine cleaner, or *bayakou,* comes only every two or three years, and then only in the middle of the night, by arrangement with a middleman, because the work is shameful and the darkness hides his identity. At one point the portable toilets and their cleaners were such a common sight that it became amusing to the foreign press corps to call Haiti's capital Port-au-Sans. Now many of the portable toilets are still in place, standing like guards shoulder to shoulder around the camps, but they are terrible festering shitholes. The cleaners' contracts ran out and were not renewed.

When the camps first started up, it seemed as if, awful as they were, they might be healthier places for Haitians to live in than the slums and popular neighborhoods they were accustomed to, with clean available water and sanitation. There was a degree of Barbara Bush–ing, the way she cooed over the amenities of the Astrodome in Houston after Hurricane Katrina. But the situation deteriorated over time, as relief ended and reconstruction began, and depopulating the camps became the underlying policy of both the Haitian government and the reconstruction effort. No one wanted the camps to be permanent, and yet, for simple practical reasons, Haitians were staying there. Reason number one: the housing, such as it was, was free. Reason number two: there was, in most cases, nowhere else better for them to go.

And, understandably, the outside world had lost its initial passionate interest in the Haitian earthquake and its victims, after the first dramatic and stirring television images of chaos and death and the astounding late rescues. Some organizations no longer had the funding to continue their work (others stayed on and raised money for the long haul). A crisis that lingers without dramatic filmable tension—and without visible heroes or villains—becomes less interesting to the world at large as well as to donors and even to the aid workers themselves, to a degree. Outsiders sometimes experience a dull alienation that has become known as "sympathy fatigue." Even though the camps, like the shantytowns, could always use relief and aid, eventually this phase of the international effort began to wind down. As water bladders were carted away, and toilets remained uncleaned, and on-site health clinics disappeared, Haitians who lived in the camps began to take responsibility for them. They were new Haitian mini-towns, with services provided by Haitians.

And the amazing part of it for Haitians living there was that the housing was free. You built it and then you lived in it: in a sense you were a homesteader—or a squatter. Each time I visited a house in the camps, its residents were eager to tell me what they had been paying for housing before the quake.

Which meant, in most cases, that these people were saving what was, before the earthquake, rent that had cost them more than half their annual income, assuming that that income hovered around $350. For some, it meant that a harsh life was a little less harsh in certain ways. I met one family living in a small shack in Toussaint Camp who had been paying three separate rents before the quake. Their living conditions now were intolerable—eleven people in a shack the size of a California king–size mattress—but they shrugged at this misery, because this misery was free. They were trying not to think about what came next.

Others were living for free in the camps while they waited for something better. I met Moïse Philippe in a camp built along the crests of a steep hillside on the side of the Canapé Vert road, between downtown and Pétionville. Philippe is a perfectly middle-class camp dweller. He wears a beige guayabera, open at the collar, and pressed black trousers, black loafers. He looks successful and well put together. His head is shaved ("to hide the gray, of course," he says). He has a version of Papa Doc spectacles on, thick-lensed and black-rimmed. He is an engineering professor who had been teaching math and sociology at a now destroyed college for many years before the quake, and who is currently teaching privately and running a printing business.

Professeur-Ingénieur Philippe was living with his wife and two teenage kids in a series of tents in the camp. In the tents were a bedroom area and a kitchen area, a fridge, a television. It wasn't a house, but in the dry season, it was pleasant enough and serviceable. Philippe's wife offered me coffee. Everything was fine, she said, until it rained, and then all was chaos and fear, and panicky covering-up of all important possessions with tarps and plastic. The hillside, Philippe pointed out, kicking a rock and watching it tumble down the ravine, was at risk of subsidence with any rain or aftershock. It was, he told me, on a known fault line. The camp residents believed that the land they were living on belonged to the state, because the family who were reputed to own it never came to kick them off it, as owners had done in some other camps—with guns and thugs.

Philippe and his family are biding their time in this camp, waiting for repairs to be completed on their earthquake-damaged house across the ravine; Philippe is having a new tin roof put up where the cement roof fell in. He's quite philosophical and fair about the role of the relief and reconstruction organizations in his small, ad hoc camp. "We got latrines," Philippe says, "but no water. Now, latrines are not nothing. There's an irresponsible state in Haiti, and they block certain things from coming into the country, like rubble-removal vehicles, and sometimes funding is also blocked for other reasons. There's a lot of corruption, of course. But basically, we're the ones who have to act. I'm not waiting for someone to come and give me a house somewhere. I'm rebuilding my old house. We have to organize ourselves. In this camp, if we hadn't known how to organize ourselves, we'd be dead."

Philippe not only is active in his camp but also participates in a group of about 250 teachers who meet regularly in the parking lot of his de-stroyed college. Together, they raised about three hundred dollars after the quake and invested it in a small water-selling business. With profits from that, the teachers bought a printing press, and now they run a print-ing business. Most of their profits are funneled back into their camps.

Philippe says there are two styles of camp. "Here, we take the five gourdes we earn or are given, and we share five gourdes. There [he ges-tures to the camp across the Canapé Vert road], they take five gourdes and make a deal and sell free stuff on the market, for a profit, but they don't invest it back in the camp. Here, the population is organized, so one or two of us could never do that, even if we wanted to." On one of my visits, we all talk peacefully in a kind of central square of packed red dirt in the middle of the little camp, sitting on plastic chairs and drinking coffee under the shade of a flamboyant tree. Our table is an ACF oil barrel from India, which is leaning up against the tree trunk (ACF is an international organization that helps with emergency relief in crisis situations). Skinny dogs wander over to our circle curiously, even hopefully, and then leave with their tails down. A small boy is squatting near us, using a ratty string to pull around a small plastic bottle, to which he's attached four red bottle caps for wheels.

Just so we understand what we're dealing with, here are some hard pre-earthquake facts about Haiti. We can assume that many of these worsened precipitously after the quake, in the affected areas, though relief services ameliorated some of the crises for a short period. Three-quarters of the Haitian population lives on less than two dollars a day. This is an easy fact to read, but a harder one to live. Imagine your nights when you know that in all likelihood, for your family of five, you'll have to scrounge up, say, at a minimum, seven dollars tomorrow for food and water and part of your rent, and yet there is no job to be had and nothing you know how to do, and you can't read or write and you're sick with TB. Speaking of water, more than half the population has no access to potable water, and in addition, many formerly decent water sources have been contaminated by cholera since the earthquake.

Speaking of work, about 95 percent of the jobs to be had are in what's called "the informal sector." This means selling in the market or on the streets, being a prostitute, cutting cane for a small cultivator, weaving straw for hampers and baskets, selling coconuts, doing sewing piecework, picking coconuts, pulling a cart, painting a sign, picking garbage and selling it—and you're lucky if you can find someone to pay you at all decently for these jobs and services. (Nowadays there are hundreds of formal jobs available for earthquake-related organizations. But for those one usually must be able to read and write; in Haiti only a little more than half the population is literate.) Haitian unemployment has been measured by USAID at about 50 percent at its lowest and 70 percent at its highest, but it is, anecdotally and visibly, much higher than 70 percent.

Only about a third of the population has access to sanitary facilities, and those are usually barely adequate. Only some 10 percent have any electrical service, and that service is sporadic when it's not nonexistent. Ninety-seven percent of the country is deforested. Four-fifths of college-educated Haitians live abroad. Around 1.2 million Haitians live in the United States and another quarter of a million or so in Francophone Canada and in France. Some 250,000 Haitian children live as household slaves called *restaveks* (stay-withs) in the homes of relatives or family friends—this figure is higher now, since the earthquake orphaned so many children and made so many homeless.

There are so many permutations. At the sad bottom of the temporary earthquake housing pile are renters. Their landlords are people who got tents and a space early in a camp. By now, those who became landlords have moved out to better housing elsewhere, or at least *other* housing elsewhere, and in many cases are renting out their space in the camp for pennies to even more unfortunate people. Where there is a way to make money, Haitians will make it.

By now, though, many people have been moved out of the camps in the central areas of the city. Sean Penn, the actor and director, came down right after the earthquake and started running a camp that people had begun putting together on the grounds of the Pétionville Club golf course, the only golf course in Haiti (tragedy for Haitian golfers, *bien sûr*) and a surreal location for a refugee camp, at the edges of the old wealthy suburb, perched on the top and sides of a hill. The Pétionville Club camp, or, as it became known, Sean Penn's camp, soon had a population of almost sixty thousand, and, like so many other outside relief officials, Penn became involved—one might say entrapped; not that he thinks of it that way—in the relocation effort. Even during the initial days after the earthquake, Penn was already thinking about how to get the refugees in his camp back to real housing and off the Pétionville Club's grounds. Needless to say, the golf course and club have an owner, who allowed the camp to remain on his grounds but who was not happy about it. It had been a lucrative and social business for him; now it was a charity.

International organizations soon pointed out to Penn that his camp was vulnerable to flooding during Haiti's torrential rainy season. Worried about this, Penn and others on his staff managed to convince about five thousand people in the camp to move out to a new refugee settlement outside of town, Corail-Cesselesse, that was being put up by various organizations in the international relief community as an interim and possibly permanent location for earthquake refugees. Once these refugees had left Penn's camp, there would be room at the golf club for the U.S. Army Corps of Engineers to put together a drainage system. Except for relocating some of the refugees in his camp to Corail, Penn was not otherwise involved with the Corail development.

According to Janet Reitman's *Rolling Stone* piece, Penn was told by officials involved in the relocation process that Corail was "less vulnerable to flooding" than his place. Penn explained to the Haitian leaders of his camp that when people moved to Corail, they would receive fifty dollars from the Red Cross "and a hygiene kit. They would also get shelter, food rations, clean water, free medical care and a school for their kids." He left the decision to the Haitians, but he strongly encouraged them to go; like everyone else, he was very concerned about the approaching rainy season. After initial skepticism, thousands agreed to depart. It seemed like a good idea to everyone: it fit in with Penn's hopes for relocation for his camp's residents; the owner of the golf club also wanted this population off his grounds; the refugees themselves did not want to be swept away by the floods; and the rest of the camp dwellers would benefit by having a new drainage system.

However, I've been to Corail. Penn, too, had visited the site before he convinced his people to move. So he knew what I knew. Corail is a gloomy desert of a hill, windblown, treeless, sunstruck, with, at the time, flapping tents in depressed rows and no central hub, no economy, no commerce, no humanity, nothing. Any Haitian, given a choice, would prefer to live in a desperate shantytown like La Saline or Cité Soleil, where there is real life, instead of in this Venusian landscape. You or I would rather live in a Port-au-Prince shantytown, too, with neighbors we know, and markets, and an organic community that has developed over generations. Not in the echoing nowhere of Corail. But Penn was promised that the area would be transformed, and soon. He believed this, or at least desperately hoped it was true. He knew that his golf-course camp—while cool and pleasant in the early mornings and late afternoons of the dry season and really, at those times, the prettiest of the camps and the most humane, with trees and groves, and roads and alleyways—could become a thundering and fatal whirlpool in the rains.

As Reitman describes it, the alternative, Corail camp, was "a denuded mountain that turned out to be as vulnerable to the elements as [Penn's] golf course." This is not quite true, but there was a meteorological problem at Corail that wasn't rain. In July 2010, belying Penn's qualified hopes for a decent refuge for his people (decent by Haitian post-earthquake standards), a windstorm swept through the unprotected hillside of Corail. This was three months after Penn's refugees had moved there. The windstorm swept through Port-au-Prince as well, and blew across the courtyards of the general hospital, where Megan Coffee's TB-weakened patients desperately clung to the ward's tent poles and canvas and somehow kept the thing from flying away.

Meanwhile, some 1,700 of the 7,000 who lived in Corail "lost their shelter to the storm," according to the *New York Times*. People were injured "by debris that flew across the exposed desert plain where rows of family-size tents sat in a grid on a graveled surface. A mother and baby were struck by lightning . . . The woman was badly burned, and the baby, taken away by ambulance, was reported by Haitian radio to have died." In other words, the new place wasn't safe. A nice big regulation tent shelter in Corail gave an illusion of protection, and it looked safe to outsiders (all those nice rectangular tents in a row); but it was an illusion—one that at the time satisfied the Haitian government, which had taken over the land there, as well as Penn's international advisers, who put up the tents and provided relief services, as well as other camp leaders who sent people there. To some, Corail looked reasonable at a glance, and it provided a place to store people when they were moved out of the central urban camps.

But anyone who had bothered to look at the place carefully, critically, beforehand or after—the real place, live and up close—would have seen Corail for what it was: a cynical answer to a cynical question. That question was how to rid Port-au-Prince of its disposable refugees, how to clear out the city quickly and efficiently, rather than fairly and humanely. And there also seemed to be an element to the way the question was posed that included a consideration of possible advantages. The greatest profit in Corail-Cesselesse was to the elite families who had owned the vacant lands around the capital for decades or more.

As Penn told Reitman, he knew Corail was in a "very vulnerable area" when he first saw it, before the group from his camp moved. But he believed the "international monitors and aid agencies" who had told him that Corail would be fine, that real transitional shelters—not blow-downable tents—would be up in a matter of months. Essentially, with the international community and the Haitian government in charge (manipulated in a sense by the landowners, as it turned out), the people who were sent to Corail were disappeared from Port-au-Prince. With the best of intentions, Penn had himself shown a sort of drummed-up passionate intensity—as described by Reitman and as he acknowledged in his response to her story (also published in *Rolling Stone*)—in convincing almost a tenth of his population to move there.

Penn was among the freest and most personally committed and involved of the reconstruction outsiders who came to save Haiti. He operates on his own terms as much as possible. But the transition to Corail-Cesselesse showed that no matter the motivation, the innocent army's most decent impulses can turn out to be wrongheaded and ill-conceived. Often the best people are left with few good choices as they try to cope and cooperate with a corrupt and abusive as well as subtle and complicated system with which they are utterly unfamiliar.

It turned out that the land on which Corail had sprouted up was owned by a consortium in which a number of Haiti's most powerful families were involved. Before the earthquake, this barren, unpopulated area had not looked too promising as a moneymaker, but after the earthquake, it was a different story. Gerard-Emile Brun, who was president of the consortium, had been chosen by the Préval government to head up the refugee relocation effort and depopulate the refugee camps around Port-au-Prince, according to Jonathan Katz of the Associated Press. In what would be a clear conflict of interest anywhere else (but in Haiti can often be seen as just good, traditional business practice), Brun made the lucrative decision to establish the Corail-Cesselesse relocation camp on land owned by the consortium he headed, which meant that basically, as a government official, he was directing the government's and Haitian aid donors' money to his consortium. According to Katz, this meant that the consortium Brun was in charge of stood "to gain part of $7 million the government [was to] spend compensating landowners." As Graham Greene wrote in *The Comedians,* "It is astonishing how much money can be made out of the poorest of the poor with a little ingenuity."

And, Katz continued, "that's just a small part of the potential payoff. [The consortium] is also a lead negotiator with South Korean garment firms to build factories that Haitian officials say will likely go into Corail-Cesselesse." That was the idea, and those garment jobs were the bait for the Corail-Cesselesse refugees and the golf-club camp authorities who urged them to move.

A deal to create the "North Industrial Park" was finally signed in January 2011 by the U.S. government, along with the Inter-American Development Bank, the Haitian government, and Sae-A Trading Co., Ltd., South Korea's premier garment manufacturer. The ultimate spot selected for the new park, however, was not in Corail or anywhere near Corail, but in the destitute northern reaches of the country, near a formerly unnavigable port called Caracol. Some believe that the land deal and the involvement of the Brun consortium had become too controversial to keep the industrial park in Corail. The Caracol press release issued by the American embassy in Port-au-Prince stated that "the North Industrial Park, which is projected to create 20,000 permanent jobs through Sae-A's investment alone, fulfills priorities . . . to create centers of economic development outside of Port-au-Prince for Haiti's future growth and to bring much needed jobs to Haiti's underserved regions."

The foundation rock for the Caracol park was laid in November 2011, at a ceremony attended by President Martelly and Bill Clinton, who shoveled some rock into a hole himself to get the thing going. The future park "shows the positive impact foreign investment can have in building Haiti back better," Clinton was quoted as saying in the press release for the event. Clinton must have felt a certain degree of pride: the plan for this industrial park—including the participation of Sae-A—dated back before the earthquake, and it had been a pet project of the Clintons (both the former president and the then secretary of state) for some time. Now earthquake reconstruction funds would be used to push it forward.

It might be wiser to wait and see how such things turn out before claiming for them a positive impact. I want Clinton to be right, but I can't bring myself to believe in his vision, in part because I recall the industrial parks of Haiti, before Aristide's rise to power frightened away conservative foreign investors; a few thousand more Haitians had jobs back then, but those workers were never paid enough to lift the next generation out of poverty. If such maquiladora projects are to be the model for Haiti's economic future, they will simply create future generations of sweatshop labor at subsistence wages. And yet one goes on hoping, and Haitians who've been unemployed for a lifetime will tell you only one thing: they want either a job, or a visa to get out of the place. Preferably the latter.

One good reason (according to my analysis) for putting the Caracol park up north near a very small town rather than in Corail, in the greater Port-au-Prince metropolitan area, is that people in the north are more cut off, more isolated, less organized, less wired to communications.

Which is to say they are more desperate and less aware of what choices they might have, and they have fewer choices; they're less organized in this remote area than Port-au-Prince residents, and less likely to kick up a fuss if things don't go the way they'd like. They're more zombie-like. Equally, they'll be largely out of reach of the international media, which for most of its visits prefers its Port-au-Prince hotels and restaurants and wireless to the hard knocks of the Haitian "road." Without a helicopter or a plane to get you there, it will take a long, rough time to get from Port-au-Prince to Caracol, and there will be no lightly sautéed salmon and no glass of white wine at the end of your hard day.

I have a friend who runs a mattress factory in Diquini, outside Port-au-Prince, and his workers are aging out. When I talk to Samuel and Jerry, the last thing they want is to slave, to use a fraught word, over mattress foam or tennis togs or yoga clothes in a huge factory with what they perceive as "other losers," and the usual unwritten Haitian workers' contract that virtually specifies that there will no benefits and no pensions, in a country where (is it too obvious to say?) there is no social security. If Jerry and Samuel are going to have no job security and no promise of future care, at the very least they don't want to waste their youth in desperate conditions for very little money.

Instead, they want to be drivers for banks, or security heavies for important businessmen. They want to figure out how to buy a motorbike and run a little taxi service. They might want to sell weed, but they're too scared of the drug traffickers, and anyway, if that's what they wanted to do, they wouldn't tell me. Samuel and Jerry wouldn't mind working in a pharmacy or a restaurant, or a radio station, or in tourism, if there were tourism. They want something, in other words, that has a whiff of freedom and a whiff of youth and excitement, because they know about such things from their life in the big city. They'd rather cut cane in the Dominican Republic than work in a factory in Diquini, even in my friend's relatively decent enterprise. And their girlfriends want to sell in the market or work for a private seamstress or get into sales or travel or banking, somehow. At the very top of all their insane hopes for the future: get out of Haiti.

~~

I went up to Péguyville late one afternoon. Péguyville is a suburb on a hillside above Pétionville, yet another step higher on the rung of elite real estate. There, on the terrace of his elegant stone house, Jean-Claude Bajeux, a gentlemanly political figure of the older generation, was holding court. Bajeux, a human-rights activist as well as a distinguished academic and briefly a minister of culture under Aristide, was having coffee and serving cocktails to a half-dozen or so guests who had assembled there in the fading day. This was six months after the earthquake. A brisk wind that threatened rain toyed with the tops of the trees on Bajeux's lush property. The air was light. A tent occupied by my friend Ira Lowenthal, who was made homeless not by the earthquake but by getting resoundingly kicked out of his house by his girlfriend, stood in the front courtyard under a tall pine. The tent standing there seemed appropriate to the times, however. I wondered whether it was a free humanitarian tent Ira had got hold of. A sunlit sky appeared and disappeared behind the veil of the piney treetops.

Bajeux was seventy-eight then. He was a light-skinned former priest with a Romance literature PhD from Princeton, a member of the elite who opposed the government of Papa Doc in the 1960s. As with many Haitians of his class, you would not necessarily have guessed that he had African ancestry. He was exiled repeatedly, and the Tonton Macoutes carried off two of his brothers, his two sisters, and his mother in the middle of the night. All were executed. I am thinking about them as the scattered clouds begin to pile up behind us in the mountains.

A servant comes and goes from the terrace, offering us decanted wine or espressos, and little bowls of olives and nuts.

Bajeux's close-cropped beard is white, and he's tall, erect, pale. He points to a copy of Jared Diamond's book *Collapse* that's sitting on his coffee table, a book about how civilizations come to an end.

"Read this," he tells his guests. "Read this, and think of Haiti." He makes the French sound that starts as a *tsk* and ends with a quick exhalation through the mouth. "They've lost all sense of the state," he says of the Haitian government.

Another friend arrives, and the guests, all older men, start talking about people they know, and people they've heard of, and they discuss how much each of those is stealing from the humanitarian effort, or how much their acquaintances are making from the earthquake and its aftermath at a number of major international organizations. "Here it's like the gold rush," Bajeux says.

He gleefully points a figurative finger at the Haitians who have tried to use the earthquake as a moneymaker—not just at the landholders who are jealously guarding their lands from earthquake refugees and engaging in real-estate speculation, hoping to attract aid-group renters and buyers, or who charge vulture prices to put up new housing on their acreage; not just at the people on whose vacant lands internally displaced persons have come to squat in camps and who want them off; but also at the officials at customs who are holding up equipment, medical necessities, and other important humanitarian material until they can extort huge fees from waiting recipients. And at politicians who are facilitating the whole mess while kowtowing to the international organizations.

The guests go on talking: which lies this one is telling about the reconstruction program. Which Haitian is getting paid off for land—and how they are sucking the life out of the international donors, their utter lack of shame and patriotism.

And the donors themselves!

"Yes, yes," Bajeux says. "It's so true. And we're going to build a city in the air, because no one will let us build on the ground without paying predator prices. We'll build in the air! It will be a city like, you know, like that artist, the one—" He gropes for the name, and someone in the group, spitting an olive pit into his hand, says, "Ah, you mean Préfète Duffaut, Jean-Claude." And that's who Bajeux means. Duffaut, who is eighty-seven, paints bright landscapes filled with microscopic Haitians living in utopian cities that extend like cartoon bubbles from the sea to the land and on up into thin air.

~

There is precedent for relocations of large numbers of the poor in Haiti. More than fifty years ago, Cité Simone, named for Papa Doc's wife (and today one of the country's most destitute shantytowns, renamed Cité Soleil after the fall of Baby Doc in 1986), was built by the Duvalier regime both to depopulate various downtown Port-au-Prince slums that had been devastated by suspicious fires, and to provide workers for Haiti's first industrial park. Like Corail, Cité Simone was envisioned, or so the Duvalier regime claimed, as a model development for workers and, along with the industrial park, was built, like Corail, on the lands of a few powerful families, with U.S. support. Those workers did move (or were moved) to the shantytown, and the shantytown grew and grew over the years, populated by thousands who came to find work in the factories and who did not find it; it's now home to more than a quarter of a million people, who live in conditions almost as intolerable as those in the earthquake camps—and in some cases worse. Most of the jobs are gone; in any case, they were just the kind of subsistence jobs that barely left workers enough to pay for transportation and lunch, much less to raise the next generation out of crushing poverty. Sewing brassieres. Making baseballs. Hemming jeans. You'd think it was horrifying if I told you that the Haitian minimum wage was 61 cents an hour. But that's what it is—by law. Foreign textile companies with Haitian shops found that a bit steep, and along with the Obama State Department (Hillary Clinton, that is), made sure that, at least for textile workers, the Haitian minimum wage would be 31 cents an hour, or about $3 for a ten-hour day. To make ends meet, the average Haitian family needs about $13 to $14 per day, which they almost never can quite manage. (The minimum wage in the United States—low in comparison with European minimum wages—is $58 per eight-hour day.)

For Sean Penn, the Corail relocation was a terrible lesson.

"I feel like shit," he told Reitman. Still, in his rebuttal to Reitman's piece,

Penn said that on the day after the storm, he went to Corail and talked to hundreds of the people who had moved there from his camp. None of them wanted to return, Penn wrote. "They preferred to stay in Corail. They salvaged their belongings, 150 new tents were distributed to them, and life, shitty as it was post-disaster, went on." In other words, for them Corail, bad as it was, was not much worse than Penn's camp, and possibly better.

What Penn is trying to point out here is that Haitians, although buffeted by poverty, earthquake, storms, and the poor planning of their own government and other outside entities, still have a degree of free will, and have the intelligence to exercise it. The fact remains, though, that their choices are severely limited, so much so that one could argue that there's no choice at all, that there is simply an illusion of free will—and that since the earthquake (and, again arguably, since before the earthquake), Haitians have been trapped in an existential quandary.

Meanwhile, Corail—where Penn's people have now, according to him, *chosen* to live, with eyes open—promises very little to its residents: not running water, not interior plumbing, not irrigation, not food distribution, not commerce, and very little schooling or medical care. After a year, there are two tiny restaurants there, and a *borlette* and a bar. It says a lot about the magnitude of the disaster and the chaos and craziness of the relief response that a place like Corail, with about a hundred thousand residents, has already become one of Haiti's ten largest cities.

7
CITIZEN HAITI

Pwasson pa wè dlo
The fish doesn't see the water

Leonard Doyle is a former journalist who used to work for the *Independent,* a British newspaper, and who was now running communications in Haiti for the International Organization for Migration. IOM, which was established in 1951, is a giant operation that employs more than 7,800 people worldwide and is in charge of more than 2,700 projects— it's got a wide reach. Its initial job was to help European nations resettle the approximately eleven million refugees created by World War II, but its mandate has since grown to deal with the refugees and internally displaced people who are the victims of war and natural disasters all over the globe. It has been operating in Haiti for almost twenty years, since back when Haiti's migratory problems were boat people leaving for the Bahamas and the United States or migrant workers heading to the Dominican Republic to cut cane. Since the earthquake, IOM in Haiti has had bigger headaches, broader agendas, and more money to spend. (Interestingly, since 1998, the heads of IOM have both been former U.S. ambassadors to Haiti.)

The organization's primary goal in Haiti right now is to depopulate the worst and most dangerous camps, as well as the most visible, such as Toussaint. It has been slowly helping other agencies to do this, here and there. The planning at first was scattershot, as with the movement of Sean Penn's people to Corail. But two years after the earthquake, IOM had developed a more organized and ambitious plan that had been created in concert with the Haitian government and with Bill Clinton's now defunct Interim Commission for the Reconstruction of Haiti.

The plan was called 16/6, and it consisted of a schedule to move people out of six targeted camps back into sixteen of their old neighborhoods. It offered each family five hundred dollars toward reconstruction or rent, the equivalent in Haiti of about a year and a half's rent for families of the lowest circumstances, which is how IOM chose the figure. (Housing for couples working for aid groups in Port-au-Prince, post-earthquake, could go as high as three thousand dollars a month, and sometimes even higher in secure, gated, luxury complexes.) Jerry, his girlfriend, and their new baby, Jefferson, born in Toussaint Camp, would eventually move out with the help of 16/6. Although the initial attempts were accompanied by a degree of skepticism on the part of those who were being moved, nonetheless people were participating. Five hundred dollars was a tidy sum for most of the camp families.

In order to get the refugees out of the targeted camps, IOM operated buses that would bring camp dwellers each morning to the new (or sometimes old) places they wanted to rent outside the camps. If the place looked plausible to IOM's representatives (who came along on the buses like a development version of Club Med's "Gentils Organisateurs"), and the landlord respectable enough, a one-year lease would be signed by all parties on the spot, and the former camp dweller, now a contracted tenant, could move out of the camp and into his or her new place, paying the landlord-to-be with IOM's five hundred dollars. In Toussaint Camp, the evidence of the depopulation campaign was obvious, more than two years after the disaster. Jerry's shack I could now find more easily. Same for the squalid digs of Jésulà Dorasme, a woman I knew who lived in Toussaint with her three kids and her boyfriend,

Wilner. Doyle says that usually, the new place that a camp dweller finds for relocation looks reasonable, although sometimes it's obvious that the camp dweller and the landlord are hoping to defraud IOM of its five hundred dollars.

In Haiti, IOM does more than simply relocate people and help with the relocation process. Doyle's communications team, in one instance, partners with a Haitian dance troupe called Tchaka Dance that is used to send messages from IOM to audiences in the camps. Tchaka does funny and charming dances in a sort of hip-hop parade to show kids how to avoid getting cholera, for example.

In his continuing attempt to get his varied messages out, Doyle has also put together a production company that is making a sitcom called *Tap-Tap*, named after the brightly colored buses that travel all around Haiti. In an email to undisclosed recipients, including me, Doyle writes that "the goal of the Tap Tap series is to represent real-life interactions in which Haitians can recognize themselves, laugh about their challenges and celebrate their vibrant culture."

Words like these are bound to create a feeling of irritation among Haitians—but the Haitians who are the audience for the *Tap-Tap* show won't hear those words or read them; they won't get Doyle's email. If they did they'd wonder why Doyle had taken it on himself, as an employee of IOM, to produce a Haitian situation comedy (the very idea is repugnant) to help Haitians "celebrate their vibrant culture" and "laugh about their challenges." I watched *Tap-Tap;* it's cute and it's directed and run by Haitians, with Haitian stars. But it doesn't respond to either the pre- or the post-earthquake situation in Haiti. Its babyish story line and its kind, friendly jokes assume that a Haitian audience is simple, simple at a level below illiteracy and penury. It assumes they are a laughing, happy people who have very little idea of their own identity or the multiple ironies of their situation.

Just ask yourself: Would you be laughing, in the conditions Haitians are living in? And if you were laughing (humans do tend to laugh at whatever material is available, and gallows humor is especially useful as a survival device), would you—a Haitian living in an earthquake camp or a shantytown, say—want Leonard Doyle, a super-sophisticated Irish media operative from the International Organization for Migration, to be paying your joke writers? To be initiating and sponsoring your entertainment? Would you want your sitcom to be "based on an original concept from International Organization for Migration (IOM)"? That's how the group's role is described in the *Tap-Tap* credits.

Well, *Tap-Tap* is *something*, I guess. There are very few computers and televisions in the shantytowns, so not a lot of entertainment comes in from the outside, and Haitian wits—of whom there must be thousands, since I personally know at least a handful—don't normally have the resources to create video entertainment. It's true that outsiders have been working with and encouraging Haitian creativity for a long time—at least since DeWitt Peters, a conscientious objector sent to Haiti to teach English when he refused to serve in World War II, established the Centre d'Art in 1944 and helped ignite the Haitian art renaissance. Obviously, outside interference in another culture is not always cynical (although in a United States Information Service film about him, made in 1950, we see Peters tooling about the country in his jaunty little Centre d'Art jeep, distributing art supplies and keeping an eye on painters and perhaps others). Certainly, the products of the Haitians with whom Peters worked did not smack of propaganda the way Doyle's products do.

Quite possibly, too, I'm being unfair and holding the new world order (represented by Doyle, who is as enthusiastic, smart, and thoughtful a person as one could ever wish to meet anywhere) to old standards of authenticity that no longer work in today's globocracy. This wouldn't surprise me. Doyle definitely seems to believe he is helping Haitians.

In any case, there's more:

This is how Doyle described the first showing of *Tap-Tap* in his email: "The first public showing took place tonight in Jalousie, a poverty-wracked community that clings to the side of the hill, above Petion Ville in Port au Prince. Several hundred people gathered to watch and enjoy the film and left asking for more." Jalousie is the hillside shantytown where all the servants, gardeners, day laborers, groundsmen, locksmiths, cobblers, seamstresses, elevator men, and porters who serve the rich Pétionville families and the new international-helper community live. *Jalousie* means jealousy in English. After having watched the eight-minute *Tap-Tap* pilot myself, I find it hard to believe the crowd was begging for more, but if that's true, it just shows how desperate the community must be for a laugh. As Doyle said a bit ruefully when I asked him in person about the show's reception, "Well, there's not much else for them to watch."

Doyle has also put together a network of community journalists called Sitwayen Ayiti, or Citizen Haiti. He is a very energetic and imaginative worker. Citizen Haiti has a radio show called *Radio Tap-Tap* (how outsiders love the sunny, fanciful Haitian tap-taps!) that is broadcast not just nationally on FM radio but also on a fleet of more than a hundred actual tap-taps that blare it through the streets (although I have never heard or seen one of these). The shows feature camp residents, who complain and tell stories, and IOM workers, who give advice and make announcements; *Radio Tap-Tap* is a new-world-order version of the Voice of America.

Under Doyle's direction, IOM has also put more than two hundred information kiosks in the camps. According to an IOM information sheet that appeared about a year after the earthquake:

> Each kiosk has a locked suggestion box and more than two thousand letters have been received to date. The letters provide a unique insight into the unfolding human tragedy the scale of which can defy the imagination. Some of the letters describe the suffering of hardworking families who have been devastated by the quake.

Doyle showed me some of the letters, and now there is a professionally produced seventy-four-page digital IOM flipbook that includes copies of some of these notes (showing the original ripped paper, envelopes, notebook leaves, et cetera, that they were written on, and the scrawl of childish print) accompanied by beautiful chiaroscuro photographs of the letter writers in their camp misery. I asked Doyle what happens to these letters once they are received. "The letters are collected and read," he told me.

> They typically ask for generalized help. We send an SMS to the letter writer, saying thanks and encouraging them to keep communication going. We try to break the expectation link between call and response to encourage communication as a right and a way to bring change. The kiosks are now being used to explain the 16/6 process, with kiosks going in camps and communities of return.

Which means that after you write a letter and put it in the kiosk, nothing much happens, except your letter might go into that nice book or a new version of it (but you've never seen the nice book; you probably didn't even write your letter yourself, because you don't know how). To me, it looked more like the letters were being collected to go into the pretty book than to get people's problems solved. The book is a powerful fundraising tool, it seemed to me. It certainly made me want to give.

In his blurb for the book, Doyle writes, "This book is testimony to the desire of Haiti's new homeless to have their voices heard and to become part of their country's national conversation." But it's unlikely that that's what the people who write the letters want (what they want is not a national conversation—which is an outsider idea—but simply, please, to get their damn problem fixed). Black Rouge put a message in a kiosk and got a text message back asking him what he needed or wanted. He says he texted back: a job, a new house, or help building one. And what he heard back after that was nothing.

"It's not so much that I mind not getting anything," he said to me as we sat in the heat of his little shack while his girlfriend watched TV. He shrugged. "But why do they bother asking, and getting our hopes up? It just makes you angry."

From the other bed, Black's cousin, who was studying his electromagnetism textbook, said, "Yeah. You *know* I'm not going to get a job when I get my degree. You just *know* it."

The problem is not that Doyle can't get them jobs; the problem is the implication—from kiosk to SMS—that he can, that IOM can. As Doyle says, "We try to break the expectation link between call and response."

They try to break it, but they also create it. Once it's established, you can't break "the expectation link." You—a giant international organiza- tion of empowered white people who live grandly in Port-au-Prince and have come here to help out with, as Haitians see it, money, jobs, and material goods—cannot ask people who live in shacks and shanties on a dollar a day what they need without their expecting or at least hop- ing that you'll help provide something for them. Much is expected or hoped for from "mobile sovereigns" like Doyle. The MIT anthropologist Erica Caple James coined that term in her book *Democratic Insecurities,* about Haiti in the mid-1990s. When she writes about mobile sover- eigns, James is referring to the foreign aid workers, anthropologists, and embassy people who work in the developing world and ride around the country in their big visible white SUVs, inspecting the situation. It seems to at least some Haitians who've participated in the kiosk-box suggestion program that the mobile sovereigns of IOM are offering Hai- tians a forum to make complaints and issue demands but that, really, it's all for show.

I shudder to think what Black would say if I showed him the seventy- four-page picture book. Its title? *Voice of the Voiceless.* It struck me funny, because that's what used to be said of Aristide, back when he was preach- ing against the Duvalier regime in the 1980s. The idea that now the voice of Haiti's voiceless is packaged in a coffee-table-style digital flipbook, the sheer unfeeling arrogance of the title, the condescension implied toward those who wrote their little scraps of pathetic notes, the use these victims are being put to—it all passes understanding. And I can tell you this right now: Leonard Doyle thinks it's a good thing, and that he's doing good. He has a lot of knowledge about Haiti; he works hard—he's no fool. He's in the job, seemingly, for all the right reasons, as well as for his paycheck and his important résumé line. He loves his job, likes Haitians, enjoys hanging out with and manipulating the press (which is his job). Still, the work he does is the old-fashioned information gathering and information dissemination that used to be done, more covertly and with less panache and brio, by intelligence agencies.

The history behind both the Haitian Revolution at the end of the eighteenth century and the rebellion against the American occupation of Haiti in the first half of the twentieth century is complicated, but one thing can be said of both: the mountains were always the rebels' friends. Up in these cloudy, cool green fastnesses, rebellion was planned. This was where the maroons camped out, where slave runaways and anti-imperialist rebels alike lived (at different times, although part of the same ongoing movement) in small, hidden villages, or *bouks,* in the high hills. During plantation times, such fugitive mountainside maroon communities were common throughout the West Indies and Latin America. The biggest and best-known cliché about Haiti, other than "poorest country in the Western Hemisphere," is the proverb *"dèyè mòn, gen mòn"*— "behind the mountains, more mountains"—which does indeed just about say it all.

Frankly, the white man, no matter his nationality, did not know the mountains of Haiti and didn't want to know them. In general, this is still true. For centuries these mountains, which rise up in powerful, majestic ridges one behind the other, sheltered and protected those who fled to their dark forests. Only a few expeditions of colonizers and occupiers have ever been successful in hunting down the Haitian enemy in the mountains. In later times, the twisted corridors, pathways, and cardboard-and-tin-walled alleys of the urban shantytowns provided a similar cover for the regimes' natural opponents, a place to hide and live for grassroots organizers and popular political movements and frightened opponents of the Duvaliers. You could hide with some ease in the shantytowns. Into these unknown and potentially threatening areas, neither the regime's nor the American embassy's reach often extended with any efficiency or regularity. Only MINUSTAH, with its heavy equipment and flak jackets, has had the nerve to storm the shantytowns, chasing down people whom its officials considered to be gangsters but who, others argued, were opposition figures; possibly they were both; some victims were neither.

The earthquake changed all that, changed the whole scenario. Given the general panic, these areas—subject to the post-seismic paradigm shift—no longer seemed off-limits to the outsiders who were coming down to Haiti (although some of the shantytowns and slums have by now made it onto the no-go lists of the humanitarian organizations). The immediate and imperative needs and demands of relief work meant that the shantytowns, and also the new earthquake camps, were open to all.

In air-conditioned offices at the UN logistics base, or "logbase," in Port-au-Prince, near the airport, and in IOM offices in the provincial town of Gonaïves as well, scores of serious, committed Haitian students and graduates have been working on a mapping project for Leonard Doyle. These are some of Haiti's smartest and most dedicated young people; now they are mappers. They are the base workers of the Humanitarian OpenStreetMap Team (HOT), which is operating with IOM Communications to provide an open, accessible map of every single place in Haiti.

These young people sitting around tables strewn with computers, printers, cables, and papers are the researchers, who, in concert with Doyle's kiosk project, are hoping to map every street and alleyway in the country, every rural path and bicycle route, down to every last corridor in the shantytowns and camps. They bend over their computers; they input the information they gathered that day as they traveled around the country on bicycle, mototaxi, and foot on their reconnaissance missions. This little alley in Raboteau, the biggest shantytown in Gonaïves, leads from the end of Avenue Egalité to a little courtyard, where there's a small Baptist church on the left-hand corner. Now it's mapped; before it existed only for those who lived there. Over here, on this map, there's a long, unnamed post-earthquake road in the Aviation earthquake camp in Port-au-Prince that extends from the old amphitheater there almost all the way to Boulevard Jean-Jacques Dessalines, commonly known as Grande Rue. Now it's mapped. *Eksetera-era,* as they say in Creole.

Concerning the mapping effort in Haiti, the directors of HOT, on their "donate" Web page, say:

> [The] missions in Haiti have been very successful, but we are aiming to not only teach OpenStreetMap skills to select Haitian people, but to equip those enthusiastic local mappers with everything they need to go on and move out into new communities. There is going to be a need to have more kits to leave behind to allow OSM communities to keep growing not only in Port Au Prince, but also in main Haitian cities like Jacmel, Leogane and Gonaive and in their hinterlands . . . HOT kits will be key to support this kind of growth. Furnishing of adequate hardware kits to Haitian mappers will also contribute to their readiness to prepare and respond to future disasters including the ongoing risk posed by cyclones.

This is just the sort of project everyone loves—I know. It seems to combine the best of new technology—those kits that HOT is soliciting funds for cost "just under $4,000" each and include a Garmin GPS device, a Canon all-in-one printer, an external hard drive, a Dell XP laptop, five SD cards, six packs of rechargeable batteries, and various cables and cases— with the contemporary obsession with knowing *everything,* and also with a desire to do good. To say nothing of really cool spy-kit portability. So you can have a map of everywhere in Haiti, and a fun GPS device (in the hands of *local* people, not outsiders), and you can also rescue future victims of future tragedies, using your maps and devices. Who doesn't like a map?

But looked at from a different angle—which is something I do reflexively in Haiti now; I can't help but look at things another way— projects like this lay Haiti open to every and any outside incursion. These minutely detailed maps do to a country what the new millimeter wave images taken at the security lines in U.S. airports do to passengers. The mapping project seems, on the face of it, like equal rights for those places that Google doesn't waste its street-side cameras on. But what it really means is that there will be no place left to hide.

These bright young Haitian mappers are, looked at this way, cheerfully doing the detail work of Big Brother, or at least of MINUSTAH or some future Tonton Macoute–style police. It used to be that the CIA, using air force reconnaissance information and, later, satellite mapping, was the best and most accurate cartographer in the world. You should see their early maps and photos of Castro's Cuba. But in Cuba, at least Castro *knew* that these planes and their bosses were his enemy. Now it's OpenStreetMap's innocent army, a battalion of smart Haitians rushing around Haiti with notebooks and cameras, going about their task with, I believe, the best will in the world.

Possibly the humanitarian aspect of these inch-by-inch maps outweighs their incursion into Haiti's secret worlds. But the real reason Haitian victims of the 2008 pre-earthquake cyclones and flooding were not always rescued or cared for was not that no one could find them, but that hardly anyone tried, at least not initially. The victims were neglected because no rescue crews came, in the early stages. This was not because they were off the beaten track in unmapped enclaves that could not be discovered; the victims gathered in large numbers on roofs of downtown Gonaïves. They were in houses and fields along the national highway. You didn't need GPS and OpenStreetMap and Google's Street View to find them. Unrescued, they were on the front page of the *New York Times,* and all over the Web.

No matter what help they receive or don't receive, no matter where they fall on the maps of secret Haitian places, an estimated 515,000 camp people at this writing are still living in precariously close quarters in an unpredictable political, international, and community situation. The camps could be called Occupy Port-au-Prince, they look so much like the Occupy movements that blossomed in the United States in 2011. Haiti has its own wealthy 1 percent, or maybe its own .001 percent, and its own 99.999 percent of the rest. The habits and houses of the rich in Haiti are shocking in a country so poor, although the disparities are equally breathtaking just a few miles in various directions from where I live in L.A. Take, for example, the 13,000-square-foot palace—with a screening room, swimming pool, guest house, gym, playground, and servants' quarters—where a producer lives in Bel Air in Los Angeles, and then contrast that with the cab of a broken-down big rig in a parking lot where a homeless man lives only a score of miles away. Haiti is not always—not even usually—so different from us as it's traditionally made out to be.

As I said earlier, Haiti's is one of the most thoroughly globalized economies in the world. It has been globalized since the slave trade brought Africans, Europeans, and Native Americans together in one place, exploited human labor in the grossest way, and exported all of its fruits.

The 1791–1804 slave uprising and revolution themselves were global phenomena, as was the destructive debt of reparations (actually an indemnity) that the new nation of Haiti agreed to pay France beginning in 1825, the first meaningful instance of developing-world debt to a superpower. It was the first and perhaps the only instance of the victor agreeing to pay reparations to the loser in war. France demanded these reparations not only for the plantations they'd lost in the revolution and for the tons of sugar that had been burned, but also for the loss of property in general, among which were counted the slave rebels themselves. For decades the victorious Haitians were paying back the loser French for the slaves' own freedom—paying the French back, essentially, for themselves, for their free bodies. The monies paid by Haiti took the country's slim revenues and placed them with French banks, thereby ending any chance that the economy of the baby nation could progress. The payment of these reparations, in other words, essentially turned the victor into the vanquished. Without the payments, however, France, which finally recognized Haiti thirty years after Dessalines declared its independence, would have continued to refuse to acknowledge its former colony or to admit the new country into any kind of world trade. Naval blockades, too, were always a threat.

The seemingly endless early-twentieth-century bickerings among the great powers over Haiti and its naval access to the Caribbean basin were also global phenomena that had to do with the biggest wars mankind had ever seen. And the late-twentieth-century infiltration of Haiti's economy, the *replacement* of its economy, by outside industries, agricultural dumping, and the American Plan for Haiti have also been global occurrences. Many of the people who live in grand mansions up on the hill in Péguyville, Bourdon, Montagne Noire, Laboule, and Pétionville have fortunes built on global trade; they are bankers and import-export merchants, but also—that most global of all trades—drug traffickers. They keep a great deal of their money outside Haiti. These are not usually people who invest in-country: it's too risky.

This lack of in-country investment by the moneymaking class is one reason Haiti has been so reliant on foreign aid, both before and after the earthquake. But in the world of foreign aid, things do not work the way most people would imagine they do. According to the Associated Press, most of the $379 million initially allocated by the United States for aid to Haiti after the earthquake did not go to Haiti or Haitians. About one-third of the money went to the U.S. military for the five thousand American troops that were sent in to help out and move rubble and keep the peace. About forty-two cents of each of those dollars ended up with big aid organizations, such as the UN's food program, Save the Children, and others. Very few cents per dollar, according to the AP investigation, went to Haitians, Haitian groups, or the government of Haiti.

A Congressional Research Service report six months after the quake showed the same pattern. The $1.6 billion that the United States promised for earthquake relief was allocated to the following U.S. government departments: $655 million to Defense; $220 million for Health and Human Services for grants to various states so that they could pay for expenses for Haitian evacuees; $350 million to USAID, for disaster assistance; $150 million to Agriculture for emergency food assistance; $15 million to Homeland Security, to pay for new, earthquake-related immigration fees. *Eksetera-era.*

When you read that, unmediated, you might feel that it was another outrage: How could the United States promise that money for Haiti, and then give it to itself? But it's not so surprising: that's how foreign aid has always worked in Haiti. What's instructive about the allocations of these funds is not that they were given to U.S. entities, but that that's how the United States—as well as other foreign governments and organizations—believes that it can help the developing world, and especially Haiti, whose government is viewed as obsessively corrupt, and whose organizations and people are often seen as some simplistic version of Fred Voodoo, a stereotype—either lying, cheating, manipulative incompetents, or silly, backward, useless children. The idea is that only through our own administration can anything be done for Haiti. The idea is that giving money to Haitian organizations is a vain enterprise. These foreign-aid figures highlight the real purpose of aid to Haiti both before and after the earthquake, which is to funnel money to the guys who, the Americans believe, can make things work here—which is to say, Americans.

In particular, that grant of $350 million to USAID stands out, for old Haiti hands, because we know that for decades, USAID—the United States Agency for International Development—received similar large portions of Haiti's American foreign aid, and achieved very little: it did not bring democracy to Haiti, it did not fix Haiti's sick political class, nor did it help build "civil society" (all of these among its aims); it did not reforest Haiti; it did not increase Haiti's agricultural output; it did not develop the Haitian school system; and one would even have a hard time arguing that it significantly relieved hunger in Haiti at any point. The positive changes in Haiti over this period came about because the world was changing: in Latin America and elsewhere moving away from dictatorship toward democracy. In fact, as the United States spent less in Latin America, democracy in different guises began to emerge and strengthen. What did USAID achieve in Haiti, then? Primarily, it kept itself alive and functioning—more or less—in Port-au-Prince.

That's not good, and it's money wasted, but at least the aim is clear: to fund ourselves to try to help Haitians, after our own fashion, while keeping our agency alive. It makes sense, given a certain worldview. What makes less sense is how the Clinton Bush Haiti Fund has disbursed its monies. This fund, as you may recall, was established at the behest of President Obama by former U.S. presidents Bill Clinton and George W. Bush to help Haiti recover in the immediate aftermath of the earthquake. In 2010, the fund raised nearly $49 million, much of it in small contributions from average Americans . . . and distributed only $7.7 million, or about 15 percent of that, in grants for Haiti. By the end of 2010, CBHF still had $40 million in its pockets. That was hard to hear for donors sucked in by the star power of the Clinton-Bush team, donors who thought that all those monies would go to ensure that there would be no more Haitians left homeless or hungry by the earthquake.

Instead, the fund has been keeping its money very tight and is no longer working on earthquake relief, but rather on its vision of a renewal of the old American plan for Haiti. Here's the latest mission statement from the CBHF website:

The previous story of Haiti has been one of aid, but now the Clinton Bush Haiti Fund is helping to change this story to one of rebuilding and thriving. We are making and encouraging smart investments that will put people back to work and create the environment for vibrant, sustainable economic growth. We focus on promoting job growth and economic opportunity primarily by:

1. Supporting microfinance institutions; 2. Providing small and growing businesses with access to financing and business services; 3. Facilitating job training and workforce development; and 4. Responding to critical, unmet needs.

There are reasons why funds that raise so much money, and then continue to raise it against the still emotionally powerful backdrop of the earthquake and its victims, have not figured out how to spend all that dough. Okay, let's just say it: it's not easy to decide how to spend giant wads of money in Haiti, although that's counterintuitive, since there is patently so much pressing need.

Here's another example: ten months after the earthquake, the United States still had not delivered any of the $1.15 billion in reconstruction funds it had, with great fanfare, promised for the relocation and transitional housing of the then more than a million camp residents. (The White House points out that the United States had spent $1.1 billion in immediate and relief funds, but that figure includes the USAID and Defense Department grants for Haiti.) To get these enormous amounts of money spent properly, you have to be organized, patient, clever, original, and thoughtful, and have a deep understanding of Haitian culture, none of which aid groups are famous for. Even old established ones like the Red Cross and USAID have very little idea what they should do in Haiti, much less relative newcomers like the Clinton-Bush fund.

After the relief effort faded, the overcrowded, destitute camps were left to their own devices, and many descended into illness and gangsterism.

A strain of cholera that had never before been seen in Haiti began devastating and decimating the country just under a year after the earthquake. At first, many suspected it had arisen in the camps because of lack of sanitation and overcrowding, two conditions cholera loves. Since it appeared, the disease has cycled along with Haiti's torrential rainy seasons. It can kill within just a few hours after symptoms present: the cure is rehydration, but to rehydrate you have to have access to clean water—which is not the case for more than three-quarters of Haiti's population.

So far, more than seven thousand people have died of the disease. The latrine situation around the camps, combined with the rainy season and unsanitary conditions in seaside shantytowns and riverine villages, is likely to keep the epidemic alive in the earthquake region, in spite of concerted efforts on the part of the Haitian Health Ministry and many international health care organizations to treat the ill and try to contain the spread. Cholera has been killing people in all of Haiti's nine departments, way up in distant, cut-off mountain villages, in the ravines, on the plains, in the valleys, at the seaside, everywhere.

I went with Leonard Doyle to Terre Neuve, a tiny, picturesque town on the way up to Haiti's northernmost tip, and saw how the Terreneuvians alerted their medical clinic to new cases of cholera. A thin, older villager in a purple Hawaiian shirt demonstrated the village's cholera warning system for us. He sat down on the roots of a tree near the town's health clinic. Next to him, lying on its side in the dirt, there happened to be the rusting but still clear remains of a small colonial cannon. The man sat back and suddenly, magically pulled a very large conch shell out from behind his back, which he proceeded to blow as if it were a ram's horn in biblical times. (A blown conch also called the rebelling Haitian slaves into battle, according to legend, and was used by the mountain rebels for the same purpose in their campaigns against the Marines.) Doyle was videotaping the performance, and soon after we returned to UN logbase, a nicely shot clip of it went up on the IOM cholera page, for fund-raising purposes. Now everyone in the world who wanted to could hear the piercing call of the cholera conch.

This cholera comes from the outside, like the European-born smallpox, measles, and even the common cold in the early days of European evangelization and colonialism in the Western Hemisphere. The saga of the disease's first appearance in post-earthquake Haiti seemed almost scripted, it fit so well into the way Haitians view themselves in relation to outsiders. International medical documentation has shown that the strain of cholera that is still killing Haitians by the hundreds was probably brought into the country by asymptomatic UN peacekeeping troops from Nepal, who came in after the earthquake. The Nepalese peacekeepers' quarters were not properly sanitized, and their cholera-contaminated waste flowed into the Artibonite River, and thence into the Haitian water system, such as it is.

This series of events—earthquake, new troops, devastating illness, national contamination—caused an uproar, because MINUSTAH, the UN's stabilization troops, is a controversial force seen by many Haitians as a foreign occupation, and now here they were, if you wanted to interpret it that way, killing thousands of Haitians with a biological weapon: a variant of the South Asian *Vibrio cholerae* El Tor serotype 01 bacterium, as it turned out. Haitians often see a purposefulness or intention in events that outsiders might assume are coincidental or happenstance. However it came about, the disease spread, and at one point people were collapsing and dying in the streets. Farmers would come down from the remote mountaintops to sell their produce, become infected at the market in the valley, and drop dead on their way back home. Their bodies, collected by family and washed, as is customary with the dead, would spread the disease to the funerary helpers and, since those women also prepared the funeral meal, to the entire family and village. All of this fed a mythomaniac national imagination that even in the best of times is historically susceptible to paranoia.

Cholera came to Haiti at a point when world enthusiasm for the earthquake as a charitable event was fading. The new crisis provided an impetus for invigorated fund-raising campaigns among the big relief and reconstruction groups. "It's tragedy upon tragedy for Haiti," Imogen Wall, acting as a spokeswoman for the UN, told CBS. "We're working on a worst-case scenario. We're planning for a national outbreak." Of course this was true, and there was eventually a national-scale outbreak, and it was the right thing to say.

But, looked at from a more jaundiced point of view—from my point of view, that is—it sounded breathless, almost eager: behind the sadness of "tragedy upon tragedy" is the possibility of more funding for aid organizations, more jobs, longer stays in this fascinating, troubled place—in nice new apartments, driving those big, air-conditioned Land Rovers. It's not as if humanitarian workers are in the business for the big cars and nice apartments, but the sweet stuff comes with the territory, and the crisis caravan is used to it. I know many aid people who say right up front that if they lived in their home countries they would never live as well as they do in disaster areas—once the harshest moment of the disaster is past, that is.

Imogen Wall is British, and her most recent stint in Haiti was to research and write a British government–funded report on the role of new communications technologies in disaster response. I kept trying to get her to explain that, over and over. Like, *what?* It seemed an obvious topic, but unexpected from the British government, an entity I'd never thought of as involved in contemporary Haiti, in any case. (I'd never thought of Thailand and Nepal as particularly involved in Haiti—or Israel, for that matter—but after the earthquake they were all there.) The British study was a job, as Wall acknowledged, and a job that let her travel around Haiti, which she adores, with some of the friends she'd made in the international humanitarian and relief community during other disasters around the world. Wall went about investigating her subject with energy and intelligence. She's a good egg, and a self-described disaster junkie who has often worked for the UN. But from now on, whenever I learn about a new Haitian crisis, I will always hear Wall, who read medieval history at Cambridge, speaking in her Oxbridge accent: "It's tragedy upon tragedy for Haiti . . ."

8

GOLF-COURSE CAMP

Bel soulyè bezwen mache a tè kanmenm
Beautiful shoes still have to walk on the ground

When I visited his refugee camp on the grounds of the Pétionville golf
course, Sean Penn was out of the country. I was taken around by an Australian, one of Penn's camp people. He was powerfully built, handsome,
with a buzz cut and some kind of World War I beret on his head: straight
out of central casting—Penn hires his people that way, his people tell
me, as long as they also have an impressive résumé. Penn was at home in
California, getting ready to shoot a movie. "That's how he finances this,"
said the Australian, gesturing down the hill at the tents, the latrines, the
women sandbagging a runoff gully next to the main thoroughfare, as if
Penn had paid for all this with his own money—which he had not. The
big deal about Penn back then was that he lived "on campus," which set
him apart from the usual Hollywood do-gooder, and in fact set him apart
from almost all of the post-earthquake relief and development people,
who lived in those expensive enclaves and compounds away from Haitians. Back then, when he was in Haiti, Penn did stay in the camp.

  In the early days, visitors would check in at the camp at a big reception tent. There were lounge chairs for the people who were employed by

the camp. Buildings and tents were erected on the tennis courts, which were conveniently flat and floor-like. Penn had a plethora of groups working in his camp, including well-known international organizations such as Oxfam, Doctors Without Borders, and Catholic Relief Services, as well as volunteers that J/P HRO, the fund-raising entity for the camp, solicits on its own account (the J/P of the name is *P* for Penn and *J* for an original donor who is no longer associated with the camp; the HRO is for Haitian Relief Organization). From the very beginning, Penn was asserting that he would disestablish the camp as soon as it could be done; he was experimenting with the Corail relocation, and he also wanted to move all the camp's residents back into new housing in their old neighborhoods. But because it was a camp with good services, new people were still coming there even as old residents were packing up.

During his first months in Haiti, Penn gave several interviews in high-profile magazines that featured him as a celebrity apart, a special person, better than Paul McCartney's ex-wife Heather Mills with her anti-landmine group and her gigantic divorce settlement; better than his own ex-wife Madonna with her failed school for Malawian girls; at least as good as Matt Damon and Angelina Jolie, who are active but who don't live on-site. Penn clearly wanted people to be aware of his profound and singular commitment to Haiti and of the good work that he was doing ("that he doesn't *have* to do," as one admirer pointed out, as if *anyone* has to work in Haiti).

Here's one example of the sycophantic, outsize praise lavished on Penn, this piece by Doniphan Blair on a website called CineSource (the article was titled "The Healing Journeys of Sean Penn"):

Penn . . . had a penchant for fisticuffs but there is no denying he is setting an excellent example for all of us . . . on how to channel intensity into productivity. It's *noblesse oblige* at the highest level of celebrity, practiced with aplomb, dedication to detail and metaphysical balance, albeit with the occasional falling off the wagon (like nicotine addiction). Regardless, Penn's efforts have led to a *massive outpouring of art and philanthropy.*

"I came to Haiti in January with the intention of spending a couple of weeks, primarily helping to deliver intravenous pain management to hospitals, not to start a nonprofit," Penn told Stephanie Strom of the "NY Times." Since then he has become *the hands-down, hands-on leader of a new "brat pack" of Hollywood talent, including Ben Stiller, Matt Damon and Ben Affleck, who are tackling intractable social problems.* [my italics]

I can't help but hope that Penn finds such articles embarrassing and beside the point. By now, I'm pretty sure he does. He cannot stand to have the word "visionary" applied to him, for instance. I like to believe that, in granting these interviews, Penn was astutely using his fame as a way to keep Haiti and its problems in the minds of the media and the world. The article quoted above, for example, was an earthquake anniversary piece on a website that—without Penn's involvement in Haiti—wouldn't be giving a lot of space to the country and its woes. Most of these pieces have photographs that show Penn in the foreground, intensely looking into the distance, on a walkie-talkie, a commanding hand descending through the air. He's usually wearing banana-republic clothes and looking weary and battle worn (of course, he looked like that before his involvement in Haiti), while Haitians go about their daily lives in the background. In photojournalism, the exotic population used as a backdrop is called "staffage." *Vanity Fair* says Penn carries a Glock pistol.

In these stories, Penn is portrayed as an angry savior who refuses to take no for an answer. In fact, it would seem, reading these pieces, that *only* Sean Penn knows how to make Haiti work. By virtue of starting out knowing nothing about Haiti, little about humanitarian work, or NGO functioning, or refugee camps, or Haitian politics or history, he managed to get things accomplished. His group has removed huge amounts of rubble; they've demolished condemned buildings; they've worked with Digicel, the cell phone company, to build new schools in Cité Soleil, far from Penn's camp. They've sent helicopters to rescue or bring hydration

salts to remote cholera victims. They've now also built scores of buildings for earthquake refugees to move into. Their medical staff has treated
more than a hundred thousand people, and Penn's group has distributed cholera treatments around the whole country. In addition, they've
trained more than two hundred Haitians, and they employ that many as
staff. That's not nothing—these are serious achievements that even skep-
tics, and even Janet Reitman, who wrote the negative *Rolling Stone* piece,
cannot deny. And Penn makes small but important things happen, too.
Megan Coffee, the American doctor at the hospital downtown, credits
Penn with finding an unfindable diphtheria antitoxin for a patient of
hers. "He came through," she says.

Ignorance is a virtue, for Penn, at least insofar as he gets himself
portrayed. His success at getting things done in a place he initially knew
nothing about, and the failure of many groups with expertise to do
the same, reminds me that often it is actually those who do remember
history who are doomed to repeat it, while those who have no idea or
who've forgotten can sometimes escape a reprise. Sometimes it's better
to know less, even though people who know more, and have more invested in that knowledge, and who think they can predict failure from
the typical indicators (people like me, that is), will always look down
on you, and will always tell you it cannot be done. Often, the experts
will be right, but sometimes they'll be wrong, especially in extraordinary
circumstances. The earthquake, combined with the fame and energy of
Sean Penn, was just such an extraordinary circumstance. He's a peculiar
and unexpected person, in an unexpected situation, and all those who
predicted failure, fuck-up, and combat fatigue for him were wrong.

Now his success was coming back to haunt him, because his camp
was too good to leave, and it was proving hard, though not impossible,
to depopulate it. The new housing had to be convincing, and Penn and
the groups he worked with were always trying to up the amount they
could appropriate for building new places and bolstering old homes that
survived the quake. (California readers: you cannot call it "rebolting," because these houses were never bolted in the first place. I've only seen one

basement in Haiti, for example. Foundations normally extend only to a six-inch or one-foot depth. Unless they are colonial dungeons.)

Much of the coverage of Penn that's come out on his work in Haiti has been celebrity suck-upping of the "isn't he a saint" type. But he's no saint, even of the gritty kind: he's Sean Penn. When Sean Penn gets things done in Haiti, it's because he's Sean Penn, and people want to do things with him and for him. He lifts up his head and money flows to him. Penn has a special value as head of a camp, because anything you do with or for him gets you publicity. He can hire very good people to work for him because he's Sean Penn, and everyone wants to work for him. Everyone wants to know him. Now that he's been in Haiti for two years, about a quarter of all conversations within the relief and development communities begin by asserting a connection to Penn or his camp. Penn himself is friendly with all the most visible players in Haiti, including the valuable, efficient, and connected Paul Farmer. Penn gets to be friends with them because . . . he's Sean Penn. And also because Farmer is Farmer, a celebrity of a sort in his own right, especially in Haiti, a person whose number Penn was able to get immediately after the earthquake from Madonna—whom Farmer knew from shared African experience. That's what's so precious about the new celebrity connection to world poverty: it lets you put Madonna and Paul Farmer in the same sentence.

Penn can get financial backers for his Haiti project because he's Sean Penn. It's not like helping Megan Coffee, for which you get a nice "thank you." If you get mattresses or tents through customs for Penn, or if you donate cots for a medical clinic at his camp, you might even get a photo op with him; at the very least you can mention that you and he have a working relationship. You might get to hang out with him on the Hotel Oloffson terrace. (Penn told me that he goes to the Oloffson only to see "friends from my community" who stay there—by "my community," he means Hollywood.) You might even see your name appear in *Vanity Fair* or the *New York Times Magazine* as one of his supporters. And in return he'll get things done for you that only Sean Penn can get done in Haiti. This still begs the essential question about Penn and Haiti, which is:

What is an American actor doing running a refugee camp, and what is it about Penn, and Haiti, that allowed such a thing to happen?

Penn has said some very astute things about outsiders in Haiti, because in his short, intense time there, he's figured some things out. "Many people in the . . . disaster-relief community," he told *Vanity Fair*, "share much with Hollywood: envy, Schadenfreude, and the cover [that] bureaucracy gives to a cult of unimaginative ambulance chasers—all of whom want to claim it was they who 'made the movie' on Haitian relief." He seems, though, to want to claim that role for himself: *he's* the one making the Haiti movie. Penn is well-known for thinking he's better at everything he does than anyone else.

And yet here is the moving (and I assume true) thing that he's said about his Haitian experience, his relationship with the people in his camp: "It's a reciprocal thing. They have returned to me something I had lost—my humility."

9
MISSIONARY STYLE

Blan bay, nèg pran
The foreigner gives, the Haitian takes

The superfamous, well-connected Sean Penn tried to do things one way in Haiti, and he succeeded. His camp is run like a movie set: Penn's the director, but he has to cooperate with scores of others. He managed over time to put together a staff of able professionals, and a highly willing cast of Haitians who are more or less happy to do whatever is required to get ahead in Penn's operation. The missionaries Heather and Gerson Nozea, who also came down to Haiti right after the quake, had other organizational models for doing good. They had ideals about community, church, belief, faith, and humanity. Now let's see which method worked better.

The Nozeas are nice people. They believe in Jesus and his teachings. They want to do good and help others. After the Haitian earthquake, they wanted to start a small community in Haiti to help victims. Heather's a small, blond-haired American, from a little town south of St. Louis. Gerson's a tall, lanky Haitian-American who grew up in Carrefour, the vivid, overcrowded, filthy, squalid, and ebullient town just outside Port-au-Prince. They're married. They met when Heather was on a mission in the northwest of Haiti for a group called Northwest Haiti Christian

Mission. Together they started a group called Growing Hope for Haiti, in 2009. Their long-term plans were to work on their own in the northwest of Haiti, separate from the mission group they'd started with. They were both good Christians, but they had some ideas of their own.

"We worked with the group," Heather says, "but we didn't get along with their ideas. We don't like handouts. Handouts create dependency and increase entitlement. And they don't fix anything; they're like a Band-Aid on a wound."

In the northwest province, the Nozeas bought a three-acre plot from a farmer and planned to create a community with solid educational facilities and sustainable agriculture. But Gerson still had another year of college to finish in the States.

Then the earthquake struck. The Nozeas weren't in Haiti at the time, but they decided they needed to come. (There's that difficult question again: Did they themselves have a need to come? Or did they think that Haiti, or Haitians, needed them to come?) Gerson got in through the Dominican Republic a week after the earthquake, and Heather came down with a church team a few days later. Along with others, they set up an instant camp of helpers in Carrefour. Heather already had a network of people back home who supported her mission work, and, as she says, she didn't even *need* to raise money. Some sixty thousand dollars poured in to support her in the first few weeks.

"There was a new openness in Haiti because of the earthquake," says Gerson. "Before the foreigners arrived, Haitians were trying to help each other. Rich Haitians were picking up bleeding victims in their fancy cars and rushing them to the hospital. That lasted about five days. After foreign aid started coming in, those same cars were being rented for a thousand dollars a week. Suddenly everyone was talking about how the earthquake was an 'opportunity.' I hate hearing that. People were already talking about how to get food for free and then sell it for profit. Everything was about business. You never heard about the injured or the dead. There was no talk about pain. Everyone was hurrying back to doing things the old way: corrupt, profit-seeking."

Heather and Gerson went and worked for about a month with a medical group near the airport, where camps were being established. Heather worked at the front desk doing triage, and Gerson was doing maintenance. They slept in tents and ate protein bars.

"We still had all this money and we were thinking about what would have the best long-term effect. We thought: let's build some permanent housing," Heather says. Working with the Fuller Center for Housing, a Christian group, the Nozeas developed what she calls a "holistic plan" for about twenty-five to fifty permanent homes, with community restrooms and micro-financing. Its target population was amputees, pregnant women, and single mothers.

They moved to a town near the earthquake's epicenter, where 80 to 90 percent of the buildings had collapsed and, according to estimates, between twenty thousand and thirty thousand people were killed. The Nozeas wanted to buy some land and start their project. Even before the earthquake, land "was like gold" in this area because of population pressures and scarcity of open turf, Gerson says. Now, with the enormous need for fast new housing to go up, land was almost priceless. In the old days, foreigners were not allowed to buy property in Haiti—this law was first promulgated by Dessalines. But it was weakened under the American Occupation, and the new constitution of 1987, which is ostensibly in force today, explicitly permits aliens to own real property.

The man from whom the Nozeas tried to buy their first piece of land—well, it turned out, from the deed they saw at the notary's office, he would have had to have been two years old when he bought the three hundred acres, and already, at two, a general in the Haitian Army whose name was on the deed. So this first guy had, in fact, nothing to do with the land he was trying to sell them.

"We tried to do things logically, and according to how you would do it in the States," Gerson says. "We knew to trust no one, but still. We'd be negotiating for a piece of land, and then, we run into someone else who is selling the *same* piece of land." There were no clear titles, he says. This is a notorious problem in Haiti, a legacy that in some cases dates back to the occupation, if not the revolution. Even the few titles that were on record were subject to debate, and in any case many such documents had disappeared in the rubble. Heather says even "normal" Haitians have to buy their land three times; it's an accepted practice, she claims. Certainly, it's not unheard of. But still, Heather says that she and her husband had "the naïve notion" that someone might make a small sacrifice and sell a piece of land for a good cause at a reasonable price to help the community. "But they were all vultures," she says.

One prospective seller, a Haitian, told the Nozeas that he was a U.S. Marine. He told them he was now working at the U.S. embassy. Oh, and he said he was also a Drug Enforcement Administration operative. The Nozeas' notary told them that this man's papers looked as if they were in order. Of course, Gerson says, "anyone can go and get fake papers, and there are no consequences. We assumed a minimal level of justice, but we were wrong." So they paid the ostensible DEA agent twenty thousand dollars for the land, and they paid their notary's fee, and they paid the squatters already cultivating small farming gardens on the land to move off, and also paid them for the crops they had already planted.

The squatters, local cultivators and peasants, told the Nozeas that actually, the land belonged to the community. The self-styled DEA agent, the squatters said, did not own it. But it turned out that the alleged DEA agent was well connected and a good friend of the local police chief. The police chief came over in his uniform, and the Nozeas and their group began clearing the land.

But as project workers were clearing the land, another guy showed up while Gerson and Heather happened to be off property. Here's where the Nozeas' tale of woe turns into a shaggy-dog story. This fellow was a white Haitian of German ancestry, according to Gerson. He told Gerson's backhoe operator to cease clearing, and left his card. Gerson called him, and the Haitian-German told him that the land belonged to *him,* that it was former sugarcane farmland. This new owner had never heard of the "DEA agent" from whom the Nozeas had already bought the land. "We wanted to get our money back from the DEA guy, and buy the land from the German," Gerson says. But the German told them, "It's not a legal matter, it's a matter of force. You'll see."

For six months, the Nozeas had been living in tents at an abandoned factory nearby. One day, while they were at the camp discussing plans with the peasants and the DEA agent, the German came to serve papers and take possession of the property.

"Well, the DEA guy takes out a gun," Gerson says. "The German pulls out a gun, too. So here's the situation: we own the land, the DEA guy owns it, the German owns it, and now the people, too, are telling us *they* own it, and thugs from the tent camp next door are saying they own it, too. The thugs get in a fight and one of them breaks the arm of a guy who tries to convince everyone to calm down—all of this in front of a fresh mission group from the States who have no idea what's going on."

Finally, the Nozeas in their confusion and desperation go to the local authorities. They complain: four different people say they own our land, which we've already bought. They look expectantly at the official over his big desk. He smiles and says, oh, don't worry, it's simple: that's government land.

"Now we had five owners," Gerson tells me. The local leader allegedly told the Nozeas that he would "fix everything" and asked for a small fee of $1,500 to get the job done. They paid him up front, the Nozeas say. But when they went back to him after there had been more squabbling, he shrugged, they say. It turned out that the land *did* belong to the German, he reportedly told them. "There's nothing I can do." He kept the $1,500, too, according to Gerson.

Heather: "We didn't come here to be in a land battle between two gunmen."

Gerson: "So we left that land."

And they found new government land, through the helpful official. But this piece was disputed, also, it turned out. The same Haitian-German claimed it as his.

Heather: "Everyone makes you feel you are so stupid for believing the others."

Finally they got settled on a third piece of land. The community there said they were pleased. After talking to the local authorities, the lawyer the Nozeas had hired said it was a good deal. They paid only four thousand dollars for this piece of land, for fees and clearing.

Now the project could begin for real. They started putting in composting toilets. But there was an issue with the tax situation, and eventually that got so complicated that the Nozeas finally threw up their hands and put the whole project on hold.

"They always thought we were trying to make money," Heather says about not just the multiple sellers of the land but also the people for whom she and her husband were trying to build housing. "People think we're sitting around trying to make money off them when actually we didn't even eat trying to help them."

The program the Nozeas had conceived required families to work for three thousand hours in the community in order to have a house there.

"But it really doesn't work," Heather says, "because so much is being handed out elsewhere that they think we're cutting our expenses by forcing them to work, and that we are keeping a profit from the money that has been donated." Gerson points out that Haitians also think he himself must be making money there, because no Haitian would leave the United States and return to Haiti voluntarily unless he was in it for profit. When Haitians didn't see them as chumps or marks, they imagined the Nozeas were parasitic profiteers, *loups-garous,* which means werewolf or vampire bloodsucker.

But, against all probability, things eventually began falling into place. The tax issue was resolved, and the Nozeas had a chance to build eight permanent houses, eight showers, and an access road . . .

It was too good to be true. One day, people whom Heather describes with a knack for Haitian mystery as "officials from the [town] office behind the [town] office" (a kind of shadow government recognized by the helpful official) decided they wanted a few of the Nozeas' acres for themselves. The Nozeas said no—there wasn't enough space for the project without that land. Then one day, the Nozeas arrived at the project to find that stakes had been driven into the earth to mark off land that allegedly did not belong to the project. This stake-driving land grab was an old tactic of the Tonton Macoutes. The people who were working at the project said the stakes were put in by people sent by the ever obliging local leader, who were claiming the land.

The Nozeas tried every recourse to reclaim the acres. They went to a legislator in Port-au-Prince; they used Gerson's family connections; they pressured their lawyer; they went back to the town office; they went to MINUSTAH; they went to the police.

But when they came back from the States after a vacation in December 2010, "we found out that every little bit of the land we had not staked out ourselves had been sold by others," Heather says. "The thugs and troublemakers and officials from the town office had built on it."

One point to be made to the Nozeas: absentee landlords do not succeed in Haiti. But that's what they became, because the tension was too much for them. They left the quarrelsome town and moved nearer to the airport. "We managed it from afar," Heather says. The few families remaining who were supposed to get houses from the Nozeas' project were already in them. Trying to anticipate problems, the Nozeas brought some of the troublemakers in the area before a judge and paid them off in front of him, so that it would be, as Heather says ruefully, "on the record."

Heather: "I believe power in Haiti in the end resides in the threat of violence."

Gerson: "We're not working here anymore because we're not willing to do what it takes."

Heather: "The problem is bigger than five hungry Haitian babies."

Because of the influx of foreign reconstruction aid, Gerson says, Haitians, on his project at least, he noticed, had begun to feel that the money to build the houses was theirs; they felt "entitled to that money," he says, "so that, from being a project we are doing for the Haitians, it turned into, really, a project we were doing to satisfy the donors, because what the Haitians seemed to want was the cash; but the donors wanted to see the houses." Metaphorically, the Nozeas and their donors wanted to buy the beggar a sandwich or a hearty cup of coffee, while the beggar had other ideas about what might constitute a satisfactory mendicant transaction.

In other words, what Gerson feels—and he is no economic analyst, incidentally—is that the economic culture spawned by foreign aid kills a sense of pride and ownership. Eventually, the town office announced to Gerson and Heather that the two of them had to remain there, on site, and finish the project.

"When, after all," Gerson says, in a tone of rumbling indignation, "it was the town office and its manipulations and land grabs that were the whole reason that we couldn't finish the project."

Gerson: "It's like we owed it to them. They think that money belongs to their town. They think we never wanted the project to succeed because we always wanted to leave with the money. They think we actually stole the money from the donors."

Anyone who has read Graham Greene's *The Comedians* will instantly recognize in the Nozeas the very type of the innocent American, in over his head. Greene's failed U.S. presidential candidate Smith and his wife come to the tortured land of Papa Doc Duvalier to establish "a vegetarian center." They love what they call "the Negro race." They are big supporters of the civil rights movement in America. And they believe what Haiti really needs is vegetarianism. They are vegetarians themselves, dining on crackers and hideous concoctions like Barmane and other brewer's yeast-ish items they bring down with them. They are sure that their vegetarian center, once firmly established, will convert Haiti in time into a happy, rational, satisfied state. Needless to say, all does not go well for their center. Downcast but wiser, the Smiths leave Haiti having achieved nothing.

Because of their disheartening experience, the Nozeas, too, have abandoned composting toilets and community-built housing, their version of the Smiths' vegetarian center. They have left Haiti for good, or at least for the foreseeable future. Late at night I think about them. The story they've told is so complicated, detailed, full of characters and meanderings and plotlines, almost like a comedic Wodehouse casino-town romp. It can't have been easy for them to recall every little bit properly, and of course I'm aware of the pitfalls of story reconstruction. The core of the Nozeas' story made immediate sense to me, however, because I have heard other stories like it over the years, though not so extreme (perhaps because those adventures didn't take place in the extremity of the earthquake's aftermath). All the corruption and conniving, the ins and outs of the deeds, and even those Duvalierist wooden stakes set down on the land when no one was watching—they strike a chord in me. But I know, too, that sometimes the minister's daughter is the one who stole Aunt Augusta's pearls; sometimes the one pleading innocence is not so innocent.

The Nozeas finally decided that foreign aid is no good for Haiti. The best way to help Haiti, Gerson says, is not to help Haiti. He points out that because of foreign aid and material coming into Haiti, the price of home-building goods has risen so dramatically that it is now impossible for Haitians to afford to build their own homes. In other words, the aid superstructure in Haiti, because of its reconstruction goals, has created exactly the circumstances in which it becomes indispensable.

Without knowing it, the Nozeas have stepped right into a heated debate that has been raging for decades over the aims, goals, and potential of foreign and humanitarian aid. They've enacted a little set piece for the experts to evaluate. Among those involved in the dispute over the value of aid are the economist William Easterly, author of *The White Man's Burden: Why the West's Efforts to Aid the Rest Have Done So Much Ill and So Little Good;* Jeffrey Sachs, the economist who is also the author of *The End of Poverty: Economic Possibilities for Our Time,* among other books, and the founder of the Millennium Promise Alliance, which seeks to put together serious funders with sustainable international development projects; David Rieff, the idiosyncratic author of *A Bed for the Night: Humanitarianism in Crisis;* Dambisa Moyo, the Zambian economist and author of *Dead Aid: Why Aid Is Not Working and How There Is a Better Way for Africa;* and Amartya Sen, the Nobel Prize–winning Indian economist and author of *Development as Freedom.*

Some of the questions raised by these experts are exactly the ones raised by the Nozeas' story of "helping Haiti": Does development aid achieve anything? Can programs conceived by outside, non-affected populations ever work? Whom exactly does aid benefit, and whom is it intended to benefit? Does Haiti have the ability to deal with and use development aid as intended by donors? Should *donors* decide how aid is to be used? If donors don't have control of what they give, will they give? Should relief and other items be distributed for free, which can lead to their being siphoned off into the informal economy for profit rather than reaching their target population? Might direct cash handouts for relief and reconstruction possibly be a better alternative than assistance *programs,* as the beneficiaries of the Nozeas' project might have argued, if they'd been asked?

One American teenager I know went down to Haiti before the earthquake to work in a clinic in a remote village. One hot morning, he and some other foreign volunteers were digging and lifting small boulders out of the clinic's future garden space. A small knot of Haitian teenagers were watching, leaning up against a fence, hooting and laughing. Finally, the volunteers turned and asked them what it was that they found so absolutely hilarious. The Haitian kids answered, "You came here to do that for *free?*" The Haitians just couldn't get over it. To them these Americans were suckers, pure and simple.

The failure of aid in Haiti is caused not only by outsider innocence or incompetence but also in many cases by Haitian corruption and the country's lack, pre- and post-earthquake, of a serious functioning government that works for the people. Many say the government is disorganized, but no one is fooled. It's organized. Actually, the Haitian kleptocracy has been organized over the years, almost purposefully, one might conclude, to be porous and incompetent, to allow for corruption.

It is a mechanism into which money is poured and then siphoned off. The Duvaliers perfected it. It's an organized disorganization, an ordered disorder. Here's this, from a pre-earthquake report on the failures of aid in Haiti by the National Academy of Public Administration:

> Lack of [government] capacity went considerably beyond poor aid administration. Haiti has dysfunctional budgetary, financial or procurement systems, making financial and aid management impossible . . . A budget reform law enacted in 1985 was never fully implemented. Offices were not created and personnel remained unassigned. Budget procedures and policies were not in place, budget data were unavailable. From 1997 through 2001, there was no approved national budget. Internal and external audits were weak. No external audits were conducted for years. Not even Parliament had access to or approved the budgets. Public procurement procedures were never fully implemented. Procurement was decentralized without controls or accountability. Government utilized sole source contracts and unadvertised bidding. Government was unwilling or unable to pay vendors for services in a timely fashion. Budget reductions and low salaries drove away most finance professionals. One-half of Government expenses were non-recurrent or discretionary, making it virtually impossible to identify fund use, beneficiaries, or impact.

Gerson Nozea says, "I have learned so much here; I have to reevaluate. You can't put a price tag on what I've learned here." He sounds like so many first-time aid workers from the huge organized groups like the UN, Catholic Relief Services, the American Red Cross, USAID, and Clinton's Global Initiative. "It's easier," he concludes, "when you don't understand as much." Weirdly, the World Bank, which understands a lot (theoretically) and has provided hundreds of millions of dollars for programs to Haiti over the decades, sounds a lot like Gerson Nozea, first-timer. An internally generated report on its role in Haiti from the fall of

Duvalier in 1986 through 2002 stated that "the outcome of the [World Bank] assistance program is rated unsatisfactory (if not highly so), the institutional development impact, negligible, and the sustainability of the few benefits that have accrued, unlikely."

As to why Haiti has come to have such an incapacitated government . . . Let's put it this way: since 1915, when the U.S. occupation of Haiti began, the powerful neighbor to the north has treated Haitian governments, at best, as rubber stamps for U.S. policy and for American businesses working in Haiti, as well as for Haitian-run businesses friendly to American interests. For almost all of the twentieth century, only U.S.-approved Haitians could be president. The embassy looked the other way at internal political repression, to say nothing of continuing starvation, as long as Haitian governments were friendly or at least anticommunist, like Papa Doc's. Only when friendly dictators became so kleptocratic that people started fleeing the island en masse for the Bahamas and Florida did the United States perk up and perform regime change, as in the case of Baby Doc. Any leader who seems to have an agenda that puts the Haitian people ahead of the tiny Haitian business elite is thrown out: viz., Aristide, twice. This is not invented, left-wing, knee-jerk interpretation. It's just true.

And it began even before the occupation. Here's a quote from Frederick Douglass's angry lecture on Haiti, the one given in Chicago in 1893:

The fault [for instability in Haiti] is not with the ignorant many, but with the educated and ambitious few. Too proud to work, and not disposed to go into commerce, they make politics a business of their country. Governed neither by love nor mercy for their country, they care not into what depths she may be plunged. No president, however virtuous, wise and patriotic, ever suits them when they themselves happen to be out of power.

I wish I could say that these are the only conspirators against the peace of Haiti, but I cannot. They have allies in the United States. Recent developments have shown that even a former United States Minister, resident and Consul General to that country, has conspired against the present government of Haiti. It so happens that we have men in this country who, to accomplish their personal and selfish ends, will fan the flame of passion between the factions in Haiti and will otherwise assist in setting revolutions afoot.

To their shame be it spoken, men in high American quarters have boasted to me of their ability to start a revolution in Haiti at pleasure. They have only to raise sufficient money, they say, with which to arm and otherwise equip the malcontents, of either faction, to effect their object. Men who have old munitions of war or old ships to sell; ships that will go down in the first storm, have an interest in stirring up strife in Haiti. It gives them a market for their worthless wares. Others of a speculative turn of mind and who have money to lend at high rates of interest are glad to conspire with revolutionary chiefs of either faction, to enable them to start a bloody insurrection. To them, the welfare of Haiti is nothing; the shedding of human blood is nothing; the success of free institutions is nothing, and the ruin of a neighboring country is nothing.

Meanwhile, foreign aid and development continued in Haiti, even as regimes were implanted and then overturned—or *dechouké*—depending on the taste and will of the United States. What Haiti needed, and needs, but still cannot get, is the overthrow of the entire corrupt system. Aristide was to be the vehicle of that overthrow, and he began intelligently, by inserting himself at the last minute into an electoral process run by the supporters of that system: the Haitian Army, the elite, and the U.S. government. In the event, they could not but accord him the office he so resoundingly won. So they waited and, as Douglass says, "fan[ned] the flame," until they could get rid of him and ensure that no real change would come to Haiti. For the system, Aristide was a glitch.

Aid and development work have often been caught up in this quest for ongoing control, and have been wielded as useful tools of what Mike Davis, the social theorist, calls "soft imperialism" in his book *Planet of Slums.* But there have undeniably been programs that have done some good for the people of Haiti. Most of these have been in health care, like Paul Farmer's Partners In Health and Jean Pape's GHESKIO, the well-established Haitian Group for the Study of Kaposi's Sarcoma and Opportunistic Infections. Other successful programs have been in the arts, or microprojects with small local and resident staffs who work with children and others making films and crafts for sale. And then there are people who begin, like the Nozeas, as individual helpers, but who figure out how to cooperate with the slender institutions that already exist and who learn the Haitian ropes. These rogue elements can eventually end up as institutions themselves, as Paul Farmer did, as Sean Penn may. They have to have persevering personalities and a certain willingness to deny themselves for a period. They have to have something concrete to offer. They have to want to work alongside Haitians. They have to learn Creole.

In other words, they have to be like Megan Coffee.

10

SPAGHETTI ROUNDS

Lespwa fe viv
Hope lets you live

Every morning for nearly a year, no matter where she happened to be living, Megan Coffee would get up early and put a huge pot of clean water on the stove to boil. She got into this habit about half a year after the earthquake, when she realized that too many of her patients weren't getting enough to eat. Every morning, she had her coffee and would dump ten or twelve pounds of spaghetti into the simmering pot, then jump into her shower—that is, when she was staying in an apartment that had a shower and when that shower was working. The shower and the boiling spaghetti took about the same amount of time to reach completion, and when Dr. Coffee came out of the shower, she'd drain the spaghetti and get dressed. Then she'd load the drained pasta into a black garbage bag, dump that into a cardboard box for more secure transport, and wait for her ride to come pick her up. By now, it would be almost 8:00 AM.

Everything Dr. Coffee needs is taken care of by friends and strangers. She has no car; she pays no rent; she makes no salary. In the morning, a friend or helper would arrive in a car, and she'd plop the box of cooked pasta onto the backseat and they'd head down from her place, this one borrowed from friends, but others sometimes rented and paid for by friends, down to the center of town, past the camps and the crowds. Sometimes, when there was unrest in the capital's streets—disputed elections usually the cause, at that time—Dr. Coffee would have to walk to work, and so she'd walk. On those days, there just might not be spaghetti.

When she gets to the hospital, she lugs the box of pasta into the small nursing tent and sticks it on top of one of a couple of filing cabinets. This is spaghetti rounds, at the hour of the morning when Haitians think it's still cool out. Here, a fan is already going. The nursing tent is about twelve feet by twelve feet. A refrigerator stocked with medications stands in one corner, topped by a dusty plastic floral arrangement, and the nurses are at their desks (there's one desk for the administrative nurse, and a table that serves as a desk for everyone else, including Dr. Coffee). At this point the tuberculosis ward established by Dr. Coffee was a rogue operation on the grounds of the general hospital, with roots in an unprecedented disaster, so everything about it was ad hoc and de facto.

Everything about Dr. Coffee's ward was privately funded, although HUEH, the state hospital, is a public institution. Her tents were donated; her medicines were donated. The doctor had cobbled together a network of aid organizations devoted to health care in Haiti, many of them long-standing, like Partners In Health and GHESKIO, to help out, mostly in kind. HUEH was supportive; it paid for her Haitian staff. Like most of what works in Haiti, Dr. Coffee's TB ward functioned as a charitable seat-of-the-pants patchwork with involved individuals, including patients and their families, contributing their energy, time, and resources. After about a year of working at the hospital, the doctor was enough of a presence on Twitter that she was able to begin a useful fund-raising drive there, as well. Her followers were not many (a few more than 1,100), but they were loyal and concerned.

It helped that her ward was never a big operation. The little tent office had three metal folding chairs and a computer for the nursing staff, as well as a laptop for Dr. Coffee. Papers seemed to fly about in a random manner as the hopeful patients clustered at the door, some carrying X-rays of their own lungs like a visa for possible entry into Dr. Coffee's healing world. Magically, for each patient who has been seen before, a file appears, floating from the administrative nurse over the file cabinets and other staffers toward the front entry and Dr. Coffee. For each new patient, a dossier is established. In the midst of what looks like chaos, there is an underlying order. "I'm glad to see all these people come back on time for their meds," Dr. Coffee says, looking out over the small crowd. She used to have to scramble to find medications for her patients, but now she gets most meds through HUEH.

Dr. Coffee takes the rubber band from around her wrist and ties up her hair. She roots around in the tent for an oversize can of generic ketchup ("*sòs tomat*," the Haitians call it, with some glorification) and her box of generic mayonnaise—both of which probably came into Haiti at some point in a humanitarian aid container. "This," she says, looking up proudly from the two condiments, "is sauce." I raise my eyebrows.

"What can I say?" she asks. "They love it." She puts on a pair of blue latex gloves, pulls down her mask, and picks up the boxed bag of pasta with the ketchup can and the mayo box on top. In we go, masked and ready for food distribution. The patients are praying and saying grace.

Each patient whose family is too poor to provide his or her own food has an improvised bowl or plate reserved for the morning distribution, and an implement of some kind. One young patient's mother assists Dr. Coffee with handing out the food.

"She's like the office manager," the doctor says.

Each patient gets a mountain-size mound of pasta with a dollop of mayonnaise and a dollop of ketchup at the summit; in my day we used to call the mix of these two Russian dressing. The pasta is served by Dr. Coffee with her begloved hands in great, cascading masses; she tips out the sauce straight from the containers onto each plate. All but her most gravely ill patients sit back on their cots, propped up with cushions and pillows, and dig in. "I like to keep them happy," Dr. Coffee says. She peels off her ketchupy gloves. There are patches of mayonnaise stains now on her scrubs. "This is one of their perks." (Another perk she offers is free consultation for friends and relatives of the nurses who work with her. Another is that family members of patients are first in line to become her driver.)

After the earthquake in Haiti, spaghetti prepared in many ways dominated what might, in another place, be called the food scene. In the weeks right after the quake, it was practically the only food available. Just after the quake, in Léogâne, the town where McKenly Gédéon lost both his hands, a fat market lady with an impromptu street restaurant was selling the stuff from a huge black slavery-era-style iron cauldron in the middle of an ad hoc displaced-persons camp. Hers was a culinary masterpiece, a byzantine confection, compared with Dr. Coffee's. It included cut-up "hot dog," or *sosis* (sausage), which is a super-preserved log of pink something—might its ingredients be Styrofoam mixed with pork offal?—that comes from the Dominican Republic shrink-wrapped in transparent plastic. This sausage is sold in the hot Haitian markets day after day and bears no physical resemblance to food; it looks more like a vital but never seen component of manufacturing or insulation. Added to the spaghetti and "hot dog" were onion, pepper, Maguy-brand bouillon cubes, and some kind of fat that looks like butter. There were a few leaves of iceberg lettuce on the side. The sauce: ketchup and mayo. (Later, it turned out, according to Haitian reports, that this *salami*, as the hot dog is also known, did contain particles of excrement.)

The *New York Times* Haiti team that same week also dined on spaghetti with a sauce that the paper's leading reporters created in the kitchen of the Park Hotel, a run-down and now half-ruined place. Their spaghetti was better than the Léogâne market lady's because it included actual tomato sauce, onion, and garlic (hold the hot dog, hold the mayo). There was "spaghetti Creole" for journalists at all the hotels that were still standing. Doctors and volunteers ate spaghetti or rice and beans. The Léogâne market lady was selling her pasta for ten Haitian dollars a serving, or $1.20. The Hotel Oloffson was selling theirs for ten times that. A number of the clients the market lady was feeding told me that because of the price, it would be their only meal that day. One little girl in shorts and a tiny bright white tank top was going to share one plate with her whole family, all six of whom were living in a shack that looked like outsider art, at the edge of the camp.

Many of Dr. Coffee's outpatients are living in conditions like that. Their poverty, she points out, compounds the illness, because you need to be strong to survive TB, even with medication. On Twitter, she has recounted story after story of her patients who, against odds that would be insurmountable in the United States—homelessness, crushing poverty, disease onset at an unthinkably early age, lack of treatment over years and years—have survived and even improved.

A seven-year-old boy appears at the nursing tent, and Dr. Coffee asks for his name. Shadwell Sherline, he says, and shoves two X-rays up at her. She takes them and looks. They seem to conflict—Dr. Coffee always reads her patients' X-rays herself. "It saves the hospital money," she says, not commenting on the hospital's radiologists. On her X-ray scripts she always writes: "Do not interpret." HUEH pays for her patients' pictures. She pays for other tests unless a patient's family has some money. "If the family has money," Dr. Coffee says, "I try to get them to pay for the tests. Otherwise I'll be bankrupted by this even sooner."

In so many ways, Dr. Coffee is the ideal foreign-aid delivery figure. She's creative; she's responsive. She lets Haiti teach her how to deal with Haiti. She doesn't care if she gives her patients spaghetti with Russian dressing in the mornings, if that's what they want, if it feeds them and helps them gain weight. She figures out how to pay for what the hospital won't pay for and her patients cannot pay for. She runs around to grocery stores buying peanut butter for her people, and notices things like the changes in the relative prices of local and foreign peanut butters. She offers people no money, and no jobs for pay. What she gives people in kind—medication—is strictly for their own use and does not come to them in bulk, so it's not worth it to resell in the marketplace, plus resale would mean not taking one's own meds. Because she offers targeted help on an individual basis with no cash or material exchange, there's almost no room in her enterprise for the kind of maneuvering, corruption, or profit-seeking that has been the ruin of so many larger, more carefully planned outsider projects in Haiti.

Another thing that makes her among the very few is that she's not in it for the glory, though she has received a measure of it: her New Jersey high school named her to its hall of fame in the spring of 2011. (The school's hall of fame includes an eclectic bunch—the actor Roy Scheider, the drummer Max Weinberg, the sexologist Alfred Kinsey, the writer Judith Viorst, and Lauryn Hill, the singer-songwriter, among them.) That's about it so far.

Her motivation is also interesting; there are not many people who would rush down into the aftermath of a major earthquake *anywhere*, much less in a country portrayed as violent and dangerous, and well-known as the poorest in the hemisphere. Like Sean Penn, she didn't *have* to do it. Then, there are even fewer who would simply stay on, doing a job. Dr. Coffee herself is less articulate than usual when she talks about her motivations. One thing she knows is that it is not spiritual in any conventional sense. She has no religion, unlike so many of the people who stay on in Haiti for longer than a month's tour of duty and who are often active missionaries or believers who will tell you that they are doing God's work. "I'm stubborn," is about as far as Dr. Coffee goes in her quest for self-knowledge. "I hate watching people starve to death and I hate watching them suffocate."

Also, she gets Haiti. She's figured out some things, things that are very important, including perhaps the most important thing: how extreme poverty works. Here's a series of her tweets:

I have learned in Haiti that someone always wants the empty box. / It makes a hard bed more comfortable for a sick patient. The floor more comfortable for the family member taking care of patient. / It organizes all the possessions of someone who has no family who wakes up from being sick on the streets in the TB ward. / So little is wasted. Except sometimes food that has no "sauce." Just not worth eating apparently even if you are hungry.

~~

When Dr. Coffee tweets from Port-au-Prince, the real city emerges from its usual faceless misery for her followers, as it has for her during the more than twenty-eight months she's lived here. She is remarkably open to the place, and seems to take in all of it. She notices every detail, every story that her path crosses, which is rare for a visitor to an exotic place where many things are inexplicable, weird, or impenetrable. It's especially rare for a doctor whose existence is circumscribed by home, hospital, and the trip to and from work. But Dr. Coffee seems to be learning all the time: about medicine, about Haiti, about humanity. She hasn't hardened yet or put up walls against the constant stream of bad news and problems, as so many development and NGO people do after a much shorter time in-country. They stop learning while they go on acting and deciding. In effect, they give up, which Dr. Coffee hasn't, and won't—the day she gives up she'll be out of there.

This continuous engagement is an important part of why Dr. Coffee has succeeded in her work at the hospital and also remained cheerful and even happy in such a difficult situation. That and the fact that she's a natural sharer, a reflexive giver. She hoards nothing, not medical assistance, not her opinion, not her observation. Well, she'd be quick to point out: she does hoard peanut butter and oxygen.

As a roving commentator, she gives her followers everything; it's Twitter as social commentary, art, philosophy, fund-raising, and matter-of-fact human understanding. She offers it all up in the least pretentious of voices: the sounds of roosters and mufflers and honking horns and gunfire; the signs for cybercafes in the camps and the incredible fact of wallpaper in the tents; the soccer-ball-size breast cancer tumors of her patients, when the disease progresses without treatment. She tweets about the steady flow of hilarity and politics on the Haitian television news; crowds in the camps shouting with joy at the victory of a new president; two of her patients trying to learn "No Woman No Cry" on a borrowed guitar; ketchup sandwiches, storms, winds, sunsets, writing on the walls;

porta-potties upended in riots during the cholera outbreak; the ward's need for sputa cups, for oxygen; a Haitian sitting alone among carousing foreigners after a hard day's work; and then always, day after day, her patients, described anonymously but in great individual detail—their illnesses, their medications, their families, their living conditions, their interests, their generosity, their probable fate. And after all that, today and every day, the drive home from the hospital, late at night, the driver arriving late, setting off through dark, silent nights down deserted boulevards, past well-known potholes ten feet deep.

11

WEREWOLVES IN THE CAMPS

Tou sa w we, se pa sa
Nothing you see is what it seems

In times of crisis in Haiti, in times like these, werewolves come out of hiding. They prowl through the popular quarters. They descend from the roofs of houses where children lie sick. They can enter your tent without your knowing it. Those strange marks on your sick baby's arm are the marks of the werewolf's teeth. Sometimes these monsters gather in one neighborhood and keep everyone awake all night with their howling.

This is when Filibert Waldeck turned up. I'd given up on him, almost. And then, one evening, I sat down for dinner at a table on the terrace of the Hotel Oloffson, and there he was. He called me "Mommy" in his hoarse voice. He was sipping gingerly at a beer that a reporter had bought for him. As one of his little sons sat in a pristine button-down shirt and a pair of pressed jeans, Filibert went on and on about the werewolves, who seemed, in his narrative, like any epidemic: they might as well have been cholera. These werewolves, he said, were living near his collapsed apartment in the weeks just after the earthquake. I'd heard about werewolves often in Haiti and had been shown their victims, who are usually small, listless children and babies suffering from disease and malnutrition. Filibert was a grown-up now but overexcited by all that had transpired. He sat very stiff and straight as he told the tale. The werewolves in his neighborhood were stealing children, giving people fevers, making nursing mothers sick. They were howling through the night. Filibert was worried for his sons; he didn't want them kidnapped. He was estranged from their mother, and afraid at the time that she might come and take them back.

In his encampment, no one could sleep.

The werewolves weren't people anyone knew, Filibert said. Usually, you'd know the werewolf who was haunting your *quartier.* But not these, Filibert said. These seemed to have emerged from the rubble.

I only half listened to his fairy-tale chatter. Grow *up,* I wanted to say to him. He was in his thirties now, not some kid who was allowed to let his imagination run rampant. I was sick of Haitian stories, of this kind of lived ethnography. I'd been coming to Haiti too long and the earthquake was *serious,* for God's sake, and Filibert, so newly rediscovered, was already giving me burnout; Filibert plus the earthquake, which itself made everything seem futile, which called into question every tiny achievement of the past twenty years and even every achievement of the two-plus centuries since Toussaint's revolution. Stop being interesting, I wanted to say to Filibert. Stop telling me quotable things. Don't talk garbage; get your act together.

I feared, too, that Filibert was telling the table of foreign journalists all this apparently interesting stuff in order to get us to buy him more beers so that we could keep him with *us*—so that we could keep getting good quotes from him, and not let him escape to other tables of competing journalists. Filibert knew his crowd, and I knew Filibert, after decades. I had served as his white man when he was little; now I was, in his eyes, a white man emeritus, a known chump, still a possible mark. The journalists at our table were old-timers, too, but more eager, perhaps, to add a paragraph or so to tomorrow's front-page earthquake story, cobbled from pertinent Fred Voodoo quotes.

Filibert continued on. He looked at me across the table as he rambled, his agile story grabbing black bats, screaming cats, a dog, death rattles, and bones out of thin air as he progressed. And I looked back. We understood each other. But because I'd heard of werewolves so many times before in Haiti, about their jealousy and destructiveness, because I'd heard even *his* stories about them before, the anecdotes filtered into my consciousness against my will, in a disjointed patter, while I thought of other things.

In Creole, as in French, the word for werewolf is *loup-garou.* Over the years, I've tried to ignore these beasts. I believe neither in magic nor in the supernatural. To begin with, I find it really hard to credit gods coming down a pole and taking control of human bodies and personalities. But at least voodoo is a complete religion, a full-fledged system of belief. *Loups-garous* are folklore, half-human animals who fly from roof to roof and stalk their victims in the night—I can't buy into it. (You can judge from these protestations of normality just how pervasive and intense and believable the unreality of Haitian myth and legend can become. Sometimes one has to wrench one's mind out of the folkloric world.)

But the pattern of the werewolves' appearance on the Haitian scene has become so clear to me that now I accept them—not as real beasts or witches, but as markers of destruction and harbingers of change. They emerge before elections, in times of food shortages, during political unrest, after fires, hurricanes, and earthquakes, and during epidemics. In villages, the werewolf comes out whenever anyone becomes too successful—she brings the community back to equilibrium, making sure no one gets above himself. A visit from a *loup-garou* who seems to threaten to steal a child can bring a person who is doing too well back into the fold of the community.

Sometimes, such a werewolf is an emissary from the village *houngan,* or voodoo priest. The *houngan* is often like an unelected mayor in these little villages, and he will use the werewolf, among other creatures and effects, as his enforcer. A visit to the *houngan,* with proper payments and obeisance, can get the werewolf off your back. Haiti can sound very weird, but if you look at ward politics in American cities in the early

1900s (and even today), you'll see something like it, corrupt and ancient as Rome, but minus the mythological bestiary.

The *loup-garou* bears little resemblance to the werewolf of horror films and eastern European tales. The Haitian werewolf is a descendant in part of French or French Canadian werewolf folk mythology, in which the beast shares habits with vampires. (One well-known tale that includes many elements of the werewolf myth is the "Little Red Riding-Hood" story.) Werewolves in Haiti are bloodsuckers and child devourers, not flesh rippers. Haitian werewolves don't slash their victims into shreds with fierce claws and teeth. Instead, they come at night and suck their victims' blood—not always all at once but often little by little—until death, sometimes over a series of days or even weeks. To outsiders unfamiliar with the stories, the victim of a werewolf can look very much like a person with a fever or a wasting disease, or a victim of starvation. And that's what the werewolf's victim is, in reality untainted by folklore and imagination.

The Haitian werewolf is almost always understood to be a woman. Usually she is childless, often elderly, and almost always something of an outsider or misfit in the life of her village or her shantytown or—today—her camp, like a witch in Puritan America. Before her rampages begin, the *loup-garou* is already well-known as an outcast. She is suspect.

You would think that such a witch figure would show herself only among the least educated or most credulous classes and would be taken seriously only by those farthest from city life and the modern world, but this is not the case. You can watch TV every night and talk on your cell phone and have relatives in Miami, and still believe in the *loup-garou* (pronounced *lou gawou* in Creole). You can have lived side by side with foreigners and the Haitian upper classes, and still believe in it—or if not *believe* in it, at least fear it. You can even be a foreigner who believes, or a member of the elite. I have heard the fanciest, best-dressed, most Paris-visiting Haitian matrons make reference to the acts of werewolves. And foreigners also. They may not believe exactly, because sophistication tells them the thing is impossible, but the *loup-garou* lingers in the back of the mind, ready to pounce.

John Engle is a serious and intelligent American missionary who married into a Haitian family, and who has lived in Haiti more or less continuously for twenty years. One night in the dark, under pine trees up in windy Pétionville, he told me a story.

After the earthquake, his wife's sister had to move into a new house, and it was quite a nice house with very high walls. "You have to have high walls," John says. Naturally, people in the neighborhood were somewhat jealous about the house—it had a wealthy aura. So anyway one night a lady from the neighborhood, an old lady—a known figure—threw a big bag of bones over the wall. A big bag, filled with bones. An old burlap sack, it was. A rice bag.

"These were not chicken bones. Or any other kind of animal. They were human bones," John told me. "I'm not joking." His eyes widened. He had seen the bones. "Fresh adult human bones," he said. I believed him; in the months after the earthquake, human bones were all too available under the rubble.

"Of course, this woman is a well-known *loup-garou,*" he said. She may also have been a local *mambo,* or voodoo priestess—John thought that that was the case (he is a missionary Christian, so the religious side of things is always present to him). Anyway, people in the neighborhood immediately knew who was behind the bag of bones, John told me. The bag of bones was taken as a threat. Who wouldn't feel threatened by a bag of fresh human bones?

"There's a high level of personal fear here in Haiti," John said. "A fear of powder and poison, I swear. Even among the bourgeoisie. You have to have security and you must show signs of force, or you'll be seen as weak. You'll be taken for a victim." John told me that after the bag came over the wall, his Haitian family responded by privately hiring heavily armed members of the Haitian National Police to guard the house. Here's what he wrote on his blog in December 2010:

I have this daily discipline of identifying things that bring me hope. It's not just a fun little exercise. It's a tool to ward off despair and cynicism in the midst of witnessing heavy daily doses of human suffering, pain and destruction. Haiti had unbelievable challenges before the earthquake and cholera. Now, it's much worse. And the legacy of violence, brutal exploitation, slavery, colonialism and the hatred that it all breeds, coats the fabric of this society. I know it. I live it. This is a place where giving one person a job and not another can lead to death. People develop unbelievably intricate ways to maintain safety for themselves and their families.

What does he think will be the *loup-garou*'s next step? I ask him.

"Anything," he responds, "anything could happen. But your biggest fear is always for the children."

Engle takes me back down the hill, but first we have to stop for gas in Pétionville in a sudden and dramatic rainstorm. All the SUVs at the gas station are performing an intricate minuet, directed by a half-toothless car-wash man who has appointed himself traffic cop and is guiding the elephantine vehicles to the pumps. John's friend Pasteur comes to meet us here, flying through the storm on his motorbike. He is going to guard us for the rest of the trip down. He always accompanies John on nighttime drives; John is careful and doesn't want to travel without protection.

The rain is violent. It slants down, blinds us. We're driving into blackness, hoping not to die. *Wap, wap, wap*—something sounds as if it's bouncing in the back of John's SUV. Pasteur and John stop the car and go out into the rain to look at what's making the noise. They secure something back there. *Pasteur* means pastor, but it's just the guy's nickname. He seems very upstanding. He's the de facto AAA of Haiti tonight.

At my corner, I have to get out. I have no choice—John can't just drive up the front path. When I go out into the rain, I am immediately taken. My shoes sink into puddles. My shirt is soaked, my jeans are sopping, my hair streaming with rain. No one's around. Streets empty. Boom—one guy with an umbrella appears across the street. Like that, he disappears.

The gingerbread tin roofs have turned into decorative fountains, scrolling water from on high off their curves and curlicues. Caribbean rain makes a thunderous sound on tin. I smell wet cement and wet dog, and then a pack of bedraggled dogs appears from behind a wall and skulks off into narrow corridors in the dark.

One day, soon after my conversation with John Engle, I went with a man named Lhérisson to a cockfight near Frère. I did not know Lhérisson well, but he is a big gambler and loves cockfights. He tapped his foot as he sat next to me in my car. He was from near Cap-Haitien but had been living in Frère for more than thirty years. Back when he arrived, Frère was just a country village near the capital, distinctive only because the Haitian Army had a base nearby, also called, metonymically, Frère. When I first lived in Haiti, I used to go to soldierly gatherings in Frère after driving several kilometers through pure countryside. I have some pictures of these in the slides I found from my first visit to Haiti. They show soldiers and soldier presidents and coup members and even the then papal nuncio, the Vatican's ambassador, gathered in front of a building that stands alone in front of field and forest.

No more. Lhérisson's Frère was a different place now. These days, whenever I didn't recognize a spot where a friend or a taxi had taken me in what I imagined was still Port-au-Prince, it would turn out I was in Frère. "*Nou nan Frè*," the driver would say, as if to imply: Where else . . . duh? Both the capital and Frère had grown so large in two decades that the formerly outlying village was now contiguous with the Port-au-Prince urban area.

Lhérisson, who came from up north but grew up in Frère, was, like millions of residents of Port-au-Prince, originally a country boy: in those decades the city tripled in size, filling up with people from the provincial towns, and with peasants coming in from dusty, ungiving rice fields that were once productive farms. In 1950, the population of Port-au-Prince was about 144,000. By 1985, when I first arrived, it was hovering around

850,000. In 2010, before the earthquake, it was estimated at more than two million. (I have seen some fairly reliable estimates that go as high as three million.)

Although he was born a provincial boy, now Lhérisson has the manners of a man from town. That afternoon when I picked him up, he was wearing a button-down shirt and black pants with a belt. I saw that he'd brought a bunch of gourdes with him for betting on the cockfight. Haitian gourdes—the national currency—are usually sorry little rags, filthy old things, noxious, covered in a viscous layer of fingergrease and pocketsweat. Lhérisson's, faded blue and faded orange, were limply cresting from one of his pockets. When he noticed me looking, he stuffed his money down. His bald head was glistening from the rising afternoon temperature. Under the buttons of his shirt, his belly was round and neat.

"I'm so happy to be getting out of the camp," Lhérisson said. He'd been living there for six months, ever since his house fell in the quake. The neighborhood had lost maybe half its population, Lhérisson said. "Not just people who died," he pointed out, but people who left seeking tents in other camps where they had friends or family. He knew at least three families who had split up in order to get more than the single tent they would have received from the humanitarian community if they'd remained together. You could go to an aid organization in a camp with your wife and five kids in tow and get one biggish tent, or you could go with three kids, and your wife could go with two, separately, and you'd get two tents.

"A lot of teenagers got tents without their parents," Lhérisson told me. Lots of girls who were too young to deal with children were pregnant now, and living in households where the oldest person was fifteen or sixteen. The social fabric was coming apart, and the werewolves were descending.

Lhérisson told me about problems in his camp up in Frère. For months, since his neighborhood set up their tents, three *loups-garous* had been terrorizing them.

"One of them came to take the babies out of their mothers' arms,"

Lhérisson said. "I could almost see her horns coming out of her head." Sometimes, he said, the *loups-garous* turn into pigs, and they walk around among the tents. He himself kicked one *loup-garou* out of his camp, he said. She had horns and was disfigured. I have decided not to be unsettled about this kind of shape-shifting in the middle of a narrative, nor to demand too literal an explanation. Wolf to pig, and with horns?

What do these *loup-garou* pigs do with the babies? I asked.

"They eat them," he said. I remembered being told that pigs will eat animal and human remains, along with all the other refuse they are willing to consume.

Now I began to understand the funny story I had heard just days before from a UN employee, an Englishman. One of the scores of studies being done in Haiti by the UN focused on children in the camps and what they feared, what was worrying them.

"Draw what you're afraid of," they told the kids.

"And what do you think?" this UN guy said to me, shaking his head. "They don't draw men with knives, or pictures of earthquake and rubble or houses falling down, or their dead mums. Instead, what we get are lots of pictures of pigs."

The UN worker assumed that this was because there *are* pigs in some of the camps, and pigs are very big and loud and pushy and six to eight times the size of the average Haitian seven-year-old. That's why *his* kid at home would be scared of a pig. But in the Haitian camps, pigs are a different breed, at least in children's imaginations. Many of these Haitian kids, living in thin tents with no protection from all that lurks outside, worry that the pigs that are snuffling for feed in the garbage trenches and gutters of the camps are *loups-garous,* out to get them. Hi, pigs.

The stage for the current situation was set during the 1915–1934 U.S. Marine occupation of Haiti, when American administrators had policy control of the Haitian government in Port-au-Prince and the Marines administered the provinces. Puppet presidents were put into power, and U.S.

agricultural, financial, and industrial interests in Haiti were backed by Marine firepower. Meanwhile, under American supervision, conscripted Haitian workers built roads and administrative buildings. Naturally, there was a rebellion—it began almost as soon as the occupation itself began and lasted, sporadically, almost as long as the occupation itself lasted.

The soldier in charge of suppressing the armed uprising against the occupation was Major Smedley Butler, who later had a change of heart and lectured against war profiteering, infamously declaring about his job in Haiti and the rest of Latin America:

> [I was] a racketeer, a gangster for capitalism. I helped make Mexico and especially Tampico safe for American oil interests in 1914. I helped make Haiti and Cuba a decent place for the National City Bank boys to collect revenues in. I helped in the raping of half a dozen Central American republics for the benefit of Wall Street. I helped purify Nicaragua for the International Banking House of Brown Brothers in 1902–1912. I brought light to the Dominican Republic for the American sugar interests in 1916. I helped make Honduras right for the American fruit companies in 1903.

The cycle continues. In a sense, the aid groups now are running Haiti as Butler and U.S. business interests once did. When Haitians hear their new president, Michel Martelly, announce that "Haiti is now open for business" (his latest clarion call), they fear—or perhaps they hope, if they're looking for jobs—that he means that Haitian workers, low on the pay scale of workers globally, are now available for outsiders' exploitation. Many of the aid groups, not a few of which were created specifically to deal with the earthquake and its aftermath, are supporting this new push for business investment. (This is especially true, as I said, of the Clinton Bush Haiti Fund. They lead the way.)

Haiti has often been called "the republic of NGOs," and the earthquake only exacerbated a situation in which ten thousand or so of these organizations, gigantic and tiny, were already operating in a country of about nine million people, a concentration that is assumed to be higher than in any other country in the world. During the early days after the earthquake, the top aid groups and funding organizations, such as the World Bank and the Inter-American Development Bank, would meet every day to discuss strategy, funding, and simply what to do; often the Haitian government was not invited, and President Préval spent disheartening hours trying to locate and penetrate these meetings. (Most were held in a secure tent at the airport.) This is how soft imperialism works. In general, the Haitian government was simply not consulted in the early days as the international community and various aid groups made policy decisions for post-quake Haiti.

The fact that the Haitian government has little left to do does not leave it idle, however. Although there have been many gifted and serious people in any given Haitian government (with perhaps the exception of the two Duvaliers' regimes and the military coup administrations), there have been many more who are not. The government's lack of governmental duties permits these latter to be highly active in the sphere of pure politics: infighting, bickering over spoils small and large, scrabbling over the awarding of government contracts; siphoning money and aid deliveries out of customs, a traditional trough of corruption; pushing lucrative land deals for relocation camps; destroying all initiatives of opposing politicians. The roaming, discontented, ravenous werewolf who sucks the blood of the local babies for sustenance is just a fairy-tale metaphor for the larger situation.

Haiti is an enigma in itself, but it can sometimes present difficult issues in very clear terms. Things are stark here, and so the place often provides glitteringly sharp outlines of whatever social or cultural or political problems you might be thinking about, whatever problems you might be seeking solutions for—although it probably won't offer up a solution. The post-quake response provided an almost perfect illustration of the problems of aid and relief. It's fair to say that one of the biggest issues to rise from the earthquake's dust is whether aid agencies and international development organizations can ever be trusted, either by the victim community or by the donors who fund them. Are they honest—do they know how to be honest; can they be honest and survive?

In the preface to *Democratic Insecurities,* which focuses on human rights abuses after the first coup against Aristide and before his restoration, Erica James, the MIT anthropologist, asserts that continuing insecurity of all kinds—political, criminal, personal—arises out of a heady mix of "political and criminal violence, economic instability, environmental vulnerability, and long histories of corruption and predation on the part of Haitians *and* foreign interveners." In Haiti, she writes, "the influx of aid [often] had the unintended consequence of exacerbating the conditions that gave rise to . . . humanitarian interventions in Haiti in the first place." In other words, the arrival of huge sums and lots of "aid groupies" (as humanitarian workers are sometimes called) can cause corruption and infighting that make a very bad situation worse.

In turn, the worsened situation can provide a further justification for continuing aid intervention and continuing fund-raising on the part of aid groups and international organizations. Haiti did not need an earthquake for observers to note that the presence of helpers with money will often generate more problems that they can then help fix with more money. Nor is Haiti the only place where this happens. In the past, situations like the one in Haiti after the earthquake have led to bizarre events, such as aid groups squabbling over rape victims. The more victims you can say you're helping, in Haiti or New Orleans or Aceh, the more money you can raise. So just as every white man has his own Haitian, every aid group has, broadly speaking, its own rape victims. Once you realize how important the victim is to the aid organization and its funding, it's impossible to take at face value victim statistics culled "in the field" in a place as complicated and nuanced, to put it nicely, as Haiti. As a high official of one international aid group said to me, "Why would anyone take down what remains of the presidential palace? A beggar needs his stump."

The whole welter of programs and plans for a new post-earthquake Haiti—the excitement the country's woes generated for outside planners—comes across in the much repeated if possibly apocryphal story about Bill Clinton's Haiti experience. As the UN's special envoy to Haiti, the poor fellow was the target of all sorts of ideas, crazed and otherwise, about how to reconstruct the new Haiti ("extravagant, outlandish imaginings," as the economist Jeffrey Sachs characterizes much of the outside fantasizing about Haitian reconstruction). All those victims and their quandary presented a thrilling intellectual challenge to those who wanted to come and help—for architects, who are notoriously dreamy and theoretical, especially.

So, as it has been told to me by aid workers at different organizations (never firsthand): Clinton's sitting in his living room in Chappaqua with a bunch of experts and reconstruction types, talking about the Haitian situation. This is supposedly just a few months after the earthquake. They're having coffee, or so the story goes. Suddenly, the fax machine begins churning out some huge document, and Clinton goes over to take a look at it. He makes some motion of dismissiveness and disgust as he looks down, and says, "If I see one more fucking blueprint for new housing in Haiti, I'm going to shoot myself."

The Haitian earthquake victims for whom those blueprints were generated have become internally displaced persons now, simple numbers on charts of hundreds of organizations. They're part of what observers of relief, human rights, aid, and recovery programs often call "the compassion economy." Depending on the bent of the nongovernmental organization that's studying these victims, the IDPs are hungry babies or rape victims. They are unemployed men or illiterate teenagers. They are cholera victims or nutritionally deficient nursing mothers or pregnant tweens. They are household slaves or starving former farmers. They are prostitutes or the indigent elderly. They are the mentally disabled. The camp residents are categorized in their victimhood and plans are made for feeding them, teaching them, curing them, providing jobs for them, housing them . . . fixing them. They become a demographic of suffering, their victimhood quantifiable and, once quantified, useful.

Not cynically or even necessarily consciously, the aid groups' commitment becomes self-serving, and finally is transformed into an unacknowledged and often unconscious commitment to self-sustaining fund-raising that safeguards jobs, housing, food, and security in Haiti—for aid workers. Haitian earthquake victims become the blood the outsiders are feeding on. Individually, aid workers justify this by believing they are doing good. Individually, many are.

To some extent all aid groups participate in this system, because they have to. It's a tautology: you can't have an orphanage without orphans; you can't collect for neediest cases without neediest cases. The American Red Cross, which had raised those hundreds of millions from its earthquake fund-raising appeal, had only fifteen or so people working in-country at the time of the earthquake. Obviously, fifteen people, no matter who they are, do not have the capacity to distribute hundreds of millions of dollars in any meaningful way—they can only hold on to the money as they cast around for what to do with it, or throw it up in the air and pray as they run away, or invest it in themselves, which is why, even after the Red Cross had scaled up for two years to meet the needs of the disaster's victims, less than half of that money had been spent or even targeted toward actual victims.

Paul Farmer's Partners In Health had been in Haiti for more than two decades and had five thousand people delivering health care in-country before the quake, most of them Haitians. PIH quickly raised a comparatively small $40 million, but was much better able to translate those funds into action on the ground because of its pre-quake commitment to resources and staff. They went on to raise more money in the following years.

Before the earthquake, PIH was already functioning in Haiti as a mini-government, with its own people designated to deal with customs, its own transport plans, its own hospital, its own network of associated clinics, its own suppliers (although of the aid groups, it is among the few that make a point of including government ministries and authorities in the mechanics of their programs as much as possible). All

nongovernmental organizations that have stayed in Haiti over long periods have been forced to create their own mini-fiefdoms to one degree or
another. Haiti's is a cycle of misrule in which all actors must participate.

They have other difficulties, too: in order to find that the problem
you are trying to fix within a population—with all your resources blaz-
ing—is nonetheless continuing to grow, you need to assert a systemic
dysfunction within that population itself (or admit fault *yourself*). Hence
the reflexive stories about Haitian corruption, incompetence, and crimi-
nality so often heard from the outsider community: there's something
wrong with them, and we keep trying to fix it, but it's hard because:
there's something wrong with them. But . . . we need to fix it.

And so the victims of a disaster like the Haitian quake became a
moneymaking tool for these groups. However, *without* those donations
and whatever filtered down to them from those monies, would Haitians
have survived the initial days and weeks after the earthquake?

Which leads to another question: Exactly how many people died in
the Haitian earthquake? The short answer is that no one really knows.
President Préval put the final toll at 316,000, but, as he has told me and
others, he did not have a data-significant or scientific source for that estimate. (As Haitians would say, in English, it was just his "feeling"—plus
an assessment, but not a strict body count, by the drivers of the trucks
who picked up the dead.) For some months, I accepted the death toll as
a given, even though I knew that statistics are unreliable in countries that
are not accustomed to keeping them. Then, one day, I began to wonder.
I was not alone.

Although 316,000 were reported dead, and another million were said
to have left town for relatives' places in the countryside, the city seemed
more crowded than ever. At first, I put this down to homelessness caused
by the earthquake. In other words, there were more people out in the
streets at all times, perhaps. Eventually, I discovered, through statistics on
cell phone usage provided to me by Digicel, that the people who had fled

the capital right after the quake had started coming back to Port-au-Prince almost as soon as the relief mission got under way—sensing that there might be money, food, or jobs to be had, in spite of all the death and destruction (or because of it). Many brought relatives from the countryside along with them. So that was another reason the city appeared crowded.

But even with these explanations, something seemed off about the high death toll. Although most people I asked had lost one relative or several, or friends, or both (or, like Black Rouge, a still-uncounted number from his densely populated neighborhood), many people I asked had lost no one: not one family member, not one friend. These were not just my friends but random individuals accosted in the streets; admittedly, not scientific at all and not a meaningful sample, but at least anecdotally mildly interesting. My friend Jacques-Richard, who sometimes works in security or as a gofer for international organizations and who travels all over for them, speculated that one reason for this counterintuitive anecdotal evidence might be that Haitian families and neighbors are so close and spend so much time all together in one room or house that entire families were crushed in the quake, and perished simultaneously, leaving no one behind to give an account. It was a murky demographic field, certainly. Some Haitians think the toll is higher than 316,000.

But I knew President Préval, the person who had announced the steeply rising death counts in the days after the quake: in the destruction, he saw a chance for his country, and after his initial personal shock, which was severe, he certainly recognized possibilities and potential for Haiti that high numbers could not hurt. As Leslie Voltaire, an urban planner and former presidential candidate, has been known to say, "A disaster is a terrible thing to waste." One foreign journalist who had covered the quake from the first days listened to me one day speculating about the death toll and said quietly: "Divide by ten. Thirty thousand."

That seemed to me insanely low, given the physical destruction of housing and public buildings and schools. But there is reason to wonder about the death count, which was always an estimate largely based on the number of trucks used to haul bodies from the wreckage and the morgue, the number of runs they made per day, and their capacity, which is to say, the number of bodies they could carry—and this estimate was not arrived at carefully, given the chaos in which the numbers were collected, if they ever were collected.

From listening to Préval when he discusses this topic, it's easy to conclude that there was no paper and little computation involved in establishing the final toll. The loss of life was incomprehensibly large, whether it was 30,000 or 316,000. But if I were a Haitian, I would want a clear accounting. Just to arrive at some theoretical number seems uncaring and disrespectful of those who lost their lives. As if it doesn't matter, really, how many Haitians died, or who they were. As if the dead were just a lump sum.

A year and a half after the earthquake, a casualty report prepared for USAID was leaked to the media, stating that between 46,000 and 85,000 had died in the earthquake. The authors of that report used statistical sampling based on door-to-door interviews, but on close scrutiny the data in the reports as well as the methods of analysis seemed to be flawed and unscientific. The writing itself was fantastically childish: "We also asked people why they left [the camps]," the report states. "Over 60% mentioned filth, chaos and noise. Crime and insecurity by which many people meant not so much crime as conflict with neighbors, was third. Mosquitoes was a big issue as was heat." It's a report filled with fascinating observations and it makes some good points, and its numbers might be right, but they might be wrong. The report feels unreliable. One can see why USAID never released it.

But when it was leaked to the press, the report caused a stir, since it had been commissioned by USAID and so seemed to have the aid organization's imprimatur; and then later, it seemed to have been suppressed by them—giving it even further legitimacy in the eyes of many. Another perhaps more reliable independent study, released around the same time, came up with a death toll of 158,000. Of course, there would have been less international interest and a lower level of charitable donation had the initial death count been closer to 46,000, rather than 200,000 and rising.

Would some $5.5 billion in pledges of monies for Haitian relief and re-construction have been raised at the March 2010 United Nations donors' conference if the death count had been 46,000? Maybe.

Interestingly, the head researcher on the project, Timothy T. Schwartz, was the author of a book called *Travesty in Haiti: A True Account of Christian Missions, Orphanages, Food Aid, Fraud and Drug Trafficking*, which challenges what Schwartz considers to be overblown victim statistics and their relationship to fund-raising charities. In any case, the leaked report came far too late to influence the course of relief. But it will probably resurface during debates about how much money Haiti needs, how much should be given.

There are other kinds of lycanthropism. For example, *Haiti: Tragedy and Hope*. That's the name of the Time Inc. quickie photo-book that was published right after the earthquake and that included, as its back cover, the portrait of Rubble Man, the guy with cement adhering to his face who tried to chase me down outside Toussaint Camp. For me, that title resonates: "*Tragedy*"—by which is meant great big pictures of *other* people dead and dying. And "*Hope*"—that is to say, as a rote cliché, that you don't have to feel too bad looking at pictures of the dead and dying, because there's always hope, whatever that means.

Above the title of the book, in a smaller but still large font, is this line, extending across the entire width of the oversize book: "A share of proceeds will benefit Haitian relief efforts." Time Inc. intended to donate about 50 percent of the profits, hoping to make around $1 per book sold, anticipating that the book would make a total of at least $150,000. Therefore, according to Joy Butts, of Time's book division, the company announced that it would contribute at least $75,000 to the relief effort. In the event, however, the Haiti book did not perform as well as Time had hoped (I could have told them *that*), and netted less than $100,000 in profit. But since they had committed to donating $75,000, they did; which meant more than 75 percent of the profit.

I've looked at this book carefully, because I contributed a piece to it. I wrote an essay on Haiti's past, called "In the Land of Memory," and I got paid for it. (Bill Clinton wrote the introduction; an involved celebrity is always part of the marketing package in a publishing situation like this— but apparently even Clinton's name can't make a Haiti picture book marketable.) So I was a participant in this project.

In fact, since the earthquake, I've made about an eighth of my income writing about Haiti and the earthquake. Without all those Haitian victims, I would not have made that money—and, in fact, all my writing about Haiti has been about a continuing human tragedy that is happening to others while I profit from it. This very book that you have in your hands is one example. No share of its proceeds will directly benefit Haitian relief efforts.

So why do the editors and publishers at Time Inc. use that line on their book? Because it's a marketing ploy, meant to convince readers that buying a book of pictures of victims of a natural disaster will help those victims. It's meant to temper your guilt while you enjoy beautiful photos of terrible things. It's meant to temper the publishers' guilt, too, at publishing this stuff for sale. It's also designed to disguise the profit motive. As Sean Penn has said: "Haiti's most recent earthquake measured one million on the magazine-sale scale." A book of pictures of the disaster is, on its face, more parasitical than any other media coverage of such a subject (except perhaps videos of Anderson Cooper "rescuing" Haitian children in his New York outfits, or photos in the *National Enquirer* of Oprah Winfrey, down in Haiti after canceling her show, traipsing through rubble holding Sean Penn's hand; or photo ops for post-quickie-marriage/divorce Kim Kardashian at a fashion show at the Karibe Hotel on a much-publicized Haiti charity trip; or *Vogue*'s "Up Front" piece on Donna Karan's "goodwill tour" and the photographs of the designer inspecting goat-horn bracelets or hugging iron sculpture or walking down a street in her designer outfit next to a nice Haitian grandmother who's carrying a bag of rice on her head), because it is the pornographic aspect of the crisis that is being used to sell copies. The essays in *Haiti: Tragedy and Hope* are like those pieces on nonsexual subjects in *Playboy* that used to flow around the pictures. There, the non-pornographic written word famously disguised the fact that pornography was the product for sale—here, too.

In 2005, Time published a similar photo book on Hurricane Katrina, called *Hurricane Katrina: The Storm That Changed America*. In this case, the involved celebrity was Wynton Marsalis, the musician, who wrote the introduction. The Katrina sell-line is a little more specific than the assertion about Haitian relief on the earthquake book. At the bottom of the Katrina book there is a small Red Cross logo and a line that reads, "5% of the cover price will support the American Red Cross."

The potent mélange of celebrity, tragedy, and charity is what sells developing-world stories to the entertainment consumers of our day. A piece I wrote for *Condé Nast Traveler* magazine on Liberia and Mali—both of which vie with Haiti in their impoverishment—would never have appeared if Matt Damon hadn't been funding an organization in Mali, and if Jeffrey Sachs, who is a kind of intellectual celebrity, hadn't been traveling there and hadn't taken Angelina Jolie on a tour of Africa earlier (a video of which can be seen, with all its unintentional comedy, on YouTube).

A piece I wrote on Haiti just before the earthquake, this one also for *Traveler,* would not have been published without an accompanying sidebar by Wyclef Jean, who had a charitable organization in the country. (Angelina has also been to Haiti.) Just as every Haitian needs his own white man, every developing nation needs its own celebrity. Matt, Angelina, Wyclef, Bill Clinton, and less glamorous experts like Jeffrey Sachs and Paul Farmer are recognized guides who can lead us from the security of our lives into the heart of darkness, and return us home safe and sound.

This is "poorism"—or poverty tourism, which used to be called slumming. Today, unbelievably, visits are led for tourists through some of the world's worst poverty; in Djakarta, Calcutta, Rio, and elsewhere. Poorism has a pretty long history. As Patrick Delatour, then Haiti's bumptious minister of tourism, said to me in 2009, just before the earthquake, "Sure, Cap-Haitien is something of a wreck. It could use some paint.

But on the other hand, you can sell 'wreck' as a tourist product. How many people in Sweden have ever seen a city in wreckage?" His prophetic words echo these days.

It's true that for the most part, aristocrats in the old days tried to remain as far away as possible from the poor, in order to avoid contamination by disease, as well as to avoid hearing jokes at their own expense, and to protect their women and children from seeing what poverty can drive men to. But in the Victorian and Edwardian eras, and even more so in the Georgian period, the rich who considered themselves brave or bohemian would occasionally tour the slums of London for an evening's entertainment. In the 1920s, George Orwell wrote a book for which he lived in and reported from the dens, shacks, garrets, and hovels of the poorest classes in Paris and London. In one memorable scene, Orwell watches from among his group of homeless tramps as a bunch of London aristocrats in their fancy dress descend into a shelter, where they feel noticeably uncomfortable. The men in the shelter, half clothed, a little tipsy, warming themselves at a fire, are meanwhile amused to the point of boisterous rudeness by the visitors' awkward presence.

Slumming may be awkward and exploitive, but it's impressive that anyone had or has courage enough to try it. At least those aristocrats had the nerve to get in there and mingle with poverty, drunkenness, and possible danger and disease—and the same can be said for tourists in Rio's favelas, no matter how much they are reassured about their security. The same can be said of Sean Penn in Haiti and Angelina in Africa. It may be that Penn's life was falling apart and he needed a new hobby, but he did something that took courage. He took a risk and came down to Haiti for his own reasons, among them, possibly, an attempt to renovate his image—although he has never seemed like a person who cared too much about having a nice public image. Most important, in doing what he did in Haiti, he was never pious or high-minded or *charitable,* as charity has come to be acted out. Slumming in its newest and purest version means living in the slum over time.

One thing that made poorism a plausible exercise for poorists was the understanding that there was an unbreachable economic and social gap between the poorist and his subject. In Victorian England, for example, something about that distance and the rigid rules of society at the time made the slummers feel safe. As in: no one would *dare*. As in: the disparity is acceptable, understood on both sides. That's how life *is*—or was.

That same perimeter of security exists today in certain places, and is part of the reason why Angelina and Madonna feel they can be safe in Africa, and Sean Penn (and I—in a different, lesser way) can feel safe in Haiti. No one would dare. Conversely, those who worry that their presence might seem wrong or who think people might find them responsible for some of the general misery feel quite vulnerable: that's why the aid groups in Haiti don't normally let their employees mix with the locals, why they have off-limits areas in Port-au-Prince, and why they try to preserve a cone of security around themselves in Haiti.

In "The Compound Life," an unpublished piece, Rowan Moore Gerety, a former aid volunteer who worked with various organizations in post-earthquake Port-au-Prince, writes about how the international aid community has cut itself off in Haiti.

> Some organizations, like the U.N. mission to Haiti, restrict their staff's social outings to a pre-approved list of stores, restaurants, and bars subject to vetting by U.N. security personnel. The result is a closely choreographed dance in which most foreign aid workers interact with Haitians exclusively in a few circumscribed patterns: colleague to colleague; patron to server; aid worker to beneficiary. Most foreigners [now] working in Port-au-Prince speak next to no [Creole], have few or no Haitian friends outside of work, and know little of the flavor of local life. In a place where [approximately] 70 percent of the economy is informal, they patronize only businesses in the formal sector, and they experience their social lives in a world that is awkwardly sealed off from the world in which they work.

The aid groups and others keep themselves cut off for security reasons that are based not so much on real security threats as on their assessment of economic disparity and on their beliefs about how Haitians might perceive their own impoverishment. The aid groups are afraid that their organizations and their employees will be blamed for what's happening around them, and that they will be punished. (This is one of the perceptions that is reflexively racist and frightened.) Their ignorance and their fear feed into the construct of what Gerety calls "the compound life."

Similarly, people these days do not really tour their own country's slums, because the gap is too obvious and too politically charged. You might work in the secure zone of a needle-exchange program or a soup kitchen, but you don't venture into red zones just to have a look. It's hard to imagine a group of yuppies from Portland flying over to tour downtown Detroit in a double-decker bus with guide. Or Mayfair bohos going for a quick dekko in Brixton. If a middle-class American from, say, Irvine, California, dips a toe into some real American poverty in, say, Santa Ana, nearby, he fears there's a chance he may get singed. (Even though, statistically, it's very unlikely; in Haiti, too, it's Haitians who are victims of Haitian violence, and only very rarely outsiders.)

A suburbanite cruising the slums near his gated community would feel like a voyeur, sucking life out of real people, "fellow Americans"— people who, he might feel, have a plausible right to his kind of life, but who instead have ended up living on a different level. Easier to go be an aid worker in Haiti, where you can feel that the home life into which you were born is so very distant from the life into which Haitians—alien beings who exist outside your security gates—were born. Or, better yet, be a complete outsider, a real voyeur, in the privacy of your own living room in Boise or Indianapolis, looking at a picture book called *Haiti: Tragedy and Hope*.

One imagines a classic, slightly overweight, not overly young *Time* reader, sprawled across his couch somewhere in a leafy suburb, in the evening after work, paging abstractedly through the pictures. His wife bought the book at the register at the supermarket, say. He's picked it up off the coffee table. The TV's on: *Mad Men*. He's having a beer or a Diet Coke, and looking absently at pictures of crumbled walls and a rescue operation, of a makeshift crematorium on an open boulevard, of a dusty body beneath a pancaked house, of a hospital courtyard with bodies piled up, of—most pornographically—four pairs of legs with blood running down them onto white cement, of people huddled in the night, searching for lost family.

He's looking at them, but they're not looking back. That makes the experience safe and unembarrassing. He's making the comparison (beer, house, TV, sofa, fridge, and bounty vs. rubble, blood, dearth, and death), but the people in the pictures cannot see the contrast. They are his material; they're making him feel better about his life while giving him the slightly uncomfortable feeling that he may be too comfortable. Overall, he's enjoying their misfortune. (That latter sensation is akin to the sexual zing some people get when they read news accounts of torture.) As Sean Penn told his old friend Douglas Brinkley, the historian who wrote about Penn's Haitian foray in his article "Welcome to Camp Penn" in the July 2010 issue of *Vanity Fair,* "There is a strength of character in [Haitian] people who have, by and large, never experienced comfort. That's exactly the character that our Main Street culture lacks and needs in the United States. In other words, *we* need *Haiti.*" Deborah Scroggins, the author of *Emma's War,* about a white woman's romance with a Sudanese warlord, writes about the pain of the white Nairobi community after Emma's death: what pained them most was "the loss of yet another intimate who shared their love affair with Africa, the bittersweet black humor that colored their relationship with the continent and gave their lives the tragic edge they could not do without."

Someone else's suffering, in other words, adds zest and focus to a life that the sofa-ensconced reader of *Haiti: Tragedy and Hope* may have come to feel is too dull, too regular, too easy. Oddly, it also sounded as though Penn himself were enjoying, or at least making the most of, the discomfort of his life in a Haitian refugee camp.

When I was new in Haiti, I hung out one evening with a bunch of Haitian women in St. Martin, a popular quarter in Port-au-Prince. There had been some political unrest that day, a demonstration, shooting. We had been in the middle of it all, me, Loune, Beatrice, and Bernadette. It was exhilarating, and now we were sitting on small, straw-seated Haitian chairs and a mattress in a room within a family complex in a warren of cinder-block buildings near a soccer field. We were chatting and relaxing as the sun came down and the city cooled off. I turned to Beatrice and said, thoughtlessly, "I love Haiti." And she lifted her soda can to me and replied, "Well, then, I will give you my Haitian citizenship, and you give me your U.S. passport. You can stay here, but I'm leaving." And she beamed at me, as if to point out my absurdity.

Her point was that poverty, or even just some discomfort, is not so bad when you know that with a snap of your fingers, it can come to an end, and you'll get up that morning, inch through the traffic to the airport, hop on your flight, take off, plunge into a well-deserved nap, and, on waking, change into fresh clothes, only to find yourself *that very evening* ordering a dozen or so small plates and drinking large cocktails with some friends from the studio in some new spot in West Hollywood that you've never been to before because you were . . . well . . . *away*. In fact, knowing you can leave the poverty and discomfort makes prolonging your stay sweeter. Even if you haven't got a private jet, if you've got the money you can still book a seat on the 9:30 American Airlines flight any morning from Port-au-Prince to Miami, have a nice lunch and dinner—perhaps a meeting with local donors—and catch the next morning's flight back to Haiti. A little R&R. What I used to call a "mental health break." As Beatrice knew back then, it required only a few hundred dollars and a foreign passport, or a visa.

Below is what William Seabrook, author of a 1929 book of quasi-nonfiction about Haiti called *The Magic Island,* wrote about an earlier version of Sean Penn—it applies pretty well to many of the other people who've come down to help out in Haiti over the years. This man's name was, improbably, Faustin Wirkus, and he's become—for me—a paradigm of the outsider in Haiti. Wirkus was a Marine who was put in charge of the island of La Gonâve, just off the Haitian shore, during the U.S. occupation. Wirkus claimed he was crowned king of La Gonâve by the Haitians living there. This is from Seabrook's introduction to Wirkus's 1931 book *The White King of La Gonâve*. Think of Sean Penn when you read it:

> Every boy ever born, if he is any good, wants, among other things, to be king of a tropical island. Every man enclosed by walls, if he isn't dead on his feet, whether they be shod in expensive spats or sewer-boots, sometimes wants to get *out* and *away*. Every man (if he isn't dead on his feet like a zombie) who has seen too many steel buildings and walked (or ridden) too much on asphalt and slept in too soft beds, wants sometimes to be among tree trunks (and not in Central Park or Westchester), wants to walk or ride trails, wants to sleep on the hard ground. Every man also, sometimes, whether millionaire or day laborer, wants to be a king, that is, a supreme ego, wants to be himself, self-dependent and dependent only on himself, instead of being a highly polished or dirty cog in a wheel. Every man (who isn't dead on his feet like a zombie) perhaps wants to be God. Most of us are continually caught in wheels, and are never the mainspring. Wirkus, for a while, was the mainspring. Wirkus for a while—for ten thousand people—was God. In addition, by the chance of it being a tropical island, by the chance that a lot of Negroes crowned him king, by the chance of his liking them and their liking him, by the chance of having a jungle paradise as a theatrical drop-set, he fulfilled a dream-wish that a lot of other kids have known but never fulfilled except vicariously in reading dime novels.

Think of Penn and remember in reading this that Seabrook, who respected the White King of Haiti so deeply, was himself one of America's last great wanderers, and an early hippie experimentalist who lived before his time. He was an occultist, an intellectual gadfly, and a self-professed cannibal (he later said he thought the meat he was gobbling up was ape) who dabbled in Swiss metaphysics. Upon returning to the States from Geneva, he founded an ad agency in Atlanta and got himself one of his three wives. (He reportedly liked to drink a quart of whiskey a day, and to chain women up, so the marriages did not last long.) Seabrook served with the French Army in World War I, and was gassed during his service. He had himself committed to an asylum for alcoholism (what we call rehab today). He wore spats and carried a cane (and this was just after graduating from college). He was, in other words, the kind of person who ends up, at one point or another, in Haiti—a typical mobile sovereign, like Penn, or Leonard Doyle of IOM, or my chain-smoking, hard-drinking USAID anthropologist friend Ira Lowenthal, in his day. The white kings of Haiti are people with charisma and character, but that charisma and character are not always adequately appreciated back in the homeland—not to their satisfaction, anyway. Seabrook committed suicide in 1945, at the age of sixty-one, with a drug overdose. His hugely popular *Magic Island* is credited with bringing the word "zombie" into common usage in the United States.

12
BLACK ROUGE'S TOUR: II

Jan w bat tanbou-a, se konsa nou danse
However you beat the drum, that's how we'll dance

One night, Black Rouge takes me into the rubble for a voodoo ceremony. We're not trying for effect, not trying for "Voodoo in the Rubble." It's just that Black's *houngan,* or voodoo priest, had his temple near Black's house, and, like the house and everything around it, the temple was almost entirely crushed in the earthquake, so there's no choice other than to have your ceremony in the rubble. Black's leading the way tonight. Although I've been to the temple ruins during the day, I would never be able to find the place again amid the debris and half-fallen walls, especially in the dark. I meet Black at his little one-room post-quake shack across the street from the detritus of his former house; his girlfriend is sitting on one of the two beds, watching a Spanish-language soap opera. She's not coming with us. She laughs and shakes her head. No way.

On the street outside, the market ladies are selling; at night it's not easy to tell their stalls from people's shacks. They're selling lemons, and charcoal in pails, and beauty products from wide baskets; you can see their wares under the lights of their little paraffin lanterns, which cast a wavering illumination in small circles. We get in my car, me and Black in front and Jerry and Samuel—glassy-eyed and giggling—in back. We have to navigate through the surging market ladies who make way for us uncomplainingly, parting and then coming back into place like seabirds. Samuel has a fever, he tells me from the back. He always seems to have a fever, but that doesn't stop him.

Eventually, though, we have to disembark, because the way becomes too narrow and you cannot climb through this rubble in this vehicle. I have a little flashlight and Black has a candle. Jerry and Samuel follow, loose-limbed and laughing, in our wake. We're all dripping with sweat even though it's night. Black takes us down one path between undestroyed walls, and back, and down another and then back. Even he can't quite tell his way. We follow the light from his candle and the shadow of his big rasta head as it bobs above broken walls and doors. Candlelight plays over his chubby, boyish, angel face, his ham hands. His head seems to float ahead of us above the rubble. Cockroaches and rats move beneath our feet, blue under my flashlight, darting and scrabbling. I have to walk carefully as I go because the ground's not stable and in my right hand I'm carrying the flashlight, in my left a bottle of rum for the *houngan*. I make an awkward explorer. It's the rainy season and there are vast puddles in some places, across which we make our way on unreliable stepping-stones.

Now we're climbing a huge hill of rubble. To our left, a mound of collected rebar is piled in a raggedy heap, like pickup sticks. To our right is another hill of rubble like the one we're ascending. Now I hear singing. There's lightning, but no rain yet, and the moon is coming up. Black's candle flickers ahead. The singing is louder now; it sounds like chanting at a revival meeting. As with all voodoo singing, there's a rumble from the men, but mostly you hear the high-pitched women, very soprano. Black's head stops its forward movement; we've arrived. In front of Black there's an opening between two walls, a rectangle of yellow light. He blows out the candle, and I step down behind him into the temple: the stairs have been assembled from a half cinder block sitting on top of a whole cinder block, and these two pieces are not cemented together. It's a precarious descent.

The small room into which we've emerged has a ceiling, which makes it exceptional in the Marché Salomon rubble. It feels very enclosed. It's half full of people, mostly in their late teens and twenties. There are two small boys, too, the *houngan's* nephews. The *houngan* himself is bent over a white enamel bowl that has four piles of cornmeal in it, and a candle burning near its center. The priest is seated on a stool for the moment, and he looks just as normal and unexceptional as he did when I met him a few days ago in the afternoon. He's a thin, middle-aged guy, graying. He's without question the oldest person in the room. He and his assistant, a bigger, stronger, younger man, are both singing, bent over the bowl, in *langage,* which is a mix of slavery-era African dialects combined with Creole; it's used only in voodoo ritual and is one of the world's few remaining wholly sacred languages.

A fat cement snake with a higher BMI than anyone in the room except for Black and the priest's assistant is carved around what remains of the temple's central pole, down which the gods will descend to possess their worshippers.

This is where voodoo practice always becomes a little strange for outsiders; that is to say, it becomes strange when the ceremony starts in earnest. Even when you know something about the religion, it's hard to tell what each individual *houngan* is up to. Tonight the *houngan* is beginning what he has told me will be a two-day ritual. The *houngan* shakes his rattle and sings; his female attendants are clapping in a weird, scattered rhythm. More congregants are arriving. It's too hot in this room. Along the snake's back, one of the women pours the rum I donated, and lights it with a lighter. The blue fire climbs up the pole. This makes me uncomfortable: I don't like fire in small, enclosed places filled with people. No one else here is disturbed by the flames. Black puts his hand into the burning rum and rubs flame and unevaporated rum on his arms. Jerry does the same. He would do anything Black does. Samuel is zonked out, leaning against the opposite wall; this whole situation cannot be comfortable in his and Jerry's condition, and yet there's something about their faces that seems content. They are glad to be here.

The fire goes out. The singing stops. Someone turns on a powerful flashlight and we hear next a strange, loud, guttural human noise. Without warning, without fanfare, here is Africa handed down from the days of the colony as, before our very eyes (in a sense), Ogoun comes down the pole from elsewhere to possess the priest. (The god could just as easily have possessed Samuel or Jerry—the gods will possess anyone among the worshippers, and you cannot know beforehand who will be possessed and by what god. They are a democratic pantheon, but *houngans* do seem to be especially susceptible.)

The two little boys are escorted out of the room by their mother, and Ogoun rises from the depth of his possession, his guttural yawp like the sound made by Haitian men in support of their rooster at a cockfight. It's not a sound heard among English or French speakers. It's macho, fierce, and seems to begin somewhere low and deep in the body.

Ogoun's attendants offer him his costume, a deep blue cowboy shirt and a red satin sash around his waist, which one of them ties for him, and some oddly crushed hat that, looked at the right way, might be three-cornered. The god's pant legs are rolled up to just below his knees, like colonial knee breeches without the stockings beneath, and each time they fall back to his ankles, as pant legs tend to do, his attendants rush forward to reroll them. Another red satin sash is tied around Ogoun's sword (an old rusted machete). I am wary of machetes and swords in voodoo ceremonies. They tend to get waved and brandished in ways I consider irresponsible.

Ogoun bugs out his eyes and goes around the room, shaking hands in a bone-crushing grasp with each person present, and looking us in the eye with a fierce, furious stare. He seems to knight some of the men with a swift, hard slap of the flat of the machete blade. He takes mouthfuls of rum and sprays the liquor out through his clenched teeth at a few of us, including me. I find this discomfiting, but it is well-known among my intimates that I am not a person cut out for voodoo worship. I don't like fire in close quarters, I have never enjoyed being spit on in any circumstance, and I don't like having my hand crushed, even by a god, even by a god who resembles Jean-Jacques Dessalines.

I don't know why anyone would like this—the fire, the spit, the bone crushing, the slap of the machete, the chanting in an unknowable language—and I don't think "like" is the word Haitians would use for how they feel during a voodoo service. It's not exactly a party—though it does share some of the ambiance of one; as at Souvenance, people are standing around, people are drinking, people are dancing. It's noisy. In fact, the service makes you realize that parties and religious ceremony are not far apart; one recalls the Greeks dancing and eating meats roasted for the gods. (Only since monotheism has religion become all plain and pure and proper.) When gods are around, humans grow excited, apparently.

Should you happen to bring yourself to believe that this *is* Ogoun, however, and not just some crabby old *houngan* consciously pretending to be the god, it's still not pleasurable to be spit on. No one likes it. But for Haitians at least it has meaning; a baptism from the god, a life-giving spray, recognition of a kind—or something.

Meanwhile, Ogoun is smoking two cigarettes. At the same time. Most people look thoughtful when smoking, and you'd imagine that a person who's smoking two of them would look doubly thoughtful, or perhaps just ridiculous—or like Paul Henreid in *Now, Voyager*. But Ogoun does not look ridiculous, or thoughtful; he looks menacing. Around the room he goes again, two cigs in the mouth, rum in one hand, the other hand out, palm up, demanding tribute.

No one refuses. Who would dare? He's god, and he's got the machete. Papa Ogoun prefers coins to bills, even though Haitian coins are virtually worthless—but it's a leftover predilection from the days of the colony with its coins made from real precious metals. I'm watching Ogoun. He's complaining: the tribute's not enough. He shakes his head. The pile should be so high, he says, and he gestures to his waist. Actually, the pile of coins does not even come up to his ankles. Also irritating to him, it's not just coins: the tribute includes as well some pieces of cooked chicken in a Styrofoam container, some root vegetables, a few extra-rickety-looking home-spun candles, and several small bottles of raw homemade rum. Watching Ogoun berate his followers, I'm reminded of Aristide. When people from around the world took to sending him charitable contributions for his projects, Aristide was not exactly grateful—far from it. Instead, he would complain about how small each check was. They were not worth cashing, he said, even though they arrived, often, by the hundreds.

A young dread-headed fellow perks up in a corner, and is making a speech about creating a community group to get food for the people of the neighborhood. Although Papa Ogoun has let the young man speak, he seems singularly uninterested in what his young follower has to say as he puffs away on his two cigarettes. His attendants dance around the central pole and sing: *"Tout nasyon gen fòt se pa nous sèl."* Every country has faults, not just us. Samuel and Jerry go out to get a breath of fresh air. Or so they say. Black's sitting with his eyes closed. As the women dance and the *houngan* smokes and watches, I'm thinking that it all seems authentic enough, the poverty of the ceremony, the sad chairs in need of prostheses, the two cigarettes, the fiery pole, Ogoun's bug eyes, his barbaric yawp, his handshake—but at the same time I am wondering.

Maybe the ceremony is so limited not because it's authentic but because it's poor, and maybe it's poor because the fairly stupid white person who asked to see it (that would be me) did not provide enough money and rum to make it plush and lively, to give it more flourishes, better costumes, more food for the god and the participants, animals to sacrifice, and not just those four sad piles of ground corn. Maybe without my request to see a ceremony, there would have been no ceremony. After all, this month was not the time of the great voodoo festivals, which come at All Saints' Day and at Easter, and in late spring and midsummer. How much of what the white man sees in Haiti is specifically a show for the white man to see—and this not just in terms of voodoo ceremonies, and not just today?

Whether this is real voodoo (whatever that means) or my personalized voodoo, what interests me most about the religion is its survival, and the survival of its archetypes. How, in the direst of circumstances, some of the worst conditions any religion has ever had to endure, it has been handed down. How durable it is, and how responsive to the bad conditions. When I think of the resilience that is always being attributed to

Haitians as the best and most amazing quality they retain in their awful situation, I think of voodoo's unbreakable strength. The astounding thing about voodoo is that it is never resigned, never supine, but always warlike and disputatious, and always certain it can resolve with divine strength and intelligence the problems of men and women.

When people talk admiringly about Haitian resilience, it often sounds as if what they really mean is resignation and survival. But voodoo is truly resilient, which is to say, capable of withstanding shock without permanent deformation or rupture, to quote Merriam-Webster. I'm still surprised, always, by the consistency of the gods' various behaviors, costumes, commentary, from cut-off mountain village to shantytown shack, after continental displacement and one century of vicious enslavement followed by two more filled with terrible poverty and continual unrest. And although the *langage* chants have changed subtly over time, there is still a continuity between the ones I'm hearing tonight in the rubble after the 2010 earthquake and what Maya Deren, the ethnographer-filmmaker, heard in the late 1940s and Alan Lomax, the ethnomusicologist, in the late 1930s; between the dances I watch now and the dances Katherine Dunham, the American choreographer and dancer, wrote about in the 1930s; between what I see and hear and all accounts of voodoo that I've read that date from the colony onward, excluding those written to make ceremonies appear lurid or demented.

To retain a tradition so strongly in a nonwritten language is like the miraculous handing down of the Homeric tales. To say nothing of voodoo's outliving the deaths of the Middle Passage and then the anti-voodoo campaigns of the colony and, later, of so many Haitian governments and of the nineteen-year American occupation. When I watch Ogoun parade around in this temple in the rubble, with his chest puffed out, spouting smoke and *langage,* I know I am witnessing something not so different from those voodoo ceremonies in the forests in 1791 from which the revolution sprang like a fierce god rising.

~

Black can't get his candle to light as we're leaving the ceremony. The wick got wet, and I can't find my little flashlight. So we grope our way out through the rubble, stumbling like blind men, falling against walls and slapping through rainwater, Jerry and Samuel laughing at our bobbles and collapses as if this were all a slapstick routine, which maybe it is— their laughter makes me laugh, too. The moon appears and disappears as if to highlight certain incidents, such as the moment when I fall backward through a door made of sheets into a room where a whole family is sleeping, and I manage to avoid tripping over them only through a painful—and ridiculous—contortion. More laughter, pointing. Black pulls me by the hand from where I've landed, seated, against a wall. I'm only faintly conscious by now—the ceremony and singing, and sleepiness and a couple of sips of rum, have done their work. I can hear the ceremony continuing sporadically behind us as we traipse along. Down the rubble we go, brick and mortar tumbling out from beneath our feet in a racket. Black stumbles over a mangy dog and kicks him lightly out of the way. From far behind us and above now, the women's high voices weave like a wind in and out over our heads, strange, harsh sounds like harpies or Valkyrie.

As it always does, the ceremony has gotten to me. After these encounters, I feel touched; not moved or transported or new or different, but disoriented, haunted, somewhat off. As if it's entirely possible that my take on reality is not the only one, or not even one at all.

13

THE VIOLENT-SEX CURE

W pa lave men-yo pou siye yo atè
You don't wash your hands to dry them in the dirt

Sometimes when it's getting dark and I'm sitting in a dirt courtyard in a Haitian camp or shantytown, gnawing on a piece of sugarcane and exchanging little jokes and pleasantries with a charcoal lady and her daughter, or drinking coconut water with a family of eleven in their tent, or a having grilled corn with a *brouette* man while he takes a break from pulling freight across town on his two-wheeled cart—as if he were an ox—or eating a piece of *dous makos,* a too-sweet treat with a pink stripe that children love, and chatting with aging orphan boys like Jerry and Samuel, I step back, in my mind, and wonder what the fuck I'm doing in this place.

This evening I'm in the shantytown called La Saline, with two girls and their mother. The mother is washing laundry in a big old paint bucket. Why am I here, I'm thinking as one of the daughters tells her mother again about a girlfriend who's misbehaving. I'm no anthropologist or ethnographer. Theoretically, I should be living in New Jersey, where I grew up. That was a possible life trajectory, certainly. I'm not a student of Afro-Caribbean history; I'm not a demographer, and I don't gather data about the world's changing urban populations. Another trajectory, arguably better than a split ranch in Fairlawn or Teaneck: I should be in front of my computer at my desk in my house in Southern California, writing fiction about American lives. I don't work for any company that needs these Haitian shantytown dwellers as consumers or workers. Nor am I on any quest. I haven't decided to become a voodoo acolyte or to walk across Haiti and the D.R. without once taking a vehicle; I'm not going to try to spend a year as a dishwasher in a Haitian hotel or to discover the compound for zombie powder. What I mean is that I have no excuse. What am I doing here, what possessed me?

Meanwhile, as the girl prattles on and the laundry gets visibly cleaner as if by miracle in the gray water, I am watching these two kids across the alley, with their dreads and sunglasses and basketball shirts and long, pulled-down shorts. They are lounging next to a small stand that sells cigarettes, matches, *klerin,* and other alcohol, as well as soap and laundry detergent and cans of sardines. They are not really kids, but—like Jerry and Samuel—as good as men; tall and rangy and clearly up to something. They are watching me with a sullen interest that I don't appreciate. They might be packing a knife or even a gun, I realize. It's almost night.

Although surrounded by people, some of whom seem to like me, some of whom affect an instant fondness, I'm profoundly alone here. No one on the outside knows where I am. As far as anyone knows who knows my name, I've already disappeared. I forgot to tell Maryse where I was going this evening; I didn't tell Loune or Jean-Robert. Jacques-Richard dropped me off in another *quartier,* earlier: he had something else to do tonight. Even Samuel and Jerry—whom I trust about zilch, but with whom at least I have a longish connection—live in Toussaint, a long way away from this shantytown.

And yet here, where I am right now, everyone knows my whereabouts, because I'm white, which makes me strange, aberrant. They don't know my name, but they can say definitively that the white woman in the filthy shoes who speaks Creole and writes in a notebook is at so-and-so's house . . . People who are five shantytown blocks away and who didn't see me arrive could tell you where I am at this very instant, whom

I'm with, what I'm doing. If I move locations, they will know within moments. It's not that they're thinking about me. They're probably playing dominoes or watching TV, feeding a baby or making coffee. But my presence in the neighborhood is duly noted. I am supremely visible, here in the dark, nowhere anyone's heard of. I'm a person of interest here. These people would know my fate, if it became interesting to know.

When this occurs to me, I feel like an idiot for being here, for thinking I'm comfortable in a place where it would be more correct for me or anyone like me to feel great waves of awkwardness, uneasiness, and possibly shame. Feeling that I belong here on this chair, eating this sweet, laughing at this joke—how stupid. Where do I get off? Who do I think I am? These are both fit questions for someone who does what I do to ask herself this evening as I sit in this courtyard, hanging out on terms of unearned equality with people who will sleep tonight three or four in a bed and possibly three or four under it, most of whom had lunch today but neither breakfast nor dinner. I'm writing their story for you, reader. I'm bringing their squalid lives into your nice house, your apartment. Why?

It's growing dark, and the boys across the way finally take off their sunglasses. They light up a big spliff and pass it back and forth. I'm writing *their* story for you, too. Why?

In Haiti, almost always, I can walk into people's lives and they will welcome me and sit me down and share their meager nothing with me, and give me a kiss goodbye, on both cheeks. They'll never know what I am doing with their stories. They'll never see any profit from their connection with me, other than perhaps a free bag of peanuts, a pack of cigarettes, or a gift of a few gourdes much later in the relationship (and even these paltry things given with a sense that I may be "violating" "journalistic" "ethics").

Most of the people I deal with are Haitians who are so poor and so beyond the reach of modern life and earthquake aid that they do not even have their own white man. They have no connection to white men, tourists, anthropologists, development workers, international aid deliverers, et cetera. I'm the closest they get, and I'm not very useful. Even when

I do things for them that, at least, might amuse them, they never get to experience it. I once put Jerry, Samuel, and Véus's music up on the Internet, but I was in the United States and their phone was dead and they don't have email, and none of my friends in Haiti could find them for me (I don't know if they even tried). The next time I saw them, the computer at the youth center was down, possibly permanently.

Once upon a time, after the earthquake, there was an American reporter who came to Haiti after being in many other disaster areas; her name was Mac McClelland and she was, at the time, the human rights reporter for *Mother Jones,* the progressive magazine published out of San Francisco. She reminded me of me when I first came to Haiti, but when she first arrived she was far more worldly than I, better traveled in the developing world, and more accustomed to people in trouble. She reminded me of me, but she also reminded me of Imogen Wall and all the other gritty, happy-go-lucky people I've met who follow disasters around the world and make a career of covering catastrophe or delivering humanitarian aid. The kind of people who can say "I met him in the tsunami, and then we were dating again when we were both posted to a refugee camp in Pakistan after the earthquake there, and then finally we broke up after the earthquake in Haiti."

So McClelland came to Port-au-Prince for the earthquake and for *Mother Jones*—and for you, reader. First she wrote a five-page camp-hopping tour of the damage, with pull lines on the *Mother Jones* website like "Next page: Inside Penn's camp: 'I'm black, and Haitian, and I wouldn't go where you're going right now, in the dark.'" Or "Next Page: Then he got me into an apartment under false pretenses, closed me in, and cornered me." It was a self-absorbed piece, but it captured something of Haiti in spite of its stereotypical white-person fascination with the danger and sex of the black republic. Such stories, which appear with regularity about Haiti, have the unintended function of reifying the country's sordid image abroad; it's not that the stories don't contain elements of truth, of course, but rather that they emphasize, almost as with a yellow highlighter or a zoom click, elements taken from very old stereotypes.

Then McClelland wrote another Haiti piece. This one appeared on a website called *GOOD,* about a year and a half after the earthquake. It was titled "I'm Gonna Need You to Fight Me on This: How Violent Sex Helped Ease My PTSD." This was McClelland's personal story, in the form of what journalists sometimes call a reporter's notebook, about covering a rape in Haiti, and the consequences for McClelland.

McClelland was following a post-quake gang-rape victim around Port-au-Prince. At some point, the rape victim, who was a camp resident and had been severely brutalized in the incident, saw one of her attackers on the street. A paroxysm of fear overcame her while she and McClelland were traveling by car, and she started to have some kind of seizure, as McClelland describes it: "We were sitting in traffic and saw one of her rapists, and she started just SCREEEAMING a few inches away from my face, her eyes wide and rolling in abject terror." Haitians have vivid and dramatic ways of expressing fear, it's true, the women especially—and I can imagine this scene, although "eyes wide and rolling" is an American antebellum cliché that's not useful. McClelland reportedly tweeted the scene live from her phone when the woman started screeeaming.

Sometime after McClelland witnessed her rape victim's fit, she found that she herself had acquired post-traumatic stress disorder. She got her PTSD, apparently, from seeing the rape victim notice her rapist through the window of the car, and also, as McClelland explains, because "there are a lot of guns in Haiti. Guns on security guards in front of banks and gas stations. Guns on kidnappers who make a living snatching rich people, guns on rich people who are afraid of kidnappers. Guns on the gang-raping monsters who prowl the flimsy encampments of the earthquake homeless."

Normally, McClelland says in her piece for *GOOD,* she copes with what she witnesses in her reporting (on the Deepwater Horizon oil spill, for example, or on Hurricane Katrina) by "inhaling the distress, then exhaling compassion." That's what we used to call "listening," or, more professionally, "interviewing." But when her rape victim started freaking, McClelland "lost the ability to locate myself in space and time in the backseat. It's called dissociation, and is a common and quite unsettling response to extreme trauma." It helped her a little, she says, when she got back to the United States and "ended up naked and panting out loud to myself in the steam room of a San Francisco spa where people get $155 facials, 'It's okay, it's okay, shhhh, you're okay.'"

One disturbing aspect of McClelland's PTSD piece and her exploitation of another woman's real trauma is how she tries to deflect possible criticisms of her personal claims in her article. She has herself asking her "brilliant" Bay Area shrink, "What kind of fucking pussy cries and pukes about getting almost hurt or having to watch bad things happen to other people?" She tells her shrink she's afraid "editors" won't want her to work for them anymore.

But she's not really worried about this. If she were, she wouldn't be writing about her PTSD and how it makes her "throw up in her mouth" in certain situations, nor about how she had to beg an old friend to simulate raping her in order to get over it. Yes, you did read that correctly. This final fake-rape scene, the climax of McClellan's *GOOD* piece, is unintentionally comic and highly improbable. It includes fake rapist (and former boyfriend) Isaac punching a pillow instead of McClelland, as well as several fake escape attempts by fake victim McClelland from fake rapist Isaac. It ends with Isaac whispering over and over in McClelland's ear, "You are so strong, you are so strong." This is homeopathy at its most hilarious.

It's a simple act of thievery: McClelland steals the rape victim's trauma and turns it into her own trauma, in order to make the story more palatable, tastier, more attractive. Bluntly: only a very few people in the United States would bother reading the first-person narrative of a Haitian camp mother's gang rape and her subsequent feelings. But the first-person narrative of a hot white journalist who's begging to be raped so she can feel good about herself again—that's another story altogether. It's so counterintuitive, so brave. In a twist that would never have occurred before the advent of the Internet and social media made such stories accessible to the occasional ordinary Haitian, the real rape victim found out about McClelland's story, and she actually had her lawyer email a letter asking McClelland not to publish. After the whole episode was over, the rape victim wrote a note to Haitian-American writer Edwidge Danticat in which she said, "Our choices about when and how our story is told must be respected." Fred Voodoo strikes back! The woman was most incensed about being identified by McClelland, and therefore endangered, she felt.

McClelland writes that her brilliant shrink in San Francisco told her that her PTSD was like the syndrome some Marines experience in wartime even if they have not been in combat. But it's not, though McClelland happily accepts the analogy. Unlike a Marine, she didn't witness the actual violence; she wasn't really afraid she was going to be hurt or killed or that she would have to hurt or kill someone; she was simply seeing someone else have a post-traumatic stress episode. She's a canny writer, though, and the piece made a pretty big splash. Even now, I'm bothering to write about her.

For decades, there have been unwritten rules about reporting, especially about foreign coverage. The first old-school rule is not to tell about your personal life, your home life, in your reporting. McClelland violates that rule all over the place. And who minds? Not me. She brings the bedroom right onto the battlefield, which in our post-feminist era seems like a reasonable idea.

All writers, even reporters, even nonfiction writers, have to choose their own material, and they each see the world through an idiosyncratic, personal prism. McClelland's prism is her sexual allure and her sense of her fun life, her interesting adventures, and all the risks she takes. Again, fine. She knows what she is doing wherever she turns up. I *still* don't have an answer to that question, for myself—or for her. One thing I know, though: it's not a simple thing to appropriate the pain of others for your own personal gain, personal gain being not just money but fame, self-glorification, moral standing.

Dr. Mark Hyman, with his "UltraWellness" and his "Haiti commitment," might be said to be guilty of some of this; Bill Clinton is a well-known "sharer" of the pain of others. It's as if Haiti attracts this sort of person, who needs to absolve himself or herself of something here, even if that thing is simply this: to have led, up until now at least, a painless, bourgeois existence, filled with water, electricity, peace, and financial security. The modern developed world provides little opportunity for pursuing notions like honor, courage, and boldness, as William Seabrook understood. Many outsiders in Haiti—not all, of course—want to feel for a moment like adventurers, explorers, heroes, saints, or mobile sovereigns, or at least to feel a little better about themselves. They want to experience the zest of committing altruism, thus the admiring comment about Sean Penn, pointing out that he's doing something in Haiti "that he doesn't *have* to do."

I know that I have felt some of this myself at different times; it's partly why Mac McClelland and her rape victim story interested me. One feels so clearly that in writing about the misery of others, one is exploiting their pain, their situation, and—even when consciously wishing not to—appropriating it, in some sense, using it. Photojournalists have this fact brought home to them in Haiti as they shoot. Haitians will turn away from the camera, not for privacy's sake but because they feel something is being stolen from them. Sometimes now in Port-au-Prince, more used to photographers than they used to be, they'll ask the photographer for money, to make the business arrangement fairer. Then the photographer must decide whether his or her "journalistic" "ethics" permit this.

Before her last trip to Haiti, McClelland tweeted that her father was worried about her safety in the midst of possible riots. She was doing something she didn't *have* to do. But it's in bad taste to mention or to hint that you're choosing bravery in the face of things Haitians can't avoid. It's ethically questionable to take someone else's rape and make it your own—not just material for your story, but your own personal trauma—in order to build your brand. When you take a hideous rape in an insecure camp in a disaster-ravaged, poverty-stricken city and turn it into a pornographic description of safe white masochistic sex in your secure San Francisco bedroom, you turn yourself into a *loup-garou*.

Dr. Coffee once told a similar story about U.S. media in a series of tweets. One day, an American television news crew came into her tuberculosis ward to film cholera victims. Even when a rather irate Dr. Coffee informed them that the thin and very ill patients they were filming were suffering not from cholera but from tuberculosis and had nothing to do with the cholera epidemic, they kept on shooting. So back in the States, that's what people saw: TB patients standing in for cholera patients. To the television crew it didn't matter, since all Haitians are Fred Voodoo, and the suffering of one type of Haitian victim can stand in for the suffering of another. In any case, the true cholera clinics out in the countryside and in far-flung shantytowns were harder to get to than the general hospital downtown.

Now, the television cameraman and certainly Mac McClelland are decent people. They don't mean to broadcast stereotype, to restate old canards: they are good and smart people who felt really sorry for those sick patients, for that poor Haitian lady who got raped. But really what journalists like this end up doing is sucking up the Haitian story to the detriment of Haitians. They're turning Haitians' pain into our entertainment, and missing important truths in order to go over old turf, the surveying of which adds to no one's understanding.

No one should co-opt someone else's pain. My rule is, don't be full of pity and charity. Don't feel sorry for them, rule number one. Be glad you're not in their situation, but don't pity. Their pain is theirs, and, in disasters and destroyed places, their pain and their survival are sometimes even important aspects of their identity. Don't pretend it's *your* story. Don't be an occupier of their narrative; don't be an imperialist in their lives; don't colonize their victimization. Be like my friend Sabina Carlson, who doesn't even notice the victimization—or chooses not to pay much attention to that aspect of the Haitian experience.

I asked Sabina why she keeps coming back to Haiti; really she virtually lives here now. Sabina looks about twelve years old; she's in her twenties and has been living for two years in the Cité Soleil shantytown, where she was originally working with IOM. Sabina said what many people say, which is that you can see and appreciate human life in Haiti in ways you cannot do in the more developed world. Sociologists would respond that the reason for this is poverty: in poor countries, especially in poor, *hot* countries, much more of life is led in public, because houses are less sheltering and because the community and family are the individual's only safety net. There's much less privacy in places like Haiti than in, say, New York or London.

Sabina, who left IOM to help create a do-it-yourself development group in Cité Soleil, told me that what keeps drawing her back to Haiti is "the functioning freedom of this place." In an email she wrote to me, she said:

> Haiti is incredibly raw, blunt, and in some ways vulnerable. If you are comparing life in Haiti with life in the States, life in Haiti is more *real* in some strange way, more vibrant and raw. More colors. Very little is hidden here. People bathe in the street, they beat their kids in the street, they march in the street, they sell plantains in the street. If you're fat, people call you fat. If you're skinny, people call you skinny. If you're missing a tooth people call you toothless. It is what it is. *Lavi-a bel, lavi-a dwol.* Life is beautiful and funny.
>
> I suppose for Americans, who are brought up with the idea that the U.S. is the land of the free but who somehow end up as slaves to the paycheck and their own social class, Haiti, or their experience of it, represents true freedom, with all of its positives and negatives. My Haitian friend was beaten up in the street with no justice to follow; a friend of mine said, "This country is free, so free that someone is free to beat up someone else just like that. If you like freedom, you swallow all of it. The good and the bad."
>
> But also, Haiti is a functioning chaos. There is order in Haitian disorder. Haiti functions not despite but because of its chaos, including the earthquake. So I would say that Haiti is that perfect intersection between chaos and order—where this crazy system somehow works every day—the *tap-taps,* the *mabi* merchants, the kids going to school,

the gangsters, the *papadap* men, the Papa Docs, the whole of it some-how works. People make it work. Even cholera and an earthquake didn't knock this country too off track. Haiti is the most organized disorder you can find.

In other words, Haiti needs to be understood in Haitian terms. Sabina would say that it's important to remember that the two swaggering kids across the way, as I sit in the shantytown in the evening, those two young self-styled gangstas with their dreads and possible knives or guns, are not there to entertain me and you and Sabina but are there to hang out and to plague their own neighbors in the shantytown, and that—like the rapist on the street—those kids will still be there in the camps and shantytowns, glowering and menacing, when I am back at the Oloffson having a rum cocktail and looking at photographs on someone's iPad, or up at Maryse's, eating a fluffy cheese omelet and having an espresso, or when McClelland is back in San Francisco on the radio, talking about such kids on NPR and then going out for a steam bath, a shrink appointment, and some wine. The kids will be there, regardless, and so will their neighbors, and so will Jerry and Samuel in the camps, and so will Sabina's cast of characters, and all the rest of the Haitian comedians, the repertory with all its theatrics. And—except when we're around to analyze and categorize them—they won't feel that their one overriding identity is that of victim, or victimizer.

14

PACT WITH THE DEVIL

Se lè koulèv mouri w konn longè-l
Only when the serpent dies can you take his measure

Here is a question that bothered me in the wake of the four hurricanes of 2008 and then the earthquake two years later: Why do some things stay up and some come down? Capricious destruction: What does it mean? Is it all in the brick and mortar, in the weak rebar and sandy, low-quality cement? Is all the death attributable to some social or cultural upheaval, like Miami rice and urban migration? Is it all because so many Haitian peasants moved to Port-au-Prince over the past thirty years? And, in the final analysis, how and why does an idea of a nation carry on, if it does indeed carry on?

After major disasters elsewhere, people going through the rubble ask the small questions (why is this movie theater still standing? why did that house get carried away?). But when there's an earthquake in Italy or Turkey or China, say, they don't ask big existential questions. No one asks, why Turkey? No one wonders whether China will endure. It's assumed that these places have a reason for existing to start out with, that their history is ongoing, and that, even when they've been visited by catastrophe, there is a point to their continuing to decorate the face of the globe. But Haiti is a different matter.

Haiti is often seen by the outside world—when they think of it at all—as a place that in some way never really had the right to exist. It's the outcome of a slave revolt, so it's being run by the descendants of slaves (weird). It got its independence from the old world in 1804, prematurely and violently, compared with Jamaica, say (1962), or Guyana (1966), or the Bahamas (1973), or Saint Martin, Bermuda, Guadeloupe and Martinique (never). It's in the wrong place (should be in Africa). Its people speak the wrong language (should speak English—or Spanish, at worst). It's always a problem, can't govern itself, and somehow, it seems fitting that it should disappear, since by now it barely exists in outside consciousness at all. It's this underlying cultural disposition, unexpressed and mostly unrecognized, that leads commentators and pundits to ask whether Haiti is "cursed," and whether it can soldier on in the face of extreme disaster. And, even more profoundly existential, whether it should. Is Haiti a failed experiment?

The American evangelist Pat Robertson is asking. God punishes those who "make a pact with the devil," he said after the earthquake, and he argued that such a pact is what the Haitian slaves made back in 1791 when they rose up against the French masters on the island and began the long struggle to end slavery. Robertson has heard that the uprising that became a revolution started at a voodoo ceremony deep in the Haitian woods. Hence, in Robertson's view, the pact with the devil (as he thinks of the gods of African animism) against the rule of the Christian white man. This is probably the only time Robertson has sided with the worldly French. His point is that Haiti is evil. This is not a new way of looking at the country.

Anne Applebaum, another political commentator, is also asking what Haiti is and whether it has a future. "There is a real possibility," she wrote, four days after the earthquake, having never, one assumes, visited Haiti, "that violent gangs will emerge . . . to control food supplies, to loot what remains to be looted. There is a real possibility, within the coming days, of epidemics, mass starvation, and civil war." All her uninformed but strongly asserted predictions ("a real possibility") made Applebaum feel bad: "I don't remember feeling this utter hopelessness about previous natural disasters," she wrote. Haiti is so depressing, so prone to violence. This is not a new way of looking at a country whose Homeric epithet in the media is "poorest nation in the hemisphere."

David Brooks, the *New York Times* columnist, is asking, too. "Haiti, like most of the world's poorest nations," Brooks writes, "suffers from a complex web of progress-resistant cultural influences. There is the influence of the voodoo religion, which spreads the message that life is capricious and planning futile. There are high levels of social mistrust. Responsibility is often not internalized. Child-rearing practices often involve neglect in the early years and harsh retribution when kids hit 9 or 10." Brooks himself did not make this stuff up about Haiti. He is relying on the word of Lawrence Harrison, whom he cites in the piece. Harrison is a disciple of Samuel Huntington, whose book *The Clash of Civilizations and the Remaking of World Order* posited—to simplify— that the world could be separated into good cultures and bad, backward cultures. (Huntington, who identified eight major civilizations in the world, classified Haiti as a "lone" civilization, not belonging to any other group—when actually, according to ethnographers, historians, anthropologists, Haitianists, Americanists, Africanists, and so many others, Haiti belongs to many civilizations, perhaps to all of Huntington's eight categories, which does make it special, peculiar, and hard to parse.)

Harrison has lived in Haiti and has many Haitian connections. A conservative social theorist and (no contradiction here) former head of USAID missions in the Dominican Republic, Guatemala, Costa Rica, Haiti, and Nicaragua, Harrison worked for the United States in the crucial, morphing years between 1969 and 1981. He and Brooks reach the same conclusion: earthquake or no earthquake, Haiti is backward.

Rather than disrupting old ways of thinking about Haiti, the earthquake allowed many commentators, political analysts, and columnists to restate what they'd always imagined to be true about the world's first black republic. The white Western world just has a tendency, when confronted by Haiti's intractable problems, to fall back on easy stereotypes and a deep-rooted, unconscious racism that suggests to them that this is all "depressing" and "hopeless," and that somehow all the problems are the fault of this irresponsible, ungovernable people, with their weird old African customs and religion. It's all Fred Voodoo's fault.

But in fact, this depression and hopelessness come from "experts" who don't understand Haiti, don't acknowledge its strengths (and don't know them), don't get its culture or are philosophically opposed to what they assume its culture is, and don't know its history in any meaningful way. I have to assume from what he has written that Lawrence Harrison lived a "compound life"—to quote Rowan Moore Gerety's phrase—when he lived in Haiti.

The earthquake was unpredictable, and its capriciousness played into Haitians' love of conspiracy and their watchful distrust of coincidence—which can look a lot like Patrobertsonianism. Robertson has an excessive belief in causality: the black revolutionary republic in some way provoked the earthquake, he argued. For many Haitians, as for Robertson, the earthquake was a perfect backdrop for both small observations and for grandiose statements and claims about cause and effect.

If you lived, like Black Rouge and so many other Haitians, in a warren of apartments and houses built by private construction, you were very likely to die when the earthquake struck at 4:53 PM, unless, like Black Rouge, you went out for a snack at 4:52. If you were driving in your car at 4:53 PM, generally, you didn't die, unless a building fell on you. If you were at home napping, like many older people, you were probably among the unlucky. If you were putting out juice and cakes and getting ready for the daily five o'clock viewing of a popular telenovela with your friends on the one television in the neighborhood, you all died. Many women and girls died because of their addiction to their favorite show—*Diablo* or *Frijolito*. If you were outside and you ran inside—to protect yourself, to save someone—you died; if you ran out from inside, maybe you didn't. But the thing is, in another dwelling, the reverse was true.

Because of poor construction and the power and shallow depth of the quake, the killing could be capricious even within a single structure. In one instance, the people in a house who ran to the left died, and those who ran to the right survived. In another, those who ran out the front door lived, but the girl who ran toward the back terrace was killed by the wall falling on her. If you were walking next to a security wall, goodbye—so many of these tall barriers fell onto passersby.

Were you having a post-work tryst with a prostitute on Grande Rue? Too bad. To give a sense of the range of Haitian reactions to the earthquake, there were many uproarious and possibly apocryphal stories told about the top floor of one of the many whorehouses there coming down on the first floor, where a couple was busily engaged, and about the two pairs of feet that people could see from the street where the building had collapsed and the wall had fallen away (one pair pointed up, one down, in case you're not following).

Working late for the government? This, too, often spelled death. Shopping for dinner? A supermarket in the wealthier section of town came down, killing scores. The market's collapse occasioned another earthquake tale told for humorous effect, this one about an old lady rescued from the debris. She's down a hole; it's been more than twenty-four hours since the earthquake. Big foreign rescuers in rescue gear are waiting at the edge of the gap to pull her up; news reporters are expectant, anticipating the miracle, cameras at the ready. And what comes out of the hole first? "Take this," comes a quavering feminine voice from below. Everyone looks down, and up comes . . . her handbag.

The Hotel Montana collapsed and killed hundreds of aid workers and visitors to Haiti of all stripes. One group of do-gooders, who are in plentiful store in Haiti even when there has been no historically devastating event, had intended to stay in a little religious *pension* on their last night in Haiti, but their guide had advised them to splurge this one time and stay at the Montana. They did, and all of them died, except for one who shut his computer after working for a few hours and went down to the poolside bar to have a beer. He ordered, got his drink, picked it up from the counter, heard a huge noise, and turned back to the hotel to find that the entire six-story building behind him had disappeared, along with his colleagues.

The national nursing school collapsed on graduating students taking their final exam: in half a minute almost all of the next generation of Haitian nurses were killed. A reporter for a wire service turned away from his desk, and his wall came down—if he hadn't moved, he might have been buried. Many people found a family member or a friend under the rubble, still alive, but couldn't pull the injured person out and had to watch as he or she slowly expired. One man knew that his wife had been killed at the little clothing store where she worked on Grande Rue, and two weeks later I found him still waiting near the wreckage, where he'd sat every day for hours in the heat, hoping to receive her remains for burial and also to get inside somehow and find the family's identity papers and a cousin's visa, which were in a suitcase his wife always left inside the store, for safekeeping.

Where I saw capriciousness and nature's indifferent hand, however, Haitians saw meaning and design, just as Pat Robertson did when he said the earthquake was a divine retribution. Haitian traditional thought is not as David Brooks characterized it. Rather than interpreting the world as capricious, and suggesting that planning is futile, the old religion here asserts an aggressive, active causality. Things don't just happen, they happen for a reason. Accidents are never entirely accidental here, and, similarly, disasters are never entirely natural. Haitians, noting the utter destruction of the Ministry of Foreign Affairs, the Ministry of Finance, the Ministry of Justice, and the Tax Bureau, as well as the legislative offices and the presidential palace, saw a purposefulness in the earthquake's thunderous hammer that had so disproportionately descended on the corrupt and the dysfunctional. The shifting plates were making a point. The quake also slammed down the headquarters of MINUSTAH in the Hotel Christopher, killing almost a hundred people, including the UN mission's special representative. The archbishop of Port-au-Prince was killed when his residence collapsed on him.

As he tweeted news from the rubble in the first minutes after the earthquake, Richard Morse, a musician and half-Haitian who runs the Hotel Oloffson, made up a name for the earthquake. He called it *Sekous Jistis*—or the Earthquake of Justice—summing up neatly Haitian attitudes about the architectural and also some of the human destruction. People noticed, from a religious point of view, that the quake pulled down about half a dozen massive nineteenth-century Catholic churches in its path, but left untouched many little shack-like Protestant churches and *houmfors,* the scattered one-story urban temples and the open-air peristyles of voodoo. One interpretation of the earthquake—taking into account casualties and destruction wrought on the Church, the government, and the UN forces—suggested that *Sekous Jistis* was an attempt on the part of the gods of voodoo to wipe out the traces white men had left in Haiti. (From a hotelier's point of view, Morse's *Sekous Jistis* was also a reasonable name for the earthquake, since his hotel stayed up while the Montana and the Christopher were destroyed.)

In Toussaint Camp, Samuel and Jerry offer their own interpretation of life's capriciousness. We're sitting under a tarp strung between a few tents that make a Haitian-style family courtyard out of the jury-rigged shelter situation. I'm balancing on another handicapped chair (missing most of a leg), and the two of them are stretched out among the roots of a tree. Smoke from weed hangs in the air.

It's even hotter in the shade of the tarp than it is outside. One of their band's DVDs, recorded on the cheap at a studio up the Delmas road, is playing on a ghetto blaster powered by electricity pirated down skinny lines from the main cable. It's "Manigèt," the same song they played for me that day outside the youth center. I'm getting to know the song. A girlfriend of someone's is suckling a baby inside one of the tents. Jerry and Samuel are quick to tell me that neither that girl nor that baby belongs to either of them.

"*Goudou-goudou* was bad," Samuel says. Jerry nods. They pass around a bunch of tiny, bite-size bananas. *Goudou-goudou* is the onomatopoeic Creole word for the earthquake. Repeat it several times in a row, quickly, and you have the shake and rattle of the earthquake, of the destruction as it tore across the city. Repeated like this, loud and fast, and with a proper Creole accent, it almost sounds like "*tuka-tuka-tuka-tuka,*" like stone on stone, shaking and rumbling.

Jerry has his sneakers on slipper-style, with the backs pushed down by his heels. He kicks one off.

"I mean, I lost people," Samuel says. Five people from his family died in the earthquake. "And now my mother's living in the countryside. I can't visit her because it costs too much to get out there. She used to make me dinner." When Haitians talk about costs that are too high, they are often referring to amounts that are as low as twenty-five cents. They live on a very tight budget. Samuel had a security job before the quake; no more. Jerry is equally impoverished. Before the earthquake, Jerry's mother was a market lady with a small business in herring, malt soda, and what he calls wine but was probably moonshine. Like so many microbusiness people, she lost her wares in the quake. Many of her clients, all of whom paid on credit, died. The six-bedroom house where she rented two rooms and sublet others was destroyed, killing an aunt and two cousins. She hasn't been able to recover yet.

"Basically what it all means is this," Samuel explains. "We were poor before *goudou-goudou.*" Samuel uses the old-fashioned phrase for being poor: we lived in misery. "And now, guess what? We are still poor." He gives a lopsided grin and shrugs. At least it's not raining. Yet. Jerry goes into one of the tents and brings out an electric desk fan, sets it on a milk crate, plugs it into the extension cord over our heads. It helps a little.

~~

I'm stirred and moved by things I see here, but I'm not sure why, and I wonder: Would you be moved? Here are the things that touch me, but a warning: they are not entirely normal. There's a house in Port-au-Prince and the bottom of it is made of brick—two stories. Then the top two stories are made of wood. In the earthquake this house did not fall down because the top was much lighter than the bottom, unlike later constructions where the roof was heavier than any other part of the building. This old house was built smart, probably in the 1930s.

I'm moved by its persistence. It reminds me of another house where my late friend Lucien Pardo, an older man and a senatorial candidate from the provinces, used to stay when he was in Port-au-Prince; his niece was renting it. The living room in that house was painted a bright dark blue. Rickety furniture filled the place; in the back was a sun-filled kitchen-like room with a table, but no one cooked there—the servants cooked outside, old-fashioned style, on a charcoal fire, even though this was an upper-middle-class place in the capital, in the late 1980s. In another room in this house, in a sitting room, there was a three-paneled screen, behind which was a ceramic commode for doing one's business. It was old Haiti, from a different time.

But I can never find Lucien's house anymore. I know it was behind a wall—back then it was one of few houses behind a wall; now, because of the spasmodic insecurity in Port-au-Prince, so many walls have been built, and so much is hidden. All of the post-earthquake groups are protected by walls, and the walls are higher now and often topped with shards of glass bottles that function as concertina wire. So the two-story half-brick house that reminds me of my friend's old house must stand in for the real, hidden house, and it brings back the memory of that other place, that other time.

Another thing that moves me: bone in a burned foot. The man sits in a broken wheelchair—he's young, maybe twenty-two. He's a friend of Jerry and Samuel's. He was riding on his motorbike in the middle of a post-quake, pre-election demonstration when a government thug, so he says, took a potshot at him. The bullet went through his abdomen, and he was in such shock that his foot got caught in the bike's muffler and burned. They took him to the general hospital, where doctors repaired the bullet's damage and left a big scar along his abdomen, which he matter-of-factly shows to anyone who asks, but the foot was left to heal on its own with no skin graft, and now, three months after the injury, you can still see the entirely exposed three inches of metatarsal bone through a blood-red hole in the top of his foot, like a peek at the guy's skeleton, as he sits there in his unwheeled wheelchair in a stony fury over his situation.

Another item in my list of what moves me here: the death of the woman who hated me. Just after the earthquake, I had a spaghetti dinner—this was the one made by the *New York Times*'s Haiti reporting team—in the kitchen of the half-destroyed Park Hotel. You had to walk under hanging cement and over broken floors to get to the lobby, and then tiptoe through the perilous lobby to the kitchen. One of the Haitians staying there, behind the rubble of the front rooms, was a Madame Coupet, an older, very light-skinned Haitian lady, *wouj*, actually, who was wearing a housedress. Her son was in America.

She had heard of the book I had published on Haiti many years earlier. How she had hated me then, she told me now—well, I had supported Aristide, she had gathered, and he was the man she held responsible for everything bad that had happened in the past twenty-five years. For this earthquake, even, it seemed. I bowed my head. What could I tell her? She wouldn't have wanted to hear what I wanted to say. But we talked about other things—her children, her family, Haiti—and in the end, we got along. She decided that I was not a demon, and that we both loved Haiti. She was surprised that I seemed nice. Polite. Well-brought-up, is how the Haitians say it.

After I left the country, I thought of Madame Coupet often, and longed to see her again. I wanted to talk to her, because I needed to hear more about old Haiti, the lost country, the country she said she loved. I thought of her mottled skin, its fairness ruined by age and the Haitian sun, of her gracious diction, and of her generosity in forgiving me for Aristide—and of mine in forgiving her for forgiving me for Aristide. When I came back to Port-au-Prince, five months after the earthquake, the middle-aged men sitting in metal chairs on the still rubble-strewn terrace of the Park Hotel, smoking cigarettes and gossiping with one another, told me the old lady had died. They wanted to tell me gently but didn't know how. So they told me bluntly: she died. Therefore, no interview. But I can still tell you what she might have said, or at any rate, what someone like her might have said. Here it is:

When I was a girl, there were lace curtains. The wind was sweet. I had a pet cat and she would chase the guinea fowl in the courtyard. I had a blue dress with a sash that only my mother knew how to tie properly. The frangipani tree in the corner of the garden smelled like my mother's perfume. There was Duvalier, sure: Papa Doc. But we children, me and my brothers, we paid very little attention. My parents tried to keep out of his way, I suppose. My father was a professor at the university, an engineer. My brothers and I, we read poetry, Durand, Rimbaud, Baudelaire, Morisseau-Leroy, Roumer, and meanwhile the bougainvillea tumbled over the front wall and there were plants in pots in the gardens and two servants, and one poor distant girl cousin who helped with chores. She was from the deep country, and did marry, finally. In summers we went to my aunt's house in the mountains and picked flowers and rode donkeys and helped make the morning coffee. I went to school in a checkered uniform that I loved. I read French literature until I met my husband, who was in the import-export business. I was beautiful, and he loved me until I grew old. We had two children, and a third who died in childbirth. Now one more is dead and the other lives in New Jersey. I prefer to be here where I understand things.

Here's something that got to me too: the last time I saw Filibert Waldeck. The last time I saw Filibert, I was standing in front of the ruined cathedral downtown. It was January 12, 2011, the first anniversary of the earth-quake. People were praying under the statue of Jesus that still stands out-side the rubble. A man rushed up and exhibited his little daughter to me. She had, to put it nicely, failure to thrive. She must have been five but she looked two, with huge eyes, reddish hair, bone-thin limbs. The man told me they'd been homeless since the earthquake. A person nearby told me, while the man was standing there in front of me with his silent child bal-anced in his arms, that that fellow came to the cathedral ruins with the kid every day looking for some visitor to beg from. Did that make his story less true? I asked myself. The crowd pressed on us and the man and his daugh-ter were shoved away. There was a band playing, and there were priests and nuns seated, waiting for the service to begin. I was standing off to the side near a white man I'd never seen before, an older man with thinning hair.

As usual with any big Haitian event, huge numbers of people were all shoved together in a giant bubbling human mass. The white man near me was at least five people away. Although we were outside, there was barely room to inhale where we stood, but uncannily, up in front of my face popped someone I recognized. At first I wasn't sure who he was, exactly. Then he spoke in his familiar growl of a voice, the same rasp he'd had as a child, only deeper. It was Filibert, wearing some kind of satanic red and silver T-shirt and old dirty jeans. He was too thin.

I said, "Filibert, what's wrong with you?" He wasn't making sense. The white man standing near me was watching. He pushed his way for-ward and took Filibert by the arm and rattled him, shook him up a bit. I was astonished. Filibert looked astonished, too, if you can look aston-ished while looking sullen. The white man, whose self-assured demeanor I now recognized as that of a lay Christian brother of some kind, was interrogating Filibert. He called him by his full name: "Filibert Waldeck, what's wrong with you?"

Filibert just shook his head, looked down at the ground. The man looked at me and back at Filibert. "You're on crack or something, aren't you?" he asked him. "I know it. I know it." The man shook his head and tried to peer into Filibert's eyes, but Filibert looked away.

"You stop that stuff, do you hear me?" The man was speaking fluent Creole.

I took Filibert aside and he began that same long rant I'd already heard about his sons and their mother and about how he had to keep them inside so she wouldn't get them, and how his motorbike had broken down and he didn't have money to get it fixed. Throughout the whole long saga, which was much more detailed and a lot less comprehensible than what I am putting down here, he would look at me sideways, slantwise, assessing my potential. Half the time he had the demeanor of a person on drugs or in the throes of mental illness of some kind, which I've always suspected with him. And the rest of the time, he looked like a smart old market lady sizing up her client. Finally, I asked him if I could help him in any way, and he just looked at me.

"Amy, you ahr my mozzer," he said to me, in English. So I gave him some money. And then he disappeared into the crowd. I saw a patch of red fading away down toward Grande Rue. My child, I thought. I tried to imagine it. I wondered if there had really ever been any connection between us, other than monetary. Because of where I was from, I had always had the power in our relationship. Because of where he was from, Filibert was always the weak one, poor, needy, desperate. Of course we each bore some responsibility for who we were and how we had ended up, but we were also prisoners of our fates, each of us locked in our individual history and geography. I was from the United States and he was from Haiti. That was it. I always had and gave money; he always did not have it and needed it. It was always my choice: Would I give him something? How much, this time? It was easy, even pleasurable, for me to give it to him; but it was all cruel for him.

The crowd around me was singing a spindly soprano hymn as the memorial service began. But where was Filibert going now? Why didn't he have a cell phone? Why didn't he have my number? And now that speck of red had vanished. I squinted into the sun, trying to find him again, but he had slipped back away into the heat and darkness, and was lost to me.

As I am writing this, at around five in the morning, I hear gunfire and screaming outside my window in Port-au-Prince. Two shots. Ridiculous. It cannot be, but it is. Freelance fire, I figure—meaningless gang shit. In the old days violence had political meaning in Haiti, but, as elsewhere in the world, now it's often pretty pointless. More gunfire now. Definitely gunfire. And screaming and a rumble of low shouting, as if a whole crowd is yelling far away. Carnival is coming, I remember; that can be a violent time. And elections are coming: that also means violence. First I get up to go to the window to look: when I peek out from a sharp sideways angle, I see a crowd down on the street below, pushing and shoving, and screaming. It's violent, and that's definitely where the shooting has been coming from. Maybe it *is* some kind of political protest, I think now. I retract my head as another round of shooting begins, and return to my desk.

Later, when I interviewed some acquaintances in the neighborhood, I discovered that the reason for the shooting and screaming and the angry nub of a crowd in the street was that the pharmacy down below my window had announced the previous day that it would be offering to fill children's prescriptions for free today, in a one-day trial program. The crowd was composed of mothers, all fighting to get in before the place stopped serving. The shooter was the pharmacy owner, trying to protect his place from the poverty-maddened consumers. I'd mistaken the mothers for a politically motivated riot. And, in a way, they were.

15

ARISTIDE'S CITADEL

Poud pa janm sevi dè fwa
Magic powder never works twice

Port-Salut is a spirited southern coastal town untouched by the earthquake. It winds around the Caribbean's beating surf, an expansive sparkle of dazzling silver and blue. Little houses sit on the mountain side of the road, and bigger ones stand across the way, on the beach. You might think for a second that you're in Jamaica or even Puerto Rico. In fact, Port-Salut reminds me of Malibu, but of course, it's nothing like Malibu—only topographically parallel. I end up at the house of former Aristide political employees—it seems to me that everyone in the town is the cousin or associate of the former president. This is his hometown, his birthplace. He used to run around the mountains here as a little kid, without any pants on. That's what they say. Just like so many other kids. In Haiti it's a clichéd description of a little boy: *sans pantalons.* Today, on the mountain side of the road, I see skinny little Haitian boys running around in this comfortable outfit. Two teeny little things are kicking a piece of plastic as if it were a soccer ball, and another is shrieking something in a high-pitched wail with his fists all balled up and his eyes closed tight. Another small, pantless one is gathering twigs in a pile. Aristide's origins were like theirs, the nonstarving poor. The nearly lower middle-class. His grandfather had some land. He left with his mother for Port-au-Prince and a better life when he was a very small boy.

I have lunch with Myrtha and her husband, Toto, and Jean-Robert and Jean-Marie, some of whom are Aristide's cousins and all of whom have long connections to him and his family. Véronique and Marc, Canadian friends of Myrtha and Toto, are also invited. We're eating salad prepared by Myrtha and Véronique, and a big plate of rice and beef prepared by Marie-Yolène, a servant who gets yelled at a lot, teasingly. Four unfairly bony and undersize dogs sit hopefully near the table but not too near. They are scaredy-dogs who can run backward and have never been petted or spoiled, and who eat garbage scraps and sometimes some dog food. That's a good life for a dog in Haiti.

The talk here at the lunch table in Port-Salut is all of the upcoming elections. After enough time in Haiti, everything (except the earthquake) seems like déjà vu. These are elections that are taking place in the rubble, the candidates running in the ruins. This impending vote is the election from which Wyclef Jean, the hip-hop musician, has already been barred by the Haitian electoral council. The people around the lunch table don't like the remaining candidates, and never liked Wyclef.

In normal times, Wyclef would not have been running for president of Haiti. Ordinarily it's just not that attractive a job for someone who is not a committed member of the Haitian political class in Port-au-Prince. But because of the earthquake, the job was now very attractive to the aging hip-hop artist: there was a world spotlight on Haiti, and it was a good backdrop for his celebrity. His plans were wrecked, though, when he was knocked out of the running because he hadn't lived in Haiti for the five years prior to the vote, having lived in New Jersey rather than in the homeland since he was nine.

While Wyclef was still running, it was pack journalism covering the election down in Port-au-Prince, and when I say pack I mean pack—a crowd of journalists and Wyclef's posse nearly suffocated as they waited in the security area outside the Plaza Hotel's lobby for someone to unlock the hotel's inner door and let them in. The Haitian crowd outside, eager for a glimpse of Wyclef, pressed on the pack from the other side of the outer door. It was like covering a rock star—it *was* covering a rock star. Following Aristide had been like that, too, in the past. The difference was in the substance of the figure, his significance.

Over the whole post-earthquake season—the relief effort, the reconstruction plans, the elections—hung the silent, distant figure of Aristide. He was still in exile in South Africa. He had shed public tears after the earthquake, and he wanted to return to Haiti. Now that he had his PhD, he was Dr. Aristide. In Haiti, the thirty- and forty-year-olds, who had grown up thinking of Aristide as a liberator of Haiti's poor, desperately wanted him back. That generation had voted for the man they called Titid, they'd elected him twice, they'd seen him pushed aside in two coups d'état, and they felt he was still their president. (Filibert Waldeck wanted Aristide back because Filibert had had a job in security at the presidential palace when Aristide was in office—which perhaps explains in part why it wasn't so hard to overthrow Aristide.) Others who had been frightened by the widespread violence during Aristide's second term were hoping he'd stay away. Among the international media, too, Aristide was a disputed figure. Some journalists worked almost as public-relations personnel for him, trundling back and forth to South Africa at his beck and call, and others referred to him privately as the Evil Black Insect.

Aristide was still, in absentia, a lightning rod for political feeling in Haiti. The very idea of his return drove many Haitians into a hopeful euphoria, while it sent others into pre-catastrophe overdrive. On the walls around Port-au-Prince, graffiti had been scrawled in Creole that read "*VIV TITID*," or "Long Live Aristide," and "*Titid Wa*," or "Aristide Is King." Running counter to that were graffiti and stencils in sunny French that said, ominously, "*Bon Retour Jean-Claude Duvalier*," as if awaiting Baby Doc the way one waits for a proud soldier returning from the front. As the election proceeded, there was a sense that another theoretical election, a shadow election, was also happening and that was the one between Aristide and Duvalier, between, that is, the people and the ruling elite, between— that is—some kind of democracy and the continuing status quo.

Instead, Michel Martelly, the singer, was elected, which meant the status quo was victorious. It was a complicated vote in which many people who should have taken part did not—the Haitian people. There was only 23 percent participation, largely because Aristide's party, Fanmi Lavalas, was excluded from the election on a technicality. Similarly, many people took part in the election who—in a normal country with sovereign structures and parameters—would usually not. The head of the UN mission, Edmond Mulet, was highly influential in certain decisions that were made by the electoral council. Digicel was interested in the elections and made those interests clear. The Organization of American States was involved. Unelected and unappointed figures from the elite were pushing the buttons and pulling the levers of power. The Americans were working it. Outgoing president Préval was in on the game, too. He was focused on putting someone from his party into the *fauteuil presidentiel* or, failing that, perhaps taking control of the parliament and getting himself appointed prime minister. His preferred presidential candidate was a cheerful, self-involved reputed womanizer who had been head of the government's construction operation.

The election was of special interest to outsiders and insiders because it was the first post-earthquake election. The people who would end up in charge of Haiti after the balloting would at least theoretically have some control of some of the monies flowing into the place. The aid organizations and the international community were looking for a "responsible partner," which, translated from aid-ese, meant someone who would agree with the aid community's guidelines and recommendations, policies and programs. And not screw things up.

By chance, I met Préval's candidate, who looked to be a sure loser, at a cabinet meeting just before his candidacy was announced. He sat stiffly in a gilded reception chair among the other ministers, while President Préval demonstrated for me—with a set of porcelain espresso cups that had been set up on a tray for his advisers—the difficulties of dealing with post-earthquake neighborhoods where some houses had remained habitable (pointing to upright cups) while others among them (turning a cup here or there over on its delicate, gold-rimmed side) were so badly damaged they would have to come down. The capriciousness of the damage was a problem for those like Préval, who understood that what people wanted most was to return to their old neighborhoods, if not their old rent payments.

A rumored five million dollars was spent on the unsuccessful campaign of Préval's favorite. On billboards, the man's grinning face presided over the sprawling camps like the eyes of Dr. T. J. Eckleburg over the wasteland in *The Great Gatsby.* The more he smiled down on them the less Haitians liked him.

The election proceeded along the usual Haitian political road, filled with dangerous potholes and the usual hairpin Haitian twists and turns, none of it guided by real popularity or the substance of a political platform. In the first round of voting, Martelly was apparently eliminated from a later final, deciding ballot. But Martelly and his backers were having none of it. Crying fraud, his followers proceeded to riot and to burn down government offices in various spots around the country. Amid the violence, the OAS was called on to investigate the preliminary balloting, and to make a determination as to who really had won it.

Somehow I got caught as a minor figure in the unspooling of the plot. I was down in Haiti a month after the first round of elections, as the OAS was finishing its investigation and completing its report. Someone I knew from the international business community had obtained a draft of the document. He had it on a flash drive and asked me if I would send it out to the international media without naming him as the source. I said yes, as long as I could also use it myself.

The next day, before any news of the report was out, I happened to have an appointment to interview Préval in his offices behind the ruins of the palace. You drive in and park, and then walk through security. There are new prefabricated buildings and some older offices still standing back there. Security and reception were in a tent for a long time. The ruins of the palace were visible from behind, crumpled and teetering, windows broken, domes down, and walls in the process of subsidence, cracks running to the ground. On this day, a brass band was practicing "The Star-Spangled Banner" in the parking lot under a tree.

Because I am a child of my era, and—I guess—reflexively hierarchical, I mistakenly assumed that *the president of Haiti* had the OAS report *about Haiti* already and already knew its still embargoed contents, so to me my conversation with Préval that day had all sorts of meaning that, afterward, I realized it had not had. He hadn't seen the report. I had it on a flash drive in my bag. During the interview, I thought he was making references to the report, but he could not have been. No one had bothered leaking it to him. In fact, it had been specifically kept from him for as long as possible.

After the main points of the report made it into the news, I heard from people in Préval's cabinet that he was outraged to have been beaten by a leak, outraged that the OAS had not given him the report before they leaked it to someone else. I was nonplussed. I loathed my unimportant part in the charade: to have been used to disseminate a report on Haitian elections before the president of the country had even seen it; to have been played like that in the white man's game, to be a white man party to the deception of a Haitian president, to trick the president, as if I were a player in Haiti's history, and he were not.

The OAS investigation, it turned out, had found that Martelly was still in the race. That's what the report said, and therefore, he was. In the final round of voting, Martelly defeated his remaining rival to become Haiti's fifty-sixth president. It was a bitter dose of realpolitik for Préval to swallow. The election of a successor had been tugged out of his control. Now, a sitting president should not be able to stage-manage the election of his successor. Nor should the OAS be in charge of that. But in Haiti, where elections and statistics are within reach of control and manipulation, someone (Haitian or not; often not) is always stepping in to try to take hold of the reins of power. Just as coups d'état don't just *happen* in Haiti, neither do presidents just *get elected*. Except, perhaps, in the cases of surprise last-minute guerrilla candidates, like Aristide.

It felt wrong to be an outsider inside something that should have been a purely Haitian affair. But who was I kidding? The whole election was an outside affair, and the biggest players were the groups inside and outside Haiti that would need to have powerful influence with the next president—earthquake aid donors, MINUSTAH, and major business figures like the one who leaked the report to me in the first place. There were a few in the elite who had supported Préval and his candidate, but they were outmaneuvered. Two of Préval's last acts as president—besides knighting an OAS official who had revealed various machinations behind the OAS report—were to allow both Duvalier and, later, Aristide to return to the country in advance of the inauguration. This was a slap in the face to the United States, which had been involved in the downfall of Duvalier in 1986 and, reportedly, in the ousting of Aristide in 1991 and 2004.

The old joke goes like this:

Question: "Why are there no coups d'état in Washington?"

Response: "No U.S. embassy."

A knight, in Haiti, is an honorary title. You don't go charging around on a horse. It's like being given an OBE or an MBE in the UK. Here's what the knighted OAS diplomat, Brazil's Ricardo Seitenfus, told *Le Temps*, a Swiss publication:

> For two hundred years, foreign troops have alternated with dictatorships. Force is what defines international relations with Haiti, and never dialogue. Haiti's original sin, on the world stage, was its liberation . . .
>
> The world has never known how to deal with Haiti, so in the end, it has simply ignored it. So began, after the revolution, two hundred years of solitude on the international scene. Today, the United Nations deploys its troops to impose its peace operation. We resolve nothing; we make things worse. We want to make of Haiti a capitalist country, a

platform for exports for the American market. It's absurd. Haiti ought to return to what it really is: that is to say, a country that is essentially agricultural and more fundamentally, a country run by customary, traditional law. Haiti is consistently described from the point of view of its violence. But, even without a state, the level of violence in Haiti is only a fraction of what it is in the countries of Latin America.

It was this interview that reportedly led to Seitenfus's recall and departure from the OAS. It was also one of the things that got him knighted by Préval, who has always leaned to the left and had a special affection for Fidel Castro and Hugo Chávez, who have returned the regard in the form of medical aid, from Castro, and cheap oil, from Chávez.

In many ways, Préval's government was like Aristide's—but without the difficult, tempestuous, and magnetic Aristide; it was undoubtedly more beneficial to the Haitian people than any preceding Haitian government, even though it was not particularly beneficial. But Préval, successful in that he served for two full terms and left office both times legally and peacefully, failed to rise even semi-adequately to the difficulties posed by the earthquake. And that is one reason he was not able to propel his power beyond his presidency. The other reason was that the international community—in the guise of the OAS—put its foot down and said no. They wanted someone who wouldn't just pretend to do what they wanted, but who would really do it. And that someone was Martelly.

In the decade between his return to Haiti in 1994 and his second forced exit in 2004, Aristide flattened the top of a hill near his birthplace in Port-Salut and began building a fortress palace along the lines of a Grecian temple–cum–medieval dungeon. This colossal structure was put up near the actual site of Aristide's birth home, a sweet little house that was razed along with the mountaintop. Having been ousted in a violent coup once, in 1991, Aristide planned never to be overthrown again (when the Clinton administration returned Aristide to Haiti three years after the

1991 coup, he reportedly told a friend that he would "no longer govern like a choirboy"—and he didn't). So this time around he was re-creating himself, and he believed, rightly, that he still had powerful enemies. Although several charges of human-rights abuses have been leveled against the turbulent second Aristide administration, which lasted from 2000 until he was overthrown in 2004, none has been proved.

Aristide's citadel is a work of grandiosity and paranoia. It was obviously planned as a stronghold to which a besieged leader could retreat safely during a prolonged attack, a place from which Aristide could theoretically have ruled if Port-au-Prince had been overrun by his foreign and domestic enemies, if the presidential palace were no longer at his disposal. Next to this mountaintop castle, Aristide put up two unremarkable buildings that were to house a hospital and a school: no better human shields than that. The hospital staff and matériel could also have been useful, one assumed, in case of a siege, and the school could have functioned as a training ground for his supporters. Of course, both would also have a real and demonstrable humanitarian use—there are not many organized schools and hospitals in the countryside in Haiti, and that's an understatement.

Unlike the tiny one- and two-room houses of its neighbors, who are all of peasant stock, Aristide's bastion had electricity wired up to the mountaintop on poles; new roads had been laid for access. Wells for the citadel's water were drilled deep into the mountain (Aristide's neighbors here have to walk for miles on steep century-old paths to get water from the spring at the bottom of the ridge). The palace also has several possible helipads; it has a secret door in the master bedroom behind which a hunted president could hide and, if necessary, climb a ladder down a thirty-foot drop to a maze of secret corridors behind solid doors. In the master suite is a long, long pink-tiled bathroom that ends in a pink bathtub—the rest of the fixtures were looted after the second coup against Aristide, in 2004. No doubt a matching pink commode serves as seating in a one-room hut somewhere on the way down the hill.

The walls of Aristide's citadel, which is made from concrete and large chunks of rubble created when the mountaintop was sliced away, are more than a foot and a half thick. It's a defensive structure, not really a place from which to launch much of an attack. The cisterns can hold water for a large household for at least several weeks' usage, it appeared when I took a walk around the grounds a few months before Aristide made his surprise 2011 return from exile.

As in Haiti's colonial fortresses, Aristide's citadel includes many cool, dark rooms that are underground. Aboveground, there are sight lines from which one can survey the southern sea and all possible land approaches. Yet the fortress is hidden from view until you come upon it, until you virtually stumble upon it—and the only way to find it is either to arrive there by arrangement in a vehicle, or to target it from the air.

It's as if one had looked into the mind of Aristide at the end of the twentieth century, and seen straight through to the thoughts and defensive strategizing of King Henri Christophe two centuries earlier. One feels that only the cannon and piles of cannonballs are missing to complete the picture. In 1804, Henri understandably feared a renewed attack, and, two hundred years later, so did Aristide. Relations with the outside had not changed so very much since the revolution.

We're driving along the shore road in Port-Salut at night, my friend Toto at the wheel of the SUV, and his wife, Myrtha, one of Aristide's Port-Salut connections, in the front passenger seat, palm fronds spinning above us like wheeling silver fireworks, banana trees flailing in our breeze, the metallic dark leaves of mango trees glistening in the headlights in pinpoint-sharp outlines. From the beach comes the sound of a distant *rara* band, herald of Carnival's approach. We arrive at Christian's; he is a French businessman from near Orléans who's lived in Haiti for a decade and who runs a little local hotel and restaurant on the beach with his wife, Catherine, a typical matter-of-fact country Frenchwoman from Bordeaux, very nice. She's hurt her leg recently, falling in a hole in the garden where there wasn't one before. She's massaging her plump knee as we sit around a table in the restaurant.

Bob Marley is on the video projector, with his family. He's wearing a dashiki. His hair fills the screen as an amateur video camera zooms in and out; he's got the kind of dreads worn now by the gangstas in Cité Soleil. "Redemption Song" filters through the club. The tables are full.

It takes a good five hours to drive to Port-Salut, because the roads are not as good as they were during Aristide's presidency, when they were maintained to presidential standards, and the traffic is unmoving in many spots. Because of its beautiful seashore, Port-Salut is a weekend refuge for Haitians from abroad, like Toto and Myrtha; some have vacation homes here. In spite of the deteriorating roads, it's even more popular now because it was untouched by the earthquake.

One of the Aristide cousins is building a new house here, by the beach. He showed it to me on the way down, when his car's air conditioner broke (at least it *had* one) and the car died. His house is just concrete, as of now, and three-quarters finished. When he makes a little money, he builds a little more. This cousin has a radio station in Port-Salut, and he intends to run for mayor. Although he swears he will never pay for votes or give the people rum on election day, he is confident of victory. "That's *why* they'll vote for me," he says. He's a bit of a dreamer. He left a family in the United States when Aristide became president. Aristide's sister moved back to Haiti then, too. Her husband became important in Port-au-Prince. Government was a family business. It always is in Haiti, as in so many other places. Papa Doc, Baby Doc. Papa Assad, Baby Assad. Papa Bhutto, Baby Bhutto. Papa Bush, Baby Bush.

On the screen, Marley is playing acoustic. The music fills me with nostalgia for the Caribbean, for breezy Kingston and the actual Caribbean Sea. I always forget in Haiti that I am in the Caribbean basin. Normally, I barely see the Caribbean when I'm here. Before the earthquake, in any case, you could see the water from Port-au-Prince only when you were right down next to the shoreline, and then it was not a pretty sight; the shantytowns run down to the water, pigs snout around in the frothy brown spume, and the water gives off a mist of shit and refuse. I used to go there often in the old days, when I was working on my first book. There's a shantytown there (built in my lifetime) called Cité de Dieu, or City of God. The surf was always something to turn away from.

Now, because the quake has swept away more than half the city, you can see the water from hillside and ridge in Port-au-Prince, from the edge of canyons and as you come around a curve, much as it must have appeared in the days of the colony, when settlers decided that this majestic bay was a port fit for princes. Looked down on from the high mountains that encircle Port-au-Prince, the sea seems to sparkle as it does elsewhere in the basin, blue and lime green. You can't see the pigs.

In fact, Haiti is a beachy island, but most of its people are not swimmers and water isn't something they adore. They're mountain people or city people. Perhaps because of its long initial isolation from the rest of the world after slavery was defeated, Haiti feels like an island turned in on itself, the mountainous countryside removed from access to the sea and the long stretches of beach looking up to the mountains rather than out over the water to *lòt bò dlo*.

It's a world apart, sometimes a reality apart. It's not a department of France, nor a protectorate of the United States—although remittances from Haitians who've emigrated to those countries and Canada help keep Haiti's economy afloat. It's not really fully Caribbean. It's not Latin American. And it's not even really African, although of all the places with which it shares history, Haiti is most like Africa and like France—indeed, most like French West Africa. That's one reason why it is often treated by outsiders who don't know it well with a dismissive Afro-pessimism—as if to say that, like the continent it came from, which according to their assessment is ruined and failed, Haiti also can never progress.

Haiti, filled with generation after generation of kidnap's offspring, was cut off from any other cultural succor after the revolution. Because the other Caribbean slave colonies never had a successful revolution, this was not true for any of them, and this peculiar, unique history—rebellion followed by abandonment—makes Haiti different, a more radical, more African entity in the Caribbean.

We can still hear Marley's "Redemption Song" as it sifts through the increasing noise and clatter in the bar. Maybe it's on a continuous loop, synced with the video. It should be. The song is pretty much the national anthem of the Caribbean nations, the Marseillaise of the West Indies. It's about the slave trade, and slave traders—"old pirates," Marley calls them—and about what that heritage means today. Toward the end of the song, Marley directly addresses the generations who bear the legacy of slavery. "We forward in this generation triumphantly," he sings. He asks them to help him sing the songs of freedom. And he asserts that those redemption songs are his only true possession, and by extension, the only true possession of his generation of African-Caribbeans, in what is a clear reference to claiming the contested ownership of one's own body and soul, or redeeming oneself as property, making a payment for liberty. Perhaps I'm giving the song too much weight, but to interpret further: the culture of a place—or broadly, its "song"—is the very tool that leads to freedom. So if that culture, developed in, for example, Haiti by Haitians over centuries, should for some reason, like development or post-disaster reconstruction, be replaced or overrun by an outside culture, it's possible to lose a nation's inherent spirit of freedom, the very basis of its liberty.

A whiskey. Catherine still in pain—her knee. We're talking about rice and beans; here in Haiti, made a certain way, it's called *riz national,* or national rice. Marley's still on the video, his family still surrounding him—I have an impression of more bright dashikis and Marley's thin face, the cancer he had. As the night deepens, the customers in the bar grow more raucous. One woman is standing, swaying, at her table and singing along with Marley. Christian mentions building Aristide's fortress. Christian and Catherine run a construction goods store, too, as well as the hotel and restaurant. Three years after they moved to Haiti, they provided all the cement for Aristide in Port-Salut. (In Haiti, a businessman cannot have his spoon in too many stews.) Christian's shock of thick white hair, his *barbe sans moustache* overcast by thick, dark eyebrows and a strong nose, all make him look like an expat from an earlier era. He reminds me of Leonard Doyle's characterization of expats in Haiti and elsewhere in the developing world: "Missionaries, mercenaries, and misfits . . . marginal men." I look at Christian—he looks like an old pirate. He fits in in Haiti, but was he always out of place in France?

And I also think, is this me, too? Sans beard, but still. All the outsiders who come to Haiti, and come again, and never absolutely leave, are expats of a kind. What is it they get out of Haiti? This is the mystery I was trying to solve, after all. What do I get out of Haiti? What draws me back, looked at unromantically?

Maybe it's just a kind of voyeurism, like the *Tragedy and Hope* reader looking at the picture book. I keep thinking of the title of Pascal Bruckner's book *The Tears of the White Man,* a right-wing tract by a French so-called *nouveau philosophe* that rejects the developed world's compassionate charity and pity for the less developed world. As the white man tools around Haiti, he can see every day how lucky he is not to have been born into the misery of this island—not to have taken part in its legacy of pariahism, abandonment, and poverty. Escaping the misery is a ritual of every day for the expatriate community. In Haiti it's important for the outsider *not* to belong. Haitian-Americans feel this, too, sometimes—the urge not to be Haitian, to lead life in one of Samuel Huntington's approved civilizations, rather than in the not-something of Haiti. Everyone in Haiti, including Haitian-Americans and including Haitians, can see the value of a life that is not Haitian, the value of a life led, in some way or another, away from this place, the value of Gerety's compound life.

But then you come away from the expat venue. You leave Christian's bar, or my friends' apartment in a gated Port-au-Prince compound. You leave Sean Penn on the Oloffson terrace, or Leonard Doyle up at O'Brasiliero restaurant. You leave Gerety's masters—and you go hang out in Cité Soleil with Mimette and her kids. You go over to Jacques-Richard's and deal with his mother-in-law and the baby and the sister-in-law and Smith, the one who was taken by zombies but is now well. The television's going in the background. You go up to the post-presidential house that René Préval is living in on the hill above the capital and listen to him rhapsodize, among fake flowers and small statuettes, about the agricultural projects in his hometown (when he was president he ran a fish-farming project behind the palace). You go out to Bassin-Bleu and watch the farmers and their families gather.

For me, that's when I feel the power of the invented place that is Haiti, the place created by Haitians, for Haitians. It's always a less exotic place than the Haiti created by outsiders for Haitians. The farther you are from the people who are not Haitian, the more you can see the value of what's Haitian. First of all, community. Now, there is plenty of infighting and jealousy inside Haitian communities—there always will be among humans when necessities are scarce. But the bonds are strong. A man or woman may resent the hell out of it, but he or she is tied to the family of the mother or father of his or her kids. People are strongly tied to their own parents, and their aunties and uncles. You bury your dead in your front garden if you can, because they are the ancestors, all—virtual domestic gods. (Aristide's Port-Salut citadel has a family cemetery out front for this reason—and because he needs to protect his ancestors from desecration during political upheaval.) Villagers have a sense of place and belonging. A hand-stitched safety net exists in villages because there is no other security provided for villagers by anyone else. Now this may not mean that men are "faithful" to their women, or women to their men, but, as Sabina Carlson would say with emphasis, they are *faithful*. In other words, in its more serious meaning: they keep faith with their community.

Other things that matter in the Haiti that is purely Haitian: humor, hierarchy, respect, deference, generosity. When you go calling on a neighbor in Haiti, in the countryside, you still shout the word "Honor" as you stand waiting outside the door, and from inside you hear your friend say, "Respect." It's like *salaam aleikum* in the Arab world, and the response, *wa aleikum a-salaam*. "Honor-respect" is an old greeting that comes down from the days of the colony. More things: propriety, boundaries, cleanliness, hospitality, eloquence, storytelling. Some others: honesty, character, your word. Of course, sometimes people lie and tell fibs and sneak off and steal and even commit murder. Their poverty can make Haitians angry or vicious or depraved, of course. As Jacques Roumain wrote in *Masters of the Dew*, "Everything was transformed or deformed by an empty stomach: love, pride, willpower and tenderness."

I say all this as an outsider; this is what I've gleaned in stolen moments of opportunistic observation, watching, as it were, from the sidelines as I sit in the provinces and shantytowns, enjoying my Haitian sweets. But almost none of these qualities remains pure once you mix the outside world into the Haitian brew, once (that is to say) you add possible access to instant cash, future jobs with aid organizations, possible visas, et cetera, into a mix whose essential broth is penury. Then corruption enters in, and no motivation is beyond question; no story remains plausible; no ownership goes unchallenged. Once Heather Nozea arrives with her blond ponytail and infectious grin, and her check and her deed to property in Haiti, all bets are off. To a Haitian she doesn't look like Pollyanna, but like a dollar sign in a cartoon. In many ways, it's a class problem that has been confused by national and racial difference. Thus, the outsider waving his money almost never can see Haitians clearly, but always through a veil of misunderstanding and misrepresentation. Similarly, it is a rare Haitian who perceives an outsider with full, human clarity.

I stayed over at Myrtha and Toto's house on the beach that night after listening to Bob Marley at Christian's bar. The surf pounded through the night, barely a hundred feet from my window. The electricity from the private generator cycled on and off. I woke frequently to fend off the gangs of mosquitoes that were treating me as disputed territory.

The next day was hot, and we were having another lunch outside under the straw roof of Myrtha and Toto's broad waterfront terrace. Marie-Yolène, Myrtha's servant, was setting things up.

Myrtha's husband, Toto, is a political commentator—self-appointed. His real full name is Jérôme Dominique. Both Myrtha and Toto were born in Haiti, but they live most of the year in Montreal. Myrtha was Aristide's secretary and scheduler for several years while he was president, so Toto and Myrtha are not simply old friends of the former president, or just Port-Salut neighbors. They were inside the circle of power.

There is red wine in a box on the lunch table, wine that Myrtha brought down from Montreal. Toto fills a few glasses for guests.

Myrtha goes through a list of all the people Aristide's not speaking to, not speaking to all the way from South Africa, including her. Including me, I point out. She tells a series of stories about being in charge of the presidential schedule in the old days. She's a sturdy, relaxed person, but a control freak. She leans back in her chair, makes a sucking noise at a too-forward dog, and calls for more lemonade from pretty Marie-Yolène. Marie-Yolène is truculent and funny. She talks back in a way I have never seen before in a Haitian servant.

"This is the problem with democracy," Toto says after one of Marie-Yolène's outbursts, in a stage aside that Marie-Yolène can hear. But he likes it, he feels proud of the way his servant acts. "She is very post-Aristide," he says. He means that she is not submissive.

Marie-Yolène behaves with Myrtha the way Butterfly McQueen behaved with Vivien Leigh after Twelve Oaks was burned and Tara was left to war's desolation, and the Yankees had marched through Georgia, and Rhett was at the cathouse, and the Confederacy was no more. I'm talking about the Civil War movie *Gone With the Wind,* made in 1939. It's almost as if Marie-Yolène has studied acting at a fantasy Butterfly McQueen Studios. The same slightly disrespectful turning away of the head; the high-pitched, sing-song voice, the idea that insouciant Marie-Yolène will do as she likes while pretending to do what the mistress has required, the sexy flirtatiousness, the feeling that the bossy mistress is actually indulgent—and, anyway, impotent.

Marie-Yolène does what McQueen did: invests a stereotypical role with the threat of rebellion. And I realize with a sudden thump of recognition that both Butterfly and Marie-Yolène are doing Erzulie Freda, the flirty, untrustworthy voodoo goddess of love. Erzulie flounces, she wriggles, she dawdles. I've seen Erzulie at so many voodoo services—Marie-Yolène doesn't wear Erzulie's tight, sexy dress or makeup, but she radiates the same unreliable female sexuality.

And the family coddles Marie-Yolène; they scold her. They smile secret smiles and pat her. It's very antebellum here in the land where every man is free.

We're eating cold ham, baked beans American-style (from the can), okra sauce, boiled plantain, baked *mazonbel,* or taro root, and a beet salad.

Myrtha is slicing plantains at the table.

"Where is that lemonade?" she asks, loudly. She shakes her head, the implicit criticism of Marie-Yolène understood by all at the table. She turns her attention back to us. Marie-Yolène slowly makes her way back to the kitchen.

"Aristide would receive people with big hugs and kisses," Myrtha says as she distributes the plantain. It would be a lovefest, she continues: how he missed them, how happy he was to see them, chuck under the chin, slap on the back, jokes told and laughed at, giggles for the children, and his visitors so glad, so relieved, still friends with the president. They'd say, "Ah, Titid, we need to see you again," and he'd say, "Oh, I'd love to, go talk to Myrtha, arrange it with Myrtha." So they'd leave him in his office, drag themselves away, and on the way out of the palace, they'd stop at Myrtha's desk to make another appointment for a month or two later. She'd pencil them in on the presidential calendar. And then, after the cheerful visitors were safely away, Aristide would emerge from his office, lean over Myrtha and the calendar, and tell her that absolutely and under no circumstances did he ever want to see those people again.

Myrtha told about the time when Titid came to her house in Port-Salut, as president, in his shirtsleeves. In his honor, they had decorated the place with the slender homemade candles associated with voodoo practice—and he was so happy, she said, because he loved everything "mystique," a Haitian way of referring to the rituals of voodoo.

And I remember that on the inside of his chasuble, back when he was still a priest, one of his female congregants had embroidered the traditional symbols, or *veve,* of all the gods in the voodoo pantheon. So while Aristide was preaching in the nave of his church, St. Jean Bosco, at the end of the Grande Rue downtown, he was clothed symbolically in voodoo. He was preaching in the white man's church, but nearer to his heart were the spirits of Africa.

16

PLASTIC WHEELCHAIRS

Kreyol pale, kreyol komprann
Creole spoken is Creole understood

The volunteers, one from Seattle and one from Baltimore, have gone off to the street to buy hot dogs for Megan Coffee's patients.

"One day they just said, no more spaghetti," Dr. Coffee says, shrugging. I am thinking perhaps it was the mixed mayo and ketchup sauce. "They told me they were sick of it." The market women who sell snacks outside the general hospital reserve their best, warmest, freshest hot dogs for Dr. Coffee's patients and her volunteers. (Dr. Coffee herself will not eat them because, arguably, the sausages could contain meat.) Hot dog lunch starts at around four in the afternoon. Some patients are lying outside the ward in the waning sunlight, on mattresses fashioned from cardboard boxes. Megan Coffee is checking oxygen levels while her nurses hand out food, sometimes a whole hot dog and sometimes a broken half.

"I give the most emaciated patients the full ones," Lori Cabahug, a registered nurse from Baltimore, says. "And then I break off pieces for the rest." The hot dogs come in buns with ketchup, but they somehow look exotic and bumpy and delicious, as if the buns were also stuffed with bits of crispy French fries or fried plantains. The patients all seem to like this food now, just the way in days past they adored the spaghetti. Maybe it all comes down to the one question: Do you like ketchup? In any case, they receive their portions with great cheer. One woman extends the green top of a water bottle as a plate for her hot dog piece. Other patients use pieces of cardboard, or metal tops from hot food containers, whatever is flat that comes readily to hand. The nurses keep each piece of hot dog scrupulously untouched by any hand other than that of the one who'll be eating it. They themselves wear latex gloves.

After two years, Megan Coffee still isn't bored or turned off or cynical. She's still tweeting her daily observations about life and stress and disease on Twitter, @doktecoffee. She said this just the other day: "From Haiti, I have watched how some drawn to aid work in setting of stress/intensity/excitement are vulnerable to manic/psychotic episodes." But she's not. Her slouchy hat bobs away among her patients, her habitual mood buoyant, kind, tireless, chipper. I look at her as at an alien being.

She lost her favorite patient, Pierre, finally, months ago, not because of any electrical outage, not because of a storm, not because of a lack of medicine. In addition to his tuberculosis, Pierre had a heart condition, and when he would take himself off oxygen, which he would do from time to time to liberate himself from the machine, it would get worse. She put him on Viagra, which helps in these cases. But then he caught a simple diarrhea. He died on Hallowe'en.

"I happened to be with this fat family, a family that kept bothering me for food. They were always bothering me," Dr. Coffee says. She does not have the patience of a saint. An observation about fat in Haiti, however, is not what it is in New York or L.A. It's a political comment, a socioeconomic analysis, often an accusation, and sometimes (in common conversation among Haitians) a compliment. In Haiti, a fat person is someone who is displaying in his or her physical self the fact that they have so much money that they can eat more than they need to. (The country's more Europeanized upper class remains obsessed with thinness.) But "fat" is not a compliment from Megan Coffee, who works among people suffering from an often fatal inability to get enough food or to metabolize it properly—the terminally skinny. And this fat family—bothering her with their requests and demands for more food—blocked Dr. Coffee's view of Pierre and halted her on her way to him while he was dying, and dying very fast. Finally she reached him and revived him, but he was already brain-dead and couldn't be saved. "I turned my back to them to try to revive Pierre," Dr. Coffee says, "and when I turned back, he was dead, and the fat family had already taken his bed." She's aware that the story of Pierre's end is tragic, with a comic element. The comic element is humanity.

Another fat problem: "When I treat young girls, they begin to gain some weight," Dr. Coffee says. "So I fatten 'em up, and ruin their lives," because then, men start paying attention to them. "They get beautiful, and guys go after them." Sometimes they get pregnant, and that presents a whole set of medical and personal problems. Once, Dr. Coffee had to cut off the WiFi at her office abutting the ward, because all the girls were going onto her Facebook page and sending her friends explicit messages and seminude photographs of themselves. "It really came as a shock to my friends," she says, raising her eyebrows. All of Dr. Coffee's Haitian stories about cures and patients and cultures coming together have surprise endings that are the results of the unintended consequences of goodness and generosity, or just of doing business in Haiti.

Dr. Coffee is living in a group home right now, with her volunteer nurses and others. "It's a hippie scene out there," she says. She prefers living alone ("I'm not a kid anymore"), but occasionally she runs out of solo housing. Living out in the group home means she has to commute to work downtown. She takes tap-taps with her nurses, and spends about two hours in these jitneys every day—Dr. Coffee's is not the compound life. Her Creole, while still accented, is almost fluent now.

Being in a tap-tap is very like being in an open human sardine can. As many people as possible are stuffed inside to make the ride more economically profitable: like the Tokyo subway or a bus in New York at rush hour, but twice as crowded. The seats, should you get one, are not exactly cushioned. And then, of course, it's very hot in Haiti. And then, of course, the shock absorbers in tap-taps are not so good. And then, of course, the exhaust from the engine comes right back into the passenger area, making everyone slightly nauseated. Also there is your neighbor on one side who is someone whose generous lap extends pretty much onto yours, and there's her teenage daughter who's sitting on her lap, and on *your* lap, and there's an old-fashioned older man next to you on the other side trying without success not to make body contact. And then, of course, there are the animals tied to the vehicle's sides, usually goats and chickens making their way to market. Sometimes on top, there are several charcoal ladies with their giant silvery-gray bags of charcoal pushing down on the roof. And then of course, there are the little street boys who attach themselves to the grillwork at the back of the tap-tap, and who cut off what little breeze there might be if the vehicle ever moved, and who ride for free, and sometimes fall off and sometimes get run over, though the risk is lowish, since almost everywhere in the capital, traffic moves at the pace of sludge.

The truly strange thing about the tap-taps in which Megan Coffee rides is that they have as a passenger the head of the general hospital's tuberculosis ward. It is strange enough and rare to see an average Haitian in an outsider's SUV. But to see an exalted foreign personage in a tap-tap—well, it's eccentric. Dr. Coffee knows this, but she doesn't care, because from her vantage point in the tap-tap (not much of a vantage point, admittedly, since it's usually dark in there and you can't see past everybody else) she gets to witness Haitian life as it is lived by Haitians. She knows that things like this keep her real. Even if, when she's commuting by tap-tap, she spends most of her time tweeting on her iPhone.

She'll tweet anything that shows what it's like to live in Haiti now. Recently she's been tweeting about her Haitian staff mispronouncing the word "hipster" and calling certain foreign visitors "hamsters." She's been looking for funny T-shirts. They're not hard to find, and she found one: a little tent boy with a T-shirt that said "I'm more of an indoor person." She notices everything. She's part healer, part observer, part commentator, part seer. While protesters in the biggest cities in the United States

were fighting over occupying space in downtown parks for their demonstrations and tent cities, for example, Dr. Coffee was tweeting from her
tap-tap about the clearing of the earthquake camps in Port-au-Prince's
biggest (formerly) green spaces. "There are statues standing near the
National Palace that I have never seen before," she tweeted. "Founding
fathers reappearing as tents recede." Now she was passing a field where
a camp had been recently depopulated: "Pastel floor tiles cemented into
the ground, the size of a small room."

One of the vagaries of traveling by tap-tap is that your property is
not really secure, and one day Dr. Coffee's iPhone was stolen. Ripped
from her hand through the side grill of the tap-tap. Driver stops the bus,
shouting, and the thief is running, the traffic crowded, and no one is able
to catch him as he disappears into the human flow. Dr. Coffee is charac-
teristically philosophical about it. She notes how often she has traveled in
that exact tap-tap, and how everyone who travels with her on her route
knows she has an iPhone, and how the person who took the iPhone was
an outsider to that tap-tap's community. Really, she argues, the tap-tap,
with its traveling community, is *more* secure than a development organization's giant white SUV, which declares to all who see it passing by that
untold riches lie within. "The tap-tap is on time," she says. "And it's safe.
People shout but they never fight. I've never been groped. In Haiti there
is safety in crowds, that's what people don't get." What you have to do in
Haiti if you want to be successful here, Dr. Coffee says, "is look at how
Haitians survive, and then imitate them." Sometimes she has lived on less
than a dollar a day in Port-au-Prince, she says—not counting her free ac-
commodation.

Outpatients and prospective patients are sitting under a tarp in the
slapped-up, roofed-over, open-air waiting room next to Dr. Coffee's office. Things have become a little more permanent, a little more formal,
now that the TB ward is an entrenched part of the hospital. Digicel has
donated cell phones to Dr. Coffee for her outpatients, and some younger
patients and former patients are making calls on these. She pays them
to call outpatients to remind them about taking their meds and about

appointments to come in for checkups. Dr. Coffee keeps a list of her outpatients' and former patients' mobile phone numbers "even though sometimes they don't answer for months" for some reason: they moved to the countryside, their phone got stolen, the person died, or he stopped paying for minutes.

"But then suddenly, they come to life," Dr. Coffee says brightly. "Sometimes family members will tell me that one of my former patients is dead, and then that person will appear in the next couple of days, in the waiting area." One outpatient, a high-school-age student, sits in a pink dress in the waiting area. She brings her notebook in every week, so that Dr. Coffee can look at her notes to make sure she's attending classes. When the girl first came to Dr. Coffee, she was sick and illiterate. Now she's much better, and she is writing in cursive—not very fluently, but the letters are coming. (The teaching, as we can see from her notebook, is in French, which the girl doesn't speak. Another shrug from Dr. Coffee; can't fix everything.)

It's the end of another long day. Dr. Coffee has finished her evening rounds and has taken off her face mask. She's washing up. Patients fold their outdoor cardboard mats and shove them under their cots on the ward. As the sun begins to set, fluorescent lights cast a blue glow over the scene. A few strands of Christmas bulbs that were put up for the holidays inside the ward have not come down, and, looped in stray festoons from the ceiling, they add a festive glow. Lori is making some Nutella sandwiches for herself and for anyone else who is still hungry. Out in back, another nurse is trying, with limited success, to devise an ad hoc rat trap for the TB ward's storage "room" out of a surgical scrub brush and a bucket filled with bleach. The storage room is a lean-to under a tarp, and more rat-accessible than it is rat-proof.

Dr. Coffee is handing out last-minute meds, and examining a few final charts. In front of the office door, a man who does not need a wheelchair is sitting in a wheelchair, one of several similar ones that have been donated to the ward. These wheelchairs are each made from a white plastic lawn chair and what looks like a pair of bicycle wheels; the push bar in back looks as if it had come originally from a supermarket cart. In red paint, the word COFFEE has been scrawled across the backs of the chairs, and the paint has dripped down and then dried on the chairs' slats like blood, leaving the indelible impression that the chairs are ghostly and deathly and you'd be better off not stealing them.

A patient in an emerald-green dress leans against the ward's green door, gazing out at the hospital's broad alleyways. She's not waiting for anything, she tells me. In a tree in the back courtyard, a sunset frenzy of birds twitters away like mad. Even here, deep within the hospital's high walls, we can hear rush hour honking from the street outside. Behind Dr. Coffee's assistants, who are closing computers and shutting file cabinets and organizing things for tomorrow, an X-ray of someone's lungs is hanging suspended in surrounding darkness, illuminated on a viewing screen and framed by black curtains that normally close off the so-called examination room.

17
MARKET OF DREAMS

Mete zwazo nan kaj pa di li mouri ladann
If you put a bird in a cage it doesn't mean he'll die there

Notwithstanding the long view—which takes into account slavery, revolution, embargoes old and new, reparations and debt that had to be paid, foreign occupations, and a continuing local rivalry with the Dominican Republic, with which Haiti shares a border—almost all discussion of the problems encountered delivering aid to Haiti (except for discussions with Dr. Coffee and Paul Farmer and a few others) eventually conforms to traditional outsider narratives about the country. This includes discussions about aid for rescue and relief, for food distribution, emergency shelter, and ongoing health care, housing, and agricultural assistance. Here's how the narrative goes: Haitians are desperate. We come down to help. They are nice people, maybe, but they're disorganized, uneducated, untrained, corrupt. We give; they steal. We are upright; they lie to us. Despite all our best intentions for them, our work here is thwarted and eventually ineffective. It's sad, but there's something wrong with them. Unless we work completely outside the bounds of Haitian culture, and the country's government and economy, we get nothing accomplished. There concludes the narrative: QED. The narrative is told with different subtle emphases, but all sorts of development people hew to it, from the most liberal to the most conservative.

When I hear this narrative, I think back to the time I met with an Asian ambassador to Liberia in his breezy Monrovia office. He was expounding on the collapse of a bridge during the rainy season in the countryside not too far from the capital. The bridge had been down for months; villagers could not get their produce to market—fruit and vegetables were rotting; a famine was expected in the area. The villagers were waiting for the foreign organization that had originally built the bridge to come back and put it up again.

"In my country," the ambassador said as a Liberian servant poured tea for him and his guests (all present, including the ambassador and the Liberian servant, spoke English), "we would not be waiting for anyone. Our villagers would get out there with mud and bamboo and homemade bricks and thatch, and slap that bridge right up again. In two days, maybe a week: done. But here . . ." The ambassador's talk was laced with a light, reflexive racism toward the Liberians, whom he repeatedly called "these people."

But his point was not entirely ill taken, and—if you removed from it his underlying racism—it wasn't about race. It was, as it always is in Haiti, too, if you deconstruct properly, about history. Liberia itself, for one thing: an outpost established for shunted-off American slaves, who then became its elite. And then, that little Liberian village. Trained for so many years to expect help from the outside, the villagers had become reliant on it, used to it, dependent—in the favorite word of development people—and they no longer trusted to their own devices or capacity or felt that fixing the bridge would be a wise expense of limited resources, since the outsiders who built it were sure to return to fix their handiwork one day. The Liberian village had grown accustomed to the kind of outsider work and "development" that imposes itself on the locals, the kind of work that will almost invariably end up being more of an overlay or an object in itself than a real development success, since real development consists strictly in training and enabling the local population to control, direct, and participate themselves in projects that they decide they need to get done.

I dislike having to say that about *real* development, because what you've just read is such a ritual statement from development pundits. In the past twenty years, it's become a commonplace, even a cliché. Nonetheless, local control of projects remains a rarity, because of the difficulty—in fact, the impossibility—of sustaining the artificial narrative, the *fiction,* of self-empowerment and local control when the money, the technical knowledge, the specialized personnel and matériel, and the development experience itself are really all coming from the outside. But it's still true that self-started projects work best for communities, and are the most enduring. Unfortunately, often even the gesture toward local participation and control is nowhere to be found in top-down foreign aid and reconstruction projects: the homegrown element is obviously missing. Also note: in Liberia, the outsider-built bridge had collapsed. So much for foreign know-how.

As in that Liberian village, outsiders have tried for decades in Haiti to fix and meddle with and run the show, with, on the whole, quite poor long-term results, both because Haitians often don't have the minimal training and life experience to keep projects going, and because the outsiders have no understanding of Haitian culture. It's like the pigs in the camp children's drawings: *Tou sa ou we, se pa sa.* Nothing you see is what it seems to be.

The most visible outsider project in Haiti since the 2010 earthquake is the renovated and meticulously reconstructed Iron Market, a flowery nineteenth-century confection that was the heart of Port-au-Prince's downtown commercial center, and that was all but destroyed by the quake and a fire during the following week. The Iron Market restoration was funded by Denis O'Brien, the Irish entrepreneur who owns Digicel, Haiti's largest mobile telephone company. Rebuilding the market appealed to O'Brien not only because the market has always been a symbol of Haitian commerce, of which he feels himself to be, and of which he is, an important part, but also because the market's original color happens to have been virtually the same bright red as all things Digicel, from the company's logo to its offices to its signs and market-stall umbrellas.

Port-au-Prince's original market, designed by a Frenchman and constructed with fine French materials, was built at the end of the nine-teenth century—in France. Even better, given its status today as a symbol of Haiti, it was originally intended to fulfill a requisition from Egypt for a new railroad station in Cairo, but the plan somehow fell through, and Haiti's then president, Florvil Hyppolite, stepped in and bought it, no doubt at a bargain-basement price.

Haiti is a country rife with historical irony. The market's twin red gingerbread towers, supposedly symbols of Haitian commerce, were them-selves an example of foreign intermingling and even domination in Haitian affairs, rising above downtown's port and banks and stores and outdoor markets with the typical insouciant whimsy of French colonial architecture. Now they were being rebuilt—again, as a symbol of Haitian commerce—by an Irish entrepreneur whose multinational company was dominating the Haitian mobile-telephone market. The only thing about the new Iron Market that was identifiably Haitian was its absolute secondhandedness, like so much in Haiti, from the subsidized U.S. rice that's sold in markets here to the cheap secondhand clothing—called *pepe* or, less commonly, *kennedy,* after the administration during which shipments from the United States began—that is sold for pennies in the open-air coastal-road market.

Soon after its reopening, there was discontent at the Iron Market. Vendors rioted from time to time. There was intermittent gunfire, in spite or because of the new security there. Vendors inside the market's walls were disconsolate. Buyers were few and far between, they said. There was not enough access for consumers, and the only successful stalls were those that were the closest to Grande Rue, the main downtown boulevard that runs past the Iron Market (its full, formal name is Boule-vard Jean-Jacques Dessalines). The vendors who used to have their stalls right up against the exterior wall of the market on Grande Rue had been shooed away, banished by the foreigners running the place, but those stalls, too, had brought foot traffic into the market in the old days.

Now many former customers were choosing to purchase their goods in the vast outdoor market that sprawls through the streets and alleys around the Iron Market and that did a brisk, anthill-like business even in the days not long after the earthquake. This outdoor market is a ceaseless, eternal maelstrom of microcapitalism, with its rickety wooden stalls and mounds of teeny toothpastes and wire-tied mini-bags of Fab detergent. Its drawers are full of Krazy Glue; its walls pinned with school notebooks and old issues of *Paris Match* and other stationery, all for sale. Heads of lilliputian garlic sit on the ground on old remnants of burlap in pixie piles, next to skinny stands of spaghetti in plastic wrap. Nearby, a generous market woman is piling lacy bras from Indonesia and Vietnam one on top of the other in pink, blue, and beige towers—next door, a pen dealer. Farther down the alley, another voluminous example of womanhood is selling clusters of huge white cabbages from the Dominican Republic, laid out on a floral piece of plastic cloth from China. At de facto corners here and there, *fritay* ladies and their daughters are selling various bits of fried food to hungry shoppers.

Down one path are giant, shining aluminum pots and colorful plastic colanders; down another, stacks of sandals and used radios and old tires. There are fans, fans, and more fans, and over nearer the main road, flats of frozen chicken defrosting *au soleil* in the ninety-degree heat. Another section of the open-air market is filled with ribbons and rubber bands, with lace and furbelows, barrettes, hair ties, and plastic mirrors, and another segment, directly opposite the Iron Market entrance, is overflowing with vendors hawking shoelaces and knockoff Nikes . . . this market just keeps going, keeps extending, keeps filling up, responding to humanity's every need—through fires, floods, hurricanes, strikes, coups d'état, food riots, earthquakes, and whatever else man and nature can throw at it. It's hard to compete with. It's a giant outdoor mall, complete with an ad hoc food court.

Another important reason for the drop-off in sales inside the new Iron Market, one vendor said, was that for the first year, there was no meat market there. The extensive meat market had been a long-standing specialty of the big red building in the old days, but the newly reestablished market initially did not have that draw. Formerly, in order to get to the meats at the back of the market, you had to walk through the rest of the vendors' stalls, presumably buying the nonmeat items on your grocery list and other odds and ends as you came in or left.

With all the force of a Proustian sense-memory (if less *délicat*), I recalled the terrible stench of the old indoor meat market, the loud incessant buzzing of the flies that gathered by the thousands above the carcasses, the animal blood dripping onto the floor—the puddles that one had to walk over or through—the large, blunt machetes used for butchering and cutting, and the total lack of refrigeration. I can still remember what the blood looked like as it pooled and dripped on gray-brown cement, the wetness, the seeping, the absolute darkness of below.

That nineteenth-century-style meat market, like a market in Dickens's Tom-all-Alone's slum in London, was not what the new directors of the new market had in mind. They were thinking more along the lines of the bright, air-conditioned warehouses of Panama's free-trade Zona Libre. At the new market there were amazing, astonishing things like working ceiling fans and giant garbage bins, some of these reserved for recycling, an almost unheard-of activity in Haiti. There was a cleanup crew every evening that was responsible for the whole market—in the past whatever cleaning up there was, was done on a stall-by-stall basis.

An endearing European concern with proper health standards was the reason the refurbished market did not immediately allow the sale of meat. Meats, sold Haitian style, amid flies and without refrigeration, did not live up to the European specifications that O'Brien and his chief executive officer at Digicel, Maarten Boute (whose brother ran the new market), were trying to achieve—laudable standards, correct standards. Once refrigeration was in place, Maarten Boute assured me, the market would sell meats.

That was what Boute said, and eventually, meat did come to the market, along with big refrigerators provided by Digicel. But the damage to the market's reputation among consumers had been done, and business was still slow; there were fewer meat vendors in the new market, all of them up against the back wall where they could plug in their freezers. During my visits, sales were slow, and the vendors told me this was generally the case. It was complicated: they had new competitors, both in the big supermarkets that serve an ever-widening consumer base and in the peripatetic frozen-meat sellers, fairly new to the scene, who wander the streets now with coolers on their heads filled with chicken breasts on the way from frozen to thawed.

Maarten Boute is a Belgian businessman; in addition to being the CEO of Digicel in Haiti, he was also the new Iron Market project's director for the company. "Belgian businessman" describes Boute about as precisely as "former Arkansas governor" describes Bill Clinton. Boute is as slender a person as Mick Jagger, and the resemblance doesn't stop there. He has a satanic cragginess uncanny in a man of his years (he's thirty-eight), a beak of a nose, and green-blue bird's eyes that peer out at you with uncommon intelligence and judgment. He's thinner than a stick and wears business suits one might associate with a natty British dresser of the 1960s, a King's Road ethos, but tasteful and possibly expensive. He wears idiosyncratic cuff links that are made out of American dimes. His hair is slicked back in a Romantic wave, as if he were Byron facing the khamsin over Patraikos Bay. He had Sean Penn's hair in Haiti even before Sean Penn.

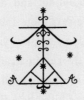

18

THE VALUE OF TALK

Kreyon bon dye pa gen gòm
God's pencil has no eraser

When I first ran into Maarten Boute, he'd broken his foot and was walking with a crutch, thus completing his props, as if directed by Tim Burton. But Boute was not an unexpected or even a singular figure in Port-au-Prince, which, as I've said, has gathered to its bosom a fair share of the world's traveling eccentrics over the centuries—and I'm not even including the kindly or in-need-of-rehab movie stars and singers who have flocked to do their bit here since the earthquake.

Boute's father trained dental health workers in Kenya, which is where Boute lived from the time he was ten to the time he was seventeen. He studied boat building, and has always wanted to move back to Mombasa and run a surf shop. Instead, for a while he worked near Lyon, in France, making fiberglass yachts. Got sick of that and went back to Belgium and worked in a call center for a company that was purchased by Orange, the French cell phone company, where he rose in the ranks until he was hired by a Russian billionaire to launch five mobile phone operations in Poland, Italy, Taiwan, Oman, and Belgium. This is all true, or at least it's the story Maarten Boute tells about himself. One almost wonders: Is Boute some kind of a spy? He certainly has the profile.

"We had all the stuff you'd expect," he says of his Russian adventure. "It was silly, exaggerated. Bling, big bowls of caviar, the best vodka, boys, girls, anything, St. Tropez, et cetera. I got sick of it."

Then he met Denis O'Brien.

O'Brien developed the Iron Market project with private, philanthropic money. It has cost him twelve million dollars so far. Haiti has been a very good business for O'Brien—he started in 2005 there with about 400,000 cellular phone customers and now has about 2.6 million, and has had a year-by-year revenue growth in Haiti of 39 percent, according to the company. Though O'Brien was personally funding the Iron Market project with private monies, Digicel was running the place in a public-private partnership that, at least for the first year, entirely excluded the government of Haiti. Instead, the "local collaboration" piece of the development project was with the municipality of Port-au-Prince, a collaboration that is supposed to continue for fifty years—a rare commitment in Haiti, both by an outside company and by a Haitian public entity. Digicel is also subsidizing the market's management at a per-year cost of about $480,000, along with a hoped-for $60,000 from vendor fees. The company says it intends to increase those fees gradually, as well as to obtain Haitian government funding (with an administration O'Brien can work with, like Martelly's), so that over the next five years O'Brien will be able to phase out his subsidy.

O'Brien is a brawny figure with the usual international man of finance's self-assurance and air of absolute command. Everyone I've spoken to at Digicel with his permission speaks with reverence of him, but everyone else talks about the usual things: his temper, his intense desire for control, the total dysfunctional management inside the company. Yet Digicel seems to work. Cell phones and Haitians mesh so fully that it's as if the cell phone had been invented for Haiti.

In Port-au-Prince there's always been a phenomenon called *teledjòl*, which means telemouth, or teletalk, and, more completely translated, means changeable gossip relayed by mouth. Rumors used to fly incredibly fast through the capital via this handy method. (Where people live so close to one another, *teledjòl* is very effective, although, as in the antique camp-circle game of Telephone, the story changes with each teller. Still, one found that the result often approximated truth pretty closely.) With the cell phone, *teledjòl* speeded up its movement into the outsider community and to Haitians living abroad. People adopted the technology in Port-au-Prince and then in the provinces as if the phones were biological extensions of the human hand and mouth; for many, it was the first experience of having easy access to a phone.

Landlines never worked well in Haiti. Access to landlines was run by Teleco, a government entity, and in order to get a line there were many officials who had to be remunerated, and amply. Even before that, you had to know someone inside Teleco to begin the long, corrupt process. The installation of a landline also required the kind of organized municipal and national infrastructure that has not often been a priority of Haitian governments. To get a landline in your house, if it hadn't been inherited from the previous homeowner, was the work of a lifetime. One head of Teleco described his own mother's circuitous journey through the wilds of the phone company, in search of a landline. He himself had worked at Teleco for decades, toiling and conniving as he made his way up the Escher-like ladder of power there.

"But it was only when I became director," he is reported to have said, not really joking, "that my mother finally got her landline."

Within a year of the mobile phone's arrival in Haiti, it was a rare Haitian you met who didn't have a cell phone or access to one; the devices were so obviously useful. The landline, as it is becoming elsewhere, was already a thing of the past in Haiti. With the arrival of cellular technology, the landline in one swoop lost its status as an aspirational device of the future and flew right into the bin of the nationally obsolete.

In April 2010, under Préval's presidency, Teleco was folded into public-private partnership with Viettel, the Vietnamese military dictatorship's telecommunications company that runs a monopoly business in Vietnam. This deal disgusted Digicel and Voilà, at the time Digicel's closest competitor in Haiti, since both wanted the contract. Viettel is to make a $99-million investment in the Haitian partnership, which has been described as the largest foreign direct investment in Haiti since the earthquake.

Maarten Boute—and, one assumes, by extension, O'Brien—was extremely irritated at President Préval and the Haitian government for choosing Viettel over Digicel as a Teleco partner; in the bargain, Viettel is to gain access to Internet bandwidth that could make it a formidable competitor for Digicel in Haiti. "We like competition," Boute says. "But it should be fair." Obviously the Préval government did not feel comfortable giving Digicel the kind of control over telecommunications that this contract would have assured it. From Préval's point of view, Digicel was already operating too broadly and with too free a hand in Haiti. In power, Préval's warm spot for leftist regimes didn't sit well with serious capitalists like O'Brien.

Boute knows that Digicel was looked upon with some mistrust by the Haitian government. "We are trying to lower our profile," he says. "The message is, we are not trying to replace the government. We're trying to help them." Apparently, Préval was not getting the message Boute was sending. Viettel now controls 60 percent of the new Teleco, the government the other 40 percent. To remain competitive, Digicel ended up buying Voilà.

Included in the Viettel contract for Haitian telecommunications is the construction of a fiber-optic international submarine cable. Word of this has come to the attention of the Haitian street, causing much confusion. Any new thing—big or little—can set off a trip wire into the politics and psychology of the slave revolt, and remind outsiders that they're dealing not just with a developing-world population coming into the twenty-first century, but also with the descendants of revolutionary slaves of the 1700s. The earthquake and the subsequent influx of thousands of foreigners into

Haiti have exacerbated Haitians' historic wariness about the outside world, and left them feeling even more than normally vulnerable to incursions. There are those, including some Europeans who have worked in Haiti for decades, who seriously believe that the earthquake itself—the actual seismic dislocation—was planned and executed by the United States.

The morning the cable deal was announced, several people described the fiber-optic cable to me as a tunnel that could secretly bring occupation troops into Haiti. *Istwa tònel,* they were calling it. The tunnel story. They wanted to know all about it. I explained that it would be hard to get a tank through a cable that's only, at its widest, about 2.7 inches across, according to the Googling I did on this over my Digicel-provided access. My interlocutors just raised their eyebrows skeptically, meaning that I, too, was probably a part of this conspiracy, or was a fool. A 2.7-inch cable, you could see them thinking . . .

This fear scenario—that foreign intervention will come from the sea—is a leftover from the days of Christophe's Citadelle. A defensive island mentality remains a defensive island mentality, and so much control has in fact been imposed on Haiti from *lòt bò dlo,* with and without actual power interventions. In the end, today's rumor-mongers will be proven correct about the Viettel fiber-optic cable, because the cable cannot help but reinforce another kind of foreign intervention in Haiti, another kind of occupation: informational, technological, cultural, economic, political.

Routes for foreign intervention into the heart of Haiti are plentiful. Two years after the earthquake, news started to appear about the discovery of gold in rural Haiti. A dispatch from the Associated Press mentioned that some fifteen days after the earthquake, "a Canadian [gold] exploration firm acquired all of the shares of the only Haitian firm holding full permits for a promising chunk of land in the northeast" of the country. Which is to say, the extractors were ready for this moment. Silver and copper are also thought to lie in plentiful millions of ounces below Haiti's fields, hills, and mountains.

I began to understand why so many people thought that the earthquake was intentional. Although there have been persistent rumors of
enormous lodes of gold under Haitian soil, and mining companies have
always kept a watchful eye on them, it was the quake that gave prospective explorers and investors a sudden, strong reason to speed their quest
for precious metals and minerals there. Apparently, every miner loves a
region assumed to possess mineral wealth that is also subject to violent
geological shifts. The seismic activity generates cracks in the earth that
form more accessible veins through which the volcanic turbulence of
lower strata may thrust out copper, silver, and gold.

No Haitian will be surprised to hear there's gold under the ground
here. Columbus knew it back when he made his first landfall in the
Americas along Haiti's northern coast. When he returned on his second
American voyage, he started up a new settlement whose administrators
enslaved large numbers of indigenous people and put them to work
extracting gold. From a "pre-contact" population that some estimate as
almost a million, the Taino or Arawak peoples were already reduced in
1514 to about 32,000, and their decline continued precipitously. A Yale
University project on genocide asserts that whose who died were killed
by "enslavement, massacre, or disease." When the Spaniards learned of
what they imagined to be far more lucrative gold deposits in Mexico, as
well as the treasures of a well-entrenched civilization, they moved on.

But gold still has a seductive allure, especially now that an ounce of
the stuff is valued at about $1,700 on international markets and has been
at or just below that level for more than a year. Speaking about Haiti's
gold not long after the earthquake, Dieuseul Anglade, a geologist and
the then-director of Haiti's bureau of mines, was widely quoted as having said that "if the mining companies are honest and if Haiti has a good
government, then here is a way for this country to move forward." When
I saw this comment, I had to laugh. Anglade seemed to me to be making
a point. Two points, really: (1) Haiti has never had a good government,
and (2) It's very hard, if not impossible, to come up with a gold mining
company that has ever experienced even a short bout of honesty.

Anglade, who was in charge of mining for Haiti's government for most of the past two decades under rapidly shifting leadership, consistently refused to sign a waiver to Haiti's current mining laws in order to permit mining to go forward in the country, and thus placed himself as a stumbling block to the mining companies that wanted to come in after the earthquake. Once a post-earthquake government came into office in Haiti, the new prime minister swiftly replaced the problematic Anglade, and told the Haitian legislature that "our subsoil is rich in minerals. Now is the time to dig them up."

One minerals exploration official called Haiti "the sleeping giant of the Caribbean." When I heard that, I remembered that at the height of the sugar-plantation slave economy, Haiti was known as "the Pearl of the Antilles." It's disturbing to think of the extraction process going forward in a place where so little attention is paid to public safety, the environment, and proper taxation. In fact, if Haiti indulges in its usual business practices when dealing with the gold companies, the only real tax on the extractors will be bribes and gifts to Haitian businessmen, landholders, and politicians. Meanwhile, Haitian peasants will be moved off their fields and exploited as cheap labor for the mining companies. Rivers and ecosystems, fragile already in the environmentally pressured country, will be poisoned or at least grossly damaged. Mining is like that.

For example, the company that is to begin mining for gold in Haiti within the next five years, should all go according to plan, is Newmont Mining, one of the world's two largest gold mining companies. Newmont makes many claims on its website about its commitment to environmentally and socially responsible mining. But as recently as July 2012, five Peruvian villagers were shot and killed during local protests over Newmont's relentless mining expansion in Cajamarca. One activist was assassinated. The Peruvian government declared a state of emergency in the area. Another activist was arrested and beaten.

Gold mining uses both cyanide and mercury in its extraction process. In Peru, Newmont has been accused of poisoning the land and waters with those substances at Yanacocha, the world's second-largest open-pit mine, which looks like the target of a repeated meteoric bombardment—a series of enormous terraced scars in the earth connected to each other over long distances by trucking trails, the craters studded with verdigris-colored pools. In 2000, the Peruvian government estimated that about 900 people in the area around Yanacocha were suffering from mercury poisoning. Newmont is also, as are all gold mining enterprises, expansionist, and Yanacocha has been creeping out from its central base in Peru in wider and wider circles. As Yanacocha nears the end of its productivity, Newmont is exploring another site for a large mine only fifteen miles away.

In Ghana, the company's record is no better. At the Ahafo mine, 5,000 families were resettled to make way for the mine, more than 9,000 farmers lost their fields, and some 3,000 hectares were taken over, with government permission but little or no discussion with villagers. The Subri River, from which a dozen or so villages used to get their water, was dammed for the mine, which is often the case in gold mining.

Now, Ghanaian villagers who used to till their small plots near the Subri must get their drinking water from company-provided tanks, to which they have to trek, and which are not always adequate. Also the drinking water from the tanks cannot be wasted to irrigate fields. In many cases, villagers who remain in the neighborhood of the mine and who previously lived off small farms have had to switch from cultivation to charcoal production in order to survive. Charcoal production involves cutting down trees in the nearby forests, which leads to deforestation (this has been true in Haiti for years, as options for survival in the countryside grow slimmer and the cash economy expands).

Pushing hard for Newmont's goals in Haiti is Ronald Baudin, Haiti's former finance minister and now (surprise) a Newmont consultant. The Haitian Bureau of Mines is to oversee all extraction, but how good a job can they do, even if they are energetic and of good will? As of late 2012, only five of the bureau's seventeen vehicles were in working order, according to various news reports. Only about 25 percent of its employees had college degrees, and most of the rest were support staff, which is to say, drivers, mechanics, secretaries, receptionists . . . The bureau works on an annual budget of around one million dollars. With possibly hundreds of millions of ounces of gold below its surface, at current market rates, Haiti stands to provide Newmont and its partners with about $20 billion. This is not to mention copper and silver deposits.

Since the earthquake, hundreds of square miles of Haitian lands have been scooped up and licensed to North American firms and their partners. Of these, Newmont is the largest and controls the most land. The square mileage in Haiti now open to exploitation by outside mineral and metal explorers and extractors is the equivalent of about 15 percent of the country's total land mass. Right now, in prospective mining areas, Haitian villagers and their children are panning for gold and digging dangerous "artisanal" mine shafts and tunnels with shovels and bare hands in the lands where they used to cultivate their small fields. On a regular basis, men in four-wheel-drive SUVs from Port-au-Prince or from the Dominican Republic come through to buy the villagers' gold at far below market prices. So far, there has been no sign of government oversight. And in some places, drilling has already begun. Natural resources have never proven healthy for countries that don't have the ability to extract them themselves—and so once again, as in its plantation era, Haiti may find itself caught up in a new kind of global net of exploitation and destruction.

It often seems as if Haiti is the perfect example of what would happen if Ronald Reagan's dream of a privatized state should become a reality. One day, years ago, when I was walking around downtown Port-au-Prince, I realized that I was living in Reagan's fantasy world. So this is what he wants, I thought. As I walked through the streets of the Belair neighborhood, I saw private schools, private water trucks, stolen and microprivatized electricity, private sanitation (the *bayakou*) when there was any. The private sector, such as it was, had taken its place in the state vacuum long before Aristide, in negotiations to get Clinton's backing for his return from exile in 1994, agreed to further privatization of Haiti's few state-run entities.

In the field of education, Haitian schools are privately run by various small nobodies and missionary groups that open their own schools, where nothing is taught—and that nothing, by rote memorization. There is no educational standardization. When I looked over Black Rouge's cousin's electromagnetism notes, they looked like notes taken in a French classroom in an era predating Madame Curie, and yet he was banking his slender hopes for the future on his electromagnetism degree. And he is a very smart and articulate person.

In the field of sanitation, garbage pickup is state run, and therefore picks up very little. The Public Works ministry has apparently discovered no useful business model for trash pickup. If they cannot figure out where in the trash cycle they can suck out some worthwhile graft, the job doesn't get done.

One sanitation project, a joint venture among Brazil, India, and South Africa, did set up a schedule of pickup and recycling for one of the capital's neighborhoods before the earthquake. It worked for the year it was funded, and then the earthquake came. Everywhere else in Port-au-Prince, huge piles of garbage collect at traditional corners familiar to my pigs, seeping away slowly when the rains come, but constantly replenished.

Water delivery is privatized, largely, so water is delivered in trucks to the slums, or purchased in supermarkets by the wealthy. It is exorbitantly expensive. The water you buy from the trucks is not trustworthy, either—as a friend of mine asked as we passed a Cristal O truck, with its long metal container for water, "How in Haiti is someone going to clean the inside of that truck?" In town, drinking water is now sold in small, gulp-size bags that are tossed down onto the curbs and streets after the water has been drunk, and never properly disposed of, much less recycled. Probably the little empty bags are swept into the sea and carried by currents into the Gulf of Mexico on the Caribbean garbage tide. In the countryside, either you are lucky enough to live near a water pump put in by an aid organization—if it's still in working condition—or you must walk miles to a river or well, as if you lived in the Central African Republic, and not a country two feet from Miami. At the river or the well, the water you collect may be cholera-tainted.

Electricity is government run, so there is very little (it, too, demands infrastructure). Haitian students gather under streetlights to do their homework. Many do night work by the light of kerosene lanterns or candles. People who want more consistent power pay for it privately, in the form of diesel, batteries, and generators. Much of the electricity of Port-au-Prince is carried to houses on wiring that is siphoned off from the government stanchions by *quartier* entrepreneurs who charge for the service. And that's Port-au-Prince. The rest of the country staggers along with almost no power.

Health care is also almost entirely privatized, so there is very little health care available in Port-au-Prince, and what is good is very expensive—mostly for the rich. Since the earthquake, some of the best-known of those expensive private Haitian hospitals, which also used to do pro bono procedures for the poor and had some of the only really up-to-date equipment in the country, have gone bankrupt. They were put out of business by the free and highly competent outsider care that suddenly became available in the disaster's wake, and stole away the private hospitals' and practices' consumers. Now those foreigner doctors and health care professionals have also left. In the countryside health care almost doesn't exist, except for what's provided—without regulation—by traditional practitioners, outsider missionaries, and a sporadic hodge-podge of international medical organizations.

One reason so much mental energy is spent on eighteenth-century concerns in Haiti is that the country is still very old-fashioned; in some parts of Haiti, farmers don't even use plows, only hoes, rakes, and shovels. In many parts of the country, herbs and traditional practice are the only medicine. But in the matter of the cell phone, those very same farmers and traditional practitioners moved into the twenty-first century immediately, without skipping a beat.

O'Brien feels he understands Haiti well, and that understanding is reflected in Digicel's corporate behavior in the country. (However, he did not understand Haiti, Préval, and Haitian intransigence well enough to get the Teleco contract.) O'Brien himself comes from Ireland, another island, formerly destitute and often corrupt and violent. As he charms and twinkles and wields language most effectively, you sense his tough-guy mentality beneath the sunny exterior—that brisk, no-nonsense attitude that comes from protecting your interests at every moment, and also from wielding power and knowing that others will do your bidding. The person most charmed and delighted by O'Brien's knifelike perceptions and intelligent banter is himself.

When he tells his friends about his continuing belief in Haiti, O'Brien says, "They think I'm fucking crazy. They say, 'Are you out of your brick?' But I have more hope for Haiti than I do for many of the other countries I invest in." Digicel has branches in more than thirty countries, many of them in the Caribbean and most of them easily classified as developing. "This place," O'Brien says of Haiti, "could be fixed in five years. I tell my friends, who think I'm crazy, to invest in Haiti themselves.

"What I've found is that outrage doesn't work here," he says about the ongoing situation after the earthquake. "If I was in charge, I could fix things. But there is no leadership. The old Haitian leadership came out of the army, but unfortunately, the army was disbanded." O'Brien is referring to what some believe was Aristide's greatest achievement, his getting rid of the overweening Haitian Armed Forces in 1995.

O'Brien winces when he talks about the inefficiencies of doing business in Haiti, and especially about the presence of the post-earthquake aid organizations. "They may all be well-intentioned, and some are doing fantastic work," he says, "but it's frustrating to watch; they can't all chase after the same client base. They should divide up the country and say we're going to get organized, instead of all these four-by-fours burning diesel all over the place. These people all living here in Port-au-Prince have inflated prices for housing and for cars. It's ridiculous. They don't have a system."

O'Brien has a highly inflected understanding of Haiti; he's no bullshitter who powers in and stomps through things, even if his personality and management style tend to sweep all obstacles out of the way. He's an organized thinker and highly observant, which is one of the reasons for his success in a place where few companies can say they've made millions. Digicel is the very peak of foreign capital investment in Haiti. You could argue that it's one of the werewolves, since the company makes a huge profit here where everyone is starving—but that's not the definition of a werewolf. Werewolves suck the lifeblood. They live off victimization.

Digicel doesn't. Like any employer in Haiti, it provides jobs for Haitians. As much could be said of any brassiere or baseball manufacturer that has operated on the island and exploited the inhumanely low Haitian minimum wage and the terrible desperation of the population. What's different about Digicel is that while exploiting low wages and the intense Haitian work ethic, it's making its money providing a service to Haitians inside the country that those Haitians want and need. Because of Digicel's innovations, Haitians can now buy micro-minutes that are sent digitally to their phone numbers; Haitian farmers can communicate with truckers and arrange pickups and deliveries (and, as a result, produce doesn't sit around rotting because it can't get to market); Haitians can communicate with relatives on the outside. Villagers can alert health care workers when they need emergency services. Soon Haitians will be able to do telebanking and telefinancing with Digicel's TchoTcho Mobile, which could change the whole fabric of the Haitian economy. (Digicel also runs similar mobile banking systems in its Fijian and Tongan markets.) Digicel innovates month by month depending on what its people perceive to be needed in the Haitian street, as does Voilà, which morphed out of Teleco and used to be owned by Trilogy International, based in Washington State, before Digicel bought it.

Digicel's "modus operandi is root and branch," O'Brien says. What he means by this is that he organizes his company vertically, so that there is the base in Port-au-Prince and then an outlying presence in the provinces. Wherever I've gone in Haiti, the one thing I can be sure to see along the road, aside from lottery-based "banks" like Solution Borlette, and tiny shack stores and microscopic produce stalls, is one quite decent-looking bright red Digicel office. Aside from the Haitian government, Digicel is Haiti's largest employer. Where Voilà is a company that incorporated existing Haitian communications networks, O'Brien came in as an exclusively foreign investor. In part this explains his somewhat cavalier and dismissive attitudes. (Although often foreign businessmen are much more respectful of Haitians and Haitian custom than are Haitian entrepreneurs.)

O'Brien could not bear to work with the Préval government. When he opened the new Iron Market, his people specifically did not invite the president of Haiti to the tape-cutting ceremony. Privately, the officers of Digicel spoke of President Préval in the most disparaging of terms.

"My other motto here," O'Brien says, "is 'Fuck the Government.' I don't have time to spend hours outside a minister's office to get permission to rebuild the market. I'm going to get things done here."

He is quick to add that he is "sensitive to the idea of Haitian sovereignty," a very delicate and nuanced way of describing his approach. He can't really bring himself to do all the diplomatic pirouetting that it would take to bring the Haitian government into the operation; for him, it's not worth the trouble and time and financial oversight, though the Haitian government could learn a lot from O'Brien's direct methods and trim efficiencies.

The two cellular telephone companies have been Haiti's biggest corporate taxpayers in recent years ("and we actually *pay* our taxes," says one Digicel employee, although a high government official told me that Digicel had to be coerced into paying all that it owed). Both phone companies support charitable projects. After the earthquake, Digicel's charitable foundation committed to building fifty schools, and they are doing it; the company backs a major Caribbean soccer competition; it gives parties and sponsors awards for local entrepreneurship, and provides grants for various projects, including the relocation of earthquake refugees from Sean Penn's camp. Penn and O'Brien adore each other, not surprisingly; Bill Clinton is another member of this informal club, a mutual admiration society, white kings of Haiti, all. Boute is a junior member. Paul Farmer is the society's professor emeritus, its éminence grise, who usually keeps himself off at a respectable remove in the countryside.

One very noticeable sign of the importance of cellular communications in Haiti came during the earthquake. Digicel's tower was toppled during the shaking, but Voilà remained in service. This meant that if you were a Voilà user, you could make calls from where you were stuck under the rubble, or tweet or text your location. Many such messages saved lives in the hours and days right after the quake. Digicel users, on the other hand, could not communicate until Digicel got its tower back up and working, which it did with admirable speed. Still, this meant that it was only after a crucial lapse of time that Digicel tweets and texts started coming from the rubble, causing a wild new optimism among relatives and friends. Unfortunately, by then, many of the people who had sent the messages were dead.

Digicel's new Iron Market was an outsider's dream, an Irishman's dream. It was a beautiful, near-perfect re-creation of another outsider's dream— a French engineer's dream—for a different colonial country, a Haitian market created from French materials for an Egyptian railroad station. But the Haitian vendors inside the dream market were waiting—like the Liberian villagers described by the ambassador. They were doing business inside the dream architecture of the colonizer, and thus they were made to live by his rules. Can one fault O'Brien's rules? Cleanliness, sanitation, security: order. It's hard to take issue with these. One wants those standards for Haiti, naturally. But still, it would be better if somehow such standards could include Haitian cultural habits and behaviors.

I don't know how this would be done, but an organic clutter and a degree of darkness and close human intimacy would be part of it. I do remember the old Iron Market. And I have an outsider's sentiment for it: it was dark, overstuffed, so hot. Insects competed with humans in it for population stats, and the insects won, as they always do. Whole families ran the stalls; children and babies were present. There was gossip among the stalls, and in certain areas of the market, vendors all came from the same village outside of town; their grandmothers had been friends and had sold at these same stalls. The sound of human voices was gigantic and overwhelming, like the noise before a show in a theater, ramped up by decibels. The stalls all ran together in a continuous overflow of buying and selling; now each stall is discrete and marked by a short wall on either side—the Haitian feeling of community property or village sharing that was present in the old days is gone.

Back then, in the half of the market where paintings and crafts were sold, Haitians who were self-styled guides followed their white men or women (or visiting diaspora Haitians) through the tumult, fending off other Haitians who might try to steal their white men away, using harsh elbows, even blows, and a stream of angry Creole invective. As a visitor, you would find yourself at the center of what felt like a moving hive, hot and human. You'd be under the control of others, without recourse— and above your head, hanging there suspended, would be the fantasies of hundreds of Haitian artists: paintings of huge, fat yellow gourds and melons, and crowds at peasant markets, jaguars sitting looking out from Haitian jungles, kitchen still lifes with weird root vegetables and salt-fish looking sorrowful, and French coffeepots steaming, and also pristine churches and parishioners flocking to their doors, and urban landscapes arching and extending right up over the sea into cerulean skies, and also peasants carrying bananas, and peasants bending over bags of charcoal, and provincial families throwing parties, and also Santa Claus—a great fat traditional one, although black—in the middle of a Haitian village filled with tiny villagers. This whole crowd of mythic figures and beasts, made of paint and canvas and somehow affixed and glowing in the dark, still, sullen air above us, looked down from frames on the human tumult flowing below. The vendors and their shills in the crowd were hoping that the visitors would buy. Really, in this crowd, the visitor had little choice: you bought. When—if—you ever emerged from this hell still breathing and with a newly unframed canvas rolled under your arm, you were grateful for air, light, oxygen. It sounds awful, but it was exhilarating. It was something to experience and survive.

Today, there are few white men and women who come to buy their souvenirs at the Iron Market, not because there are fewer white men and women in Haiti today—oh, far from it—but because the white men and women stay on UN logbase or at the headquarters of whatever organization they work for, living the compound life and buying trinkets for their families from the clever Haitians who have set up stands against walls nearby. Because of strict orders about where they can and cannot go—there is a changing map of red zones—even the less fearful outsiders are likely to cave in to efficiency, and buy their stuff nearby.

Dr. Coffee can buy near the hospital, for example. Up in Pétionville, where many aid groups are based, people can buy at the central square that is ringed with canvases. At UN logbase, you can buy outside on the street facing the entry, or inside, at the logbase's very own Haitian crafts market. Who needs the arts-and-crafts half of the new Iron Market? The arts section is barely filled. The artwork is mass-produced, in "schools" around town (paintings of the presidential palace before the earthquake are very popular; so are paintings of the collapsed structure—the one you might select depends on your attitude). Traditional trinkets, voodoo charms, spirit bottles, ritual kerchiefs, and other actual Haitian souvenirs—homemade candles and peasant aprons among them—are not much in evidence, while in a sweltering alley back behind the sparkling market, all sorts of authentic local items can be found.

On the day I was to attend the opening of the renovated Iron Market, I went into that back alley and bought a small bottle decorated with three red horns, the iconography that signifies Bossou, the voodoo bull god, who in my mind resembles the Minotaur of Knossos. The bottle was for a friend back in Los Angeles who had told me she wanted something *real*. The man I bought it from runs a little stall; he's a voodoo priest, but also a motorcycle repairman, he told me. I stuffed the bottle into my purse and went around the tall fence of the market to the entrance. A crowd was gathering for the opening ceremony. Grande Rue, out front, had been cleared of traffic, and only official cars and special tap-taps, whose colorful decoration had been commissioned by Digicel, sat outside.

Who was there to see the bright Digicel-red ribbon cut on the dais between columns upon which were painted the words PAIX and TRAVAIL (peace and work)? Edwidge Danticat, the Haitian-American writer, had flown in from Miami. Edmond Mulet, the outgoing head of MINUS-TAH, was there. Richard Morse, hotelier, musician, and cousin of the soon-to-be president Micky Martelly. Dr. Reginald Boulos, of the old Haitian Syrio-Lebanese import-export family, who has been connected to the U.S. embassy for decades, and who enthusiastically opposed Aristide and all he stood for. Mac McClelland was there, too, I discovered later from one of her tweets. There was Denis O'Brien, and Maarten Boute, of course—with his cane. And arriving last but not least, as Leonard Cohen's "Hallelujah" sounded from the loudspeakers, the UN special envoy, Bill Clinton, who was to do the ribbon-cutting.

History presents us with all sorts of photographs. If you were to study the imaginary album of the Haitian earthquake and its aftermath, you would see certain kinds. These are real pictures that I am now assembling into a pretend picture book, a future picture book. *Haiti: The Earthquake's Legacy*, say (hint to Time Inc. Books). There would be the formal pictures of future quake victims, before the earthquake struck. There is, for example, the pre-meeting snapshot of the UN administrative delegation to Haiti, men and women in suits. Almost all of them died shortly after the picture was taken. Old pictures, too, of the earthquake dead of note: Micha Gaillard, the longtime political figure; Hédi Annabi, head of the UN mission; Archbishop Joseph Miot; the three Haitian womens' leaders Myriam Merlet, Magalie Marcelin, and Anne-Marie Coriolan; the geographer-demographer Georges Anglade. Pictures from the earthquake would include Rubble Man, and also water-bucket-carrying woman, walking through the debris: these are the two photo icons of this disaster.

All the pictures from *Tragedy and Hope* would be included in the historic photographic record. The album would have to display the spectacular pictures of downed government buildings, especially the three domes of the presidential palace as they crumbled and then sank farther and farther into the ground with every passing day, like three old, useless drunken friends stumbling and clutching one another in stupor and impotence.

As time passes and the palace sinks away, you'd begin to see other kinds of pictures in this imaginary album, of white people giving Haitians vaccinations. Of Dr. Mark Hyman with his headlamp. Of white people looking on proudly as Haitians who lost limbs walked on their new prostheses. Of white people surveying camps and transitional housing. Of Dr. Megan Coffee. Of white people in huge white aid-organization vans, riding to their outposts in the countryside. Of nice white ladies kissing Haitian children. And of the opening of the new Iron Market, with Clinton and O'Brien on the stage, the scissors in Clinton's right hand, the red ribbon in his left, a cornucopia of flowers and vegetables strewn decoratively at their feet, and there, in the crowd below, like a dark smudge in the left-hand corner, the back of my head.

19

GHOSTS BY DAYLIGHT

Si syel-la te tonbe, yo ta ramase zetwal
If the sky fell, they'd scoop up the stars

I'm standing in the rubble one day taking a call from L.A.

I'd been having lunch at Presse Café up in Pétionville with Lorraine Mangones, the daughter of a legendary Haitian architect. We were talking about the millions of designs being proposed for new shelters for the internally displaced earthquake homeless, and Lorraine—who takes after her acerbic father when describing the Haitian landscape—was on the attack. We were laughing about a particularly ridiculous shelter concept, made of tires, when my cell phone rang. It was a friend calling from outside a courtroom back in Los Angeles.

I left Lorraine and went outside into the dust and chaos of Pétionville, which hadn't been as hard-hit as downtown but was still strewn with debris and involved in the disaster. And I'm listening to Los Angeles on my cell phone as I stand in the shattered remains. Cars are picking their way down the street. It's so hot out. Lorraine is waiting for me inside where there are fans going. The preliminary hearing in the courtroom in L.A. is for a murder case; in July 2009, my friends' daughter was murdered in one of those killings that has a right to be called senseless and pointless. A perfect, lovely young girl, and a brutal criminal, out on the street, violating the terms of his parole. Now her parents and all my other friends and my husband are at the hearing, listening to evidence. The voice at my ear was telling me all of this while I was standing in the wreckage that had killed who knew how many thousands of people. And all that mattered to me right then was that girl and what had happened to her. Amid all this death, the one death.

She was on my mind a lot as I went around town, both before the phone call and certainly after. I felt guilty about it, about focusing on her, when there was so much horror around me. I thought about the old journalists' equation, that one American death equals one hundred European deaths equals one thousand Latin American deaths equals ten thousand Asian deaths equals one hundred thousand African deaths.

Then one morning, I went to find my old friend Milfort Bruno, who had helped me get around during my first wild days in Haiti so many years ago, as Duvalier was falling. Milfort was wearing a jaunty hat and sitting on a balustrade at the Hotel Oloffson, hoping I would come by. He didn't look jaunty, in spite of the hat. He gave me a personal tour that, by showing me what he was experiencing, helped me understand better what I was feeling.

Milfort was born in Port-au-Prince in a courtyard near the Iron Market, and he worked for Carnival Cruise Lines as a young man, doing night cleaning on a ship; he got $135 every two weeks, but then the cruise ships stopped using him. "Otherwise, now I would be rich," he says.

One day, when he was twelve years old, he found a lost *blan* wandering downtown, and he helped the man get back to his hotel. This hotel turned out to be the Oloffson, a place Milfort had never seen before although it was less than three miles from his birthplace. There at the hotel Milfort discovered a treasure trove of white men. He started working there as a guide immediately and attached himself to the hotel so successfully that—although he did his brief stint at sea—he was back at the Oloffson more than twenty years later when I showed up to become one of the *blan* in his long ledger.

The day I found Milfort in his hat, he and I left the Oloffson and drove over to his house, not far away, in Carrefour Feuilles, a *quartier populaire*. Milfort had had two grown daughters and one grown son, Harry. Harry was always the big problem in Milfort's life.

Harry has been mentally incapacitated since he was run over by a car at the age of four. The story is like a rich fable from de Maupassant or even Hugo: One day, the darling boy was given a bit of change by his adoring father. It was too little to buy anything, even a piece of gum, but the coins were shiny and the boy knew nothing of the value of money, so he ran out in his little shorts to buy himself a piece of candy, like a big kid. Out came a beautiful new car from nowhere, as the boy, coins clutched in his hand, skittered off from the curb. The car smashed him, catching him in the axle mechanism and dragging him down the street. The boy was so small the driver didn't even know he'd hit someone, and the whole neighborhood was screaming at him from ledges and windows and doors, "Stop, stop!"

And the driver stopped. He was a wealthy, light-colored young man, Milfort says. Horrified at what had happened, he took Milfort's boy and Milfort to the hospital. Although Harry's chest was half crushed, doctors who looked at the boy back then said he'd be fine. The man with the car gave Milfort a thousand dollars; even now, Milfort remembers how sorry the man was. And Harry *was* fine, except for the fact that invisible trauma to his brain had caused severe cerebral injuries, and he never recovered from his untreated cranial wounds. A later *eskran*, or scan, showed irremediable damage. Otherwise, the child was in perfect health.

Now twenty-four years old, Harry sits out in a rocking chair in a little cement courtyard behind a locked gate all day long, wearing a pair of yellow shorts, when Milfort can convince him to wear anything at all. He's sedated by pills prescribed by a doctor Milfort calls the *sikat*, or psychiatrist. Milfort keeps Harry at home because otherwise he'd be out in the street in a minute, and lost perhaps forever. Also, the boy's condition shames him.

Milfort told me then that one of his daughters had died in the earthquake. He looked down at his old hands, and I remembered that this daughter in particular had been his great support, his right-hand girl. She was the one who took care of Harry while Milfort and the other daughter tried to make some money every day. (Milfort's wife had died many years earlier of a lupus-like disease.) And I realized, suddenly (though you'd imagine I would have realized it already), that the way I'd been thinking of my friends' lost daughter, the way I'd been obsessing over her fate, going through all kinds of possibilities for rescue that one shouldn't ever have to consider, was the way each Haitian who had lost someone in the earthquake was thinking about that person, or those people. Every time I thought of this girl as I went about my business in Haiti, my heart began to pound with anger and loss, and the terrible frustration of impotence, the feeling that I was somehow responsible, that I would have saved her if I could. And now, watching Milfort rock Harry's chair as Harry looked off into the blank nowhere into which his sister had disappeared, I saw that the people around me were feeling these same things, too.

But I had moments in Haiti of emotional retreat, as well. While it was happening I didn't even recognize it. After and before this moment at Milfort's, I'd wandered through the wreckage of this city I'd lived in for two years and visited for twenty, moving through the destruction with a hard heart, a very hard heart. I felt sometimes that I was inured to Haiti—I'd grown a shell against it; it could no longer touch me—hunger, tragedy, disease, waste, ruin. Nothing. It was a survival instinct, I suppose. It was the way some Haitians faced Haiti, too, I knew. Just keep moving. Don't react.

One day, right after the quake, I'd gone looking for Edgard Jean-Louis, an old voodoo priest and a maker of bright voodoo flags, an artist. The photojournalist Maggie Steber was with me. We finally found Edgard, sitting on a white plastic chair with a few members of his family. Behind them was their ruined house. Behind that was the ruined voodoo temple he had shared with other priests; it had partially collapsed in the earthquake and then it had been burned, mysteriously. Behind Edgard's personal wreckage was the whole neighborhood of Belair—where so many years ago, before Aristide was first elected, I had hidden in the alleyways with fleeing demonstrators as the Haitian Army tried to hunt them down—now crushed and heaving under the mountains of debris. Nothing came to me, nothing occurred to me to feel. I simply thought: Where is everything? It was as if the whole city had become a lost memory, like a sudden onset of dementia.

Edgard I hadn't seen in a few years, but he was an imposing, statue-like old man with a white halo of hair and a face, on this day, like the mask of tragedy. Maggie, who is notoriously susceptible to emotion—it's true— knelt down in front of Edgard, took both his hands in hers, and began to cry. All that she'd seen in my company, over the past few days, and over many past years, rose up inside her before this man who looked like a god of Africa, this person we'd known for so long. Everything he meant to her, everything Haiti meant to her, she was feeling and releasing as she held on to his hands, her face wet with tears, him smiling now—while I stood off to the side, mentally tapping my foot at the display of emotion, willing us on to whatever would be the next thing that we would see.

And I was also wondering: What can Edgard make of this? I was, as I have so often been, embarrassed by the sentimentality and muddleheaded- ness of my race, of us in Haiti. But to diagnose the scene properly: this was my friend Maggie feeling real emotions about a specific person and the earth- quake. And this was me, not feeling that—this was me amid all the death.

Try walking through the concentration camps of the Balkans, the kill- ing fields of the Khmer Rouge, the excavated mass graves of El Mozote, downtown Dresden, the outer circles of Hiroshima. That's what it was like in Port-au-Prince in those days. To me no emotion seemed proper. I couldn't find one or feel one that was fitting, that was up to the level of what I was seeing. There was a disconnect between eyes and heart. To Maggie, waves of sadness and tears, with some joy at human survival, some laughter over visible human frailties, felt appropriate. I walked around with flat affect, I think it's called. I could feel that, a flatline. Here's this leg sticking out of that pancaked school; here's that bloated hand under the motorcycle repair shop, the former motorcycle repair shop. Walking on, walking on. Here's the palace where I interviewed Aristide, and Prosper Avril, and Henri Namphy, and René Préval—figures from history, and the building's crushed. Walking on. Here are the survivors in their camps, their hungry babies, here's little McKenly Gédéon without his hands. I've achieved precisely nothing for him, with my froth of activity and carrying him to and fro, from doctor to doctor. Walking on.

At night, lying on my mattress under the stars next to the pool at the Oloffson, I can hear the wailing and praying of survivors. The ground lifts and rocks beneath us in huge cracking aftershocks. I'm thinking about mosquitoes and reaching for my pile of nighttime survival items next to the mattress: bug juice, a flashlight, Valium, a bottle of rum. I sit up and reslather the bug juice. Other journalists and relief workers are lying under sheets along the driveway, one next to another like corpses under the light of the stars. I lie back down and the scenes from the day shift through my mind: Edgard; the stray limbs; spaghetti meals; McKenly's stumps; the camp on the soccer field; a young girl crying inconsolably about something, something she wouldn't say, not looking at me; and the rickety Madame Coupet in her housedress telling her old stories under the remaining fluorescent bulb at the half-fallen-down Park Hotel.

Oh, Mac McClelland, I understand it now. Your need for violent sex after hearing about a rape, that's your version of what I'm feeling now. Did I say feeling? I meant: of what I'm *not* feeling now. When I say now I mean *now*, as in while I am writing this book. Mac, this book is my version of violent sex—it's what I'm doing to relieve the pain. Putting down these marks across my computer screen: I can feel the release.

I read a book recently by a foreign correspondent named Janine di Giovanni. The book was called *Ghosts by Daylight,* and it was all about imagining that one can go through war or disaster and remain untouched. Di Giovanni covered the war in Bosnia, and thought she had come out untouched, but her husband, a photographer (like Maggie, I

cannot help saying), was undone by it, and then di Giovanni realized
that she was, too, and that she and all her friends who'd been through the
siege of Sarajevo and other horrors of the 1990s and 2000s were wrecks.
This in spite of the fact that she lives in a nice apartment in Paris; her
wreckage is of a different kind, a different order, from the wreckage that
the Sarajevans—and the Haitians—have had to live with.

I read *Ghosts* and said to my husband, so why don't I have post-
traumatic stress disorder?

Maybe it's a generational thing, he said. No older reporters have it.
Only younger people.

In the old days, he explained, a reporter was supposed to be removed
from emotion, was supposed to shed light on events. It was even hoped
that one could be clinical, honest, objective, and not a sobbing wreck
who had to take to her bed for one reason or another. Imagine if Maggie
had fallen apart when remnants of the Tonton Macoutes (wearing red
armbands, incidentally) came into Aristide's church and killed thirteen
congregants and tried to assassinate Aristide. The macoutes tried to hold
her back by her dress, which got torn, but even Maggie, the emotionally available, the feelingly sentimental, did not have PTSD afterward.
Instead she had pictures.

Here's what Virginia Woolf wrote in *Mrs. Dalloway,* in one of the
first serious literary contemplations of shell shock, the old name for
post-traumatic stress disorder. Her characters are Evans and Septimus,
two British soldiers from World War I (note also the element of survivor
guilt):

> When Evans was killed, just before the Armistice, in Italy, Septimus,
> far from showing any emotion or recognising that here was an end of
> a friendship, congratulated himself upon feeling very little and very
> reasonably. The war had taught him. It was sublime. He had gone
> through the whole show, friendship, European War, death, had won
> promotion, was still under thirty and was bound to survive. He was

right there. The last shells missed him. He watched them explode with indifference . . . [N]ow that it was all over, truce signed, and the dead buried, he had, especially in the evening, these sudden thunder-claps of fear. He could not feel . . . There were moments of waking in the early morning. The bed was falling; he was falling.

Well. As I write, with *Mrs. Dalloway* open on my desk, let me just say that it is 4:51 in the morning on a Saturday, and I've been writing for two hours. Was the bed falling? Was I falling?

Of course, I want to be a hero. Who doesn't? But after years of being schooled by Haiti, I've come to understand that, like Woolf's Septimus, I am a survivor, not a hero. (Yes, yes . . . *Dalloway* spoiler alert: I do know that Septimus kills himself eventually.) I'm not going to save anyone, not going to fix things, not going to be able to mitigate the disaster for even one Haitian, much less the country—that grandiose idea that still plagues Bill Clinton, who has more power than a measly writer to effect change. Sure, I've gotten people visas, I've paid for kids, I have introduced people to others who can help them. Some of my Haitian friends have benefited from knowing me, I hope. But the benefit is very direct. I give them something, I make a connection for them, I get them into a job interview, I write a visa recommendation. And they do things for me, in turn.

I had dreams. I wanted to be an activist (how the word depresses me now) on a peasant collective (how the word depresses me now) outside of Hinche, a provincial town. I thought: it's a choice. Today, I respect the activists, including the outsiders, but I see I could never have done what they do; the only way I could have participated in some kind of solidarity movement with Haitians would have been with doctors, the people who get real results for individuals. I would never have been able to believe in myself as an activist. It's a personality thing: I feared I'd be useless, but that I'd have to go on pretending meanwhile to be useful. Yet what I've done in Haiti, what I've achieved with marks on paper, I cannot help but feel is useless, especially in the wake of this terrible disaster.

I mean: first there was the earthquake, and now, Duvalier has returned! My whole involvement in Haiti was based on the end of Duvalierism, and now the fat little playboy scion, heir to the legacies of Papa Doc and Uncle Bag, has come back, with his long-term girlfriend (a virtual double for his first wife) and at least one of his children. He's living up in a mountain retreat, perhaps in the very same house I saw the Haitian people destroy back in 1986, when I was taking my bad pictures.

Seeing Jean-Claude return to Haiti after twenty-five years with barely a protest and hardly any personal consequences for at least a long initial period has made me reflect on my work as a documenter of the Haitian scene, of Haiti's *déroulement*. Jean-Claude imprisoned my friends; he sent Haiti's best and brightest into exile; he ruined so many people's lives. His return to Haiti was the last straw for Jean-Claude Bajeux, the old intellectual who pointed to Jared Diamond's *Collapse* as a kind of Haitian Bible. Bajeux died a few months after Duvalier's *rentrée*. Almost everyone I knew in Haiti—from the top of the hill down to the midst of the shantytowns—had participated in one way or another in the years-long effort to oust him. Everything I'd done in Haiti, everything I'd written about Haiti, was degraded by Duvalier's virtually uncontested return. My first book was all about the fall of Duvalier and the freeing of Haiti from his dynasty's net of terror and totalitarianism. Now he was back, free, blessed by the new president, getting his picture in the paper at graduations and opening ceremonies.

I met a man once in Miragoâne whose name was Initil. That's what his parents called him, and it means "useless" (as in Useless to Complain to God About the Arrival of Yet Another Mouth to Feed). Sometimes I think that that should be my pen name. "Initil P. Ayiti." It has a nice ring to it. Useless for Haiti.

To lose all hope is nihilism, however, and extremely unrewarding as a political and psychological mechanism. A Haitian said to me, "To redevelop Port-au-Prince now is like washing your hands and then drying them in the dirt," a play on an old Haitian proverb. That's too hopeless even for me. A huge seismic event should be an astringent learning tool, as long as you're not buried beneath its detritus. The earthquake and cholera were the worst things one could imagine, "tragedy upon tragedy." But they energized certain people. The tragedies seemed to provide a shattering catharsis for the country. They excited the imaginations of so many committed outsiders, but they had simply stopped me in my tracks.

That's because when I used to try to imagine a new Haiti, it was a country rebuilt, reconstructed, and reimagined by Haitians. In late 2009, just before the earthquake, the country seemed to be teeter-tottering toward a new era, as it had when Aristide was first elected, but this time without the ebullience of that period. But the new Haiti that's being put into place now is a Haiti reimagined by us. And it's only by dint of an enormous suspension of disbelief—which I do suspend every day in order to get up and out and keep writing and thinking—that I can see Haitians managing to wrest control of their fate once again from the white man. No disrespect to the white man.

I think of Aristide often now. He's back, too. Well, you couldn't let Duvalier return and keep Aristide out, although the Obama administration tried. So Aristide is back in Haiti in a redoubt up the hill too, like Duvalier. He's silent. This is a man who never shuts up, and he's silent. Did he bargain away his speech in order to be allowed to come back? WikiLeaks shows how implacably the United States under Obama fought to stop his return from South Africa, even as Duvalier was strutting through the streets of Pétionville; was Aristide forced to make promises? It's possible that the era of his influence is over in any case—a new generation is rising—but still, to have him back and not speaking is strange. It's as though a ghost has returned.

Perhaps silence is the appropriate voice for the voiceless right now. Aristide used to say that there was such a thing as "*un silence éloquent.*" If Haitian history shows one thing, it is that Haiti—and Haitians—are exceptional, especially in extremis. So it's possible, just marginally possible, that Haiti's voiceless will start speaking for themselves again soon—not through Aristide, perhaps, and certainly not through Leonard Doyle's suggestion box, not through IOM's radio stations, not in my books or on

Anderson Cooper's show or in Jonathan Demme's documentaries, but in some new Haitian way invented by Haitians like the Haitian Revolution, in some new Haitian way that you and I cannot predict.

Maarten Boute has stopped working for Digicel. "It was tiring, and getting boring," he says. But few believe you'd leave a job like Boute's at Digicel before you had another to replace it. Something must have happened, a rupture or a deal. Anyway, Boute is still around. He haunts Port-au-Prince. He has patched back up his personal life and parked his Belgian wife and their little son in Miami, close by.

Boute stays up late, as always, traveling through the empty streets of the capital with friends, hanging out at people's houses. He knows a whole generation of late-nighters, both outsiders and Haitians. He says he often goes over to the Flamingo in Pétionville to chat with the lady in charge there, Mère Yannick. "I go there to talk with Yannick; she knows everything about this place. But her girls are ugly," Boute says. Boute is a character invented by Graham Greene. Every time I see him I am transported into riffling pages and literature.

He's looking for a new job.

Where? In Haiti, of course.

"I can't go back to Belgium," Boute says, laughing. His hair flows in Beethoven-like crests above the furrowed brow. His white button-down shirt looks designer today, as he wraps his arms tightly around his skinny self. You can see why Haitians call him "Bono." O'Brien has allowed Boute to keep his Digicel cell phones and his Digicel email address, for now. Boute doesn't seem shattered by his Digicel divorce. Maybe he'll go into energy, he says. There's always something for a white man to do in Haiti—there's a lot of room for energy projects in this electricity-deprived country, Boute points out. And Boute is pretty good friends with President Martelly, too, which can't hurt, although he doesn't say that. Sometimes, Boute goes to wake Martelly up in the mornings, helps the president get his day started. Martelly is not an early bird.

"I can't go back to Belgium and become some kind of numbers man," Boute continues. "I'd turn into a drug addict or an alcoholic, and I'd have to kill myself." Again, here's Haiti as rehab for the nonconformist First World person, Haiti as a world the eccentric Westerner can bear to live in, like Greece for the disgraced Lord Byron, a place where you can have a cause to work for and a society that respects you. A welcoming, accepting place where you can be yourself instead of the kind of person your bourgeois, fully formed, super-developed homeland demands that you be. From the outsider's point of view, a place like Haiti—where rules are not rules, at least for the interloper—provides a nice empty canvas on which to paint a freewheeling future. Even today, a person who's not perhaps so beloved at home, not so content with the everyday in the developed world, can spread his wings here and impose himself, by reason of money and connections, and create his own kind of kingdom.

20
WESLANDIA

Kenbe kabrit nwè avan-l fè nwa
Bring the black goat in before nightfall

Haiti after the earthquake was extremely appealing for outsiders—once they got over their fears and plunged in. For me, no matter the circumstances, it's normal to be here, doing what I do—the earthquake didn't change how I work in Haiti. Here, I have the rare and precious writer's opportunity to talk to people about their lives, as they experience them, and about how they are confronting some of the harshest things: hunger, disease, joblessness, rooflessness, foodlessness, schoollessness, waterlessness, powerlessness (in every sense), and all the other attributes and accessories of poverty. And then I get to go back to a Haitian friend's house or a hotel and have a nice dinner, hang out with friends, check the email. All the development people are doing their version of this, too, running out to survey misery in the morning, and then retiring back in the evening into their compound life. That's what it's like in Haiti now—for almost all the outsiders.

For instance: one night I'm having dinner on the Hotel Oloffson's terrace with Megan Coffee. Only here for a few days on this trip, I've decided to stay at the convenient Oloffson, instead of with friends. I transported Dr. Coffee from the hospital, after some convincing, and she has brought along a dress she stuffed in her bag that morning, for the occasion. Dr. Coffee doesn't do the compound life. The dress was given to her by a visiting woman doctor who just couldn't stand to see Megan go out to dinner, on those rare occasions when she would agree to do so, wearing her (one has to say, profoundly unfashionable) work clothes. So Dr. Coffee came with me and changed into her evening dress in the Oloffson bathroom. The simple jersey T-shirt dress, belonging as it did to someone else, was a little small and short on her, but cute and—comparatively—like something worn on the red carpet. So we have dinner, Dr. Coffee picking at her salad and telling me about her extended Catholic family and her mathematical upbringing, and how, as she says, she does not want "to live life as a nun." She's planning to develop a foundation to keep running her work in Haiti, so that one day she'll be able to spend some time outside the country.

The next night, I've come back from the most distant camps. I'm sunburned and dusty. I'm grabbing a plate of food as the band sets up on the same old terrace. It's RAM night, which is the night when Richard Morse and his wife, Lunise, usually perform at the hotel with RAM, their band. So I'm sitting with my plate of chicken and rice in front of me and some old friends beside me, and Sean Penn comes in—immediately there's a feeling of entourage, people sidling up to the celebrity aura. It's a feeling I recognize from having lived for years now near Hollywood. Penn hasn't come for RAM night. He's come to have a drink with a Danish director he has worked with. Penn seems to be wearing a black pleather jacket, and he looks like a reduced version of Maarten Boute. He comes and sits at my table, where the Danish director is having dinner. It's always catch-as-catch-can at this place. Anyway, I'm ready for bed.

I stop on the way to my room to listen to the band. I'm standing near the stairs next to Daniel Morel, a Haitian photographer, who's muttering in my ear as the band plays its "roots" music on bamboo, iron cowbells, a Seuss-like three-tubed tri-horn, and metal scrapers—all traditional instruments of Carnival parades. Lunise is dancing and swinging her hundreds of long African-style braids and singing; the band is marching like a voodoo procession around the back terrace area. The crowd is Haitian and foreign.

In my ear, I feel Daniel's warm breath and I hear this: "The problem with Haiti is a Haitian problem."

Okay, I think.

I am so eager to be asleep.

Daniel says: "The white people think that Haitians are stupid."

I'm just listening to the music.

He says: "But Haitians are smarter than the white people."

The drums are so loud.

"All of these white people," Daniel says, gesturing to the whole crowd, "they're soldiers of fortune, mercenaries. Out to make a buck in Haiti."

Penn passes by. "Not him," says Morel.

But then, what *is* Penn doing here?

The question is not what Penn has *done* in Haiti, because he's done plenty and his work at his earthquake camp has been solid and thorough, and generally as good as or better than the work of other, more established relief and development groups (with many of which Penn's group works). He helped get his camp going (almost by accident), helped organize it. He worked with others to make it as decent as possible, and then—most important—he began to depopulate and deconstruct it.

The question for me, then, is not what he has done, but why he has done it. What drove him to it and kept him at it? It's not different from the question of why Megan Coffee does what she does. For Penn, the usual bad-boy movie star story doesn't really work.

Penn fits into one of my types of Haiti expats, what he calls "the endless-struggle lovers," though it's unclear whether he puts himself in that category. (I put myself into it. I have no choice.) You wonder about Penn the way you wonder about all outsiders here. What draws them in, and what makes them stay? I wonder about Penn the way I wonder about the early French planters. About the Polish soldiers who fought on the side of the slaves during the revolution and to whom Dessalines granted Haitian citizenship, and who stayed on to create a little region in Haiti where one still to this day finds Haitians with blue eyes. I wonder about him the way I wonder about the Syrians who came here and stayed. For these three groups, though, one part of the answer is that the money was good. I wonder, too, about my friends Tom and Lance, North Americans who have businesses and live here. About Paul Farmer, although after devoting twenty-plus years to Haiti, he is not in-country as much as one would imagine. Penn is around more, and is more visible. I wonder about Penn the way I wonder about Megan Coffee. Megan's answer comes easier: her work is here. Professionally, it makes sense. With Penn, not so easy to see. Now, for many of the outsiders who stay and who have stayed, the initial or prolonging reason why is simple: love. Lance and Tom married Haitians; so did Paul Farmer. But I haven't heard about love where either Coffee or Penn is concerned.

I wonder about Penn's connection the way I wonder about my own, though Penn at least is a doer and a helper. Whereas I think of myself in a more clinical way: an observer, or (on a bad day) a leech.

Penn says that he's in Haiti in part because of a sense of "duty," and that this sense of duty is coupled with a kind of narcissism.

"We all believe that our time is a particular time, and that in that time, the wheel can be especially reinvented, maybe by us," he says. He's in his bedroom in the house he rents across from his headquarters, both buildings that did not fall during the earthquake. They're right behind his camp in the Delmas neighborhood. He no longer stays in the camp. "I came here by pure accident," Penn says. "I'm a victim of optimism." He'd done work in New Orleans after Hurricane Katrina, and so he had what he likes to call "a handy little crew." He was watching what was happening in Haiti, and he decided, he says, "Let's get it done yesterday." He scrambled for a landing slot at the airport, and brought in 350,000 vials of morphine (so that Dr. Hyman and others would no longer have to use vodka for amputations). Except for having had to listen to Jonathan

Demme, the film director and confirmed Haitianophile, ramble on about the place over the years, Penn says, "I knew nothing about Haiti."

He's sitting on his bed. The bedroom is tiny, like a *restavek*'s room; it's really a portion of a room that's been walled off. His single bed is unmade, and it's got rumpled, daisy-patterned sheets on it. I've seen these same sheets on beds in tents in various camps. The black pleather jacket from the night before is lying on improvised shelves. I can see by the label that it is Armani, and probably leather with no *p*. Penn talks on and on, cogently, about visiting Aristide, and seeing movies about Haiti and reading books about it now, and about his camp's relationships with international organizations, how those relationships soured, about attempts to sabotage "our work," about how various international groups felt that their work was being "usurped by that actor and his camp of gypsies." He puts another cigarette out on the tile floor next to his bed; that's the fifth cigarette so far this morning.

"I found Haiti was more raw than Hollywood," he says, smiling at the joke, except his point is that Hollywood is fucking raw. He lights another cigarette. An empty bottle of Guinness sits on his bedside table. A big waterproof black rain suit is hanging from a peg on the wall; in its domination of the scene, the bulky, glistening suit reminds me of the Tonton Macoute effigy in Aristide's similarly tiny office, in the old days. In a way, the little room feels as if it's the handiwork of a set director— the sheer mass of stuff seems to elucidate Penn's character and his role here in that specific, "filmic" way. Pairs of reading glasses punctuate the undifferentiated mess. Pairs of much-used boots, similar to my crap camp shoes, stand under the shelves. The nightstand is piled with books, two BlackBerrys, many tubes of ChapStick and packets of Trident. A half-dome tent is rolled up on the floor. Thick extension cables lie in coils nearby. A pinup of Miss Haiti (whose mother, a conservative attorney, was assassinated during the Aristide-Préval era) has been plastered on the wall, the room's only decoration. It's signed, Penn points out, and is a joke between him and a friend who is also a donor to the camp and who happens to be Miss Haiti's boyfriend. Across from his bed, next to the bunched-up Armani jacket, is a big black Sentry safe. I imagine it holds a wad of cash, Penn's passport, his supposed Glock, and some rounds of ammunition. Next to the bed, a tiny, formerly magenta rug that looks more like a moth-eaten bathmat provides a touch of warmth. Next to this, the butts and cinders of Penn's now six crushed-out cigarettes lie in a serendipitous ring like dancers exhausted after some miniature Busby Berkeley romp. Each time Penn puts out a cigarette there, I am wondering about the Haitian who's going to clean up after him. But knowing Penn, he probably picks up the butts himself.

Penn lights another cigarette, and leans back on his bed with his oceanic hair scrunched up into a corner. He's telling a long story he's told before about how some local guys made off with some of the camp's equipment, and how he got it back. It's a funny story, but he doesn't want it published because he has to work with those very people all the time. While he's telling the story, his toes play with the safe's handle. That's how small the room is. He gets to the end of his tale, where the equipment is bashfully returned by a man whom one would never think of as bashful. "We work with these guys, a lot, now," Penn says. "I think they have a kind of vision."

People tend to have a kind of vision, according to Penn—if he can work with them, I'm thinking, as I sit on a metal chair, the only other piece of furniture besides the bed. I'm squeezed into a small area at the foot of the bed, the chair's back almost right up against the door to the room. My pen and my notebook, open on my lap, feel to me like ridiculously formal accessories. I should have my feet up on Penn's bed and be smoking a joint or something. When I'm with outsiders in Haiti, half the time, I'm in a book by Greene, but the other half, I'm in a movie by Altman.

"Oh, shit, I have to take a shower now," Penn says, quashing another cigarette. "I've got Senator Dodd—oh, *former* Senator Dodd—coming in, gotta get him at the airport. I ran into him at Sundance." Penn's conversation is studded with little gems of disjunction like that one. I ask him if his friends in Hollywood will listen to him talk about Haiti.

"Are you kidding?" Penn says, laughing. "They have no choice, man." I ask if they care about Haiti. He responds indirectly: "I have periods of compassion for Californians."

In Haiti, Penn says, people from development organizations tend to talk to him as if he's mentally deficient. "They always want to have talks with me that are like 'Development 1A,'" he says. "They want to tell you how you work from the community up. You know? They're always trying to remind me of things we're already doing." He gives a short laugh. "But a lot of them have left."

A lot of refugees have left Penn's camp by now, too. By the winter of 2012, only about twenty thousand of the original sixty thousand remained. The tennis courts are cleared. Throughout the camp are pockets where the slapped-up shanties and fortified tents have been abandoned. Most of his people, Penn says, have left the camp for rebuilt or renovated housing in their old neighborhoods on the Delmas road. His group has been working with IOM on the relocations.

Penn can be cuttingly dismissive, but he's an enthusiast at heart, and, like Boute, he's looking for a place that will accept him and let him be active, helpful, and worthy—and give him a little *meaning,* too. That's an extra, after building the camp and clearing the camp and building the houses and clearing the rubble. Another extra is the fun; in part the fun of doing something that's worthwhile and in part the fun of just being free and in Haiti. Probably running a refugee camp in Haiti after an earthquake should be a requirement on the curriculum of any rehab center, any wellness center—like Dr. Mark Hyman's UltraWellness Center in Lenox, Massachusetts.

Don't you think?

I often think that all the outsiders here—or at least the Americans—are in rehab, seeking redemption, some kind of laissez-passer for being safe and bourgeois in a world that also contains Haiti. That they are seeking forgiveness for living in a country whose wealth and peace are intimately connected—historically, economically, politically, and perhaps even spiritually—to Haiti's lack of same. It's most obvious when the outsiders are celebrities like Charlie Sheen or Kim Kardashian, both of whom visited Haiti after moments of disgrace at home.

"We *need* Haiti," as Penn has said to other reporters. He means it profoundly, as in, America needs Haiti, or one's soul needs Haiti, but it could equally be said for the kinds of need Haiti serves with the likes of Kardashian.

"Look, I feel productive here," Penn tells me now. "That's the long and short of it."

One sign of Penn's ongoing commitment to Haiti is that President Martelly, in a show of his continuing confidence in and intimacy with Penn, named the actor/development worker to the position of ambassador at large for the Haitian government. Penn has a Haitian diplomatic email address now. Penn's group is set to begin demolishing the ruins of the presidential palace. Like Ricardo Seitenfus, the disloyal OAS official, Penn has also been knighted, which is just hard to imagine. As ambassador, Penn travels around Latin America helping President Martelly to find funding for various projects. He meets with heads of state. He takes the job very seriously—indeed, "very serious" about Haiti is something that comes naturally to Penn, although he can be lighthearted. One day I email him and his response is "Greetings from Bolivia!" He's there for Martelly.

Mr. Ambassador.

Here are two other Haitian ambassadors at large: Wyclef Jean and Donna Karan, the fashion designer who helped found a mission to Haiti after the earthquake. "I believe that where there is creativity, there is hope," Karan wrote on the *Huffington Post* on the second anniversary of the earthquake. "Hope is all over Haiti. Hope is Haiti." She and other outsiders who work with her in Haiti, she says, are hoping "to bring together a conscious community of leaders in music, fashion, film, finance and art to become agents of change for the renewal of Haiti."

Another sign of Penn's commitment is that he has a Haitian Creole–learning application on his iPad.

~~

I have two friends in Los Angeles, architects who, through a complicated series of personal and professional coincidences, became involved in the Haiti reconstruction effort. They were responsible for at least one of the kinds of faxed blueprint to which Bill Clinton was said to have reacted with such irritation. One day, they asked me over to their hip offices in a hypercool L.A. neighborhood to look at their project before they handed it in. It was a really nice project, again supposed to be a housing development for earthquake victims, who were to be transformed into suburban residents as well as employees in a foreign-owned manufacturing plant of some kind near the new development. Each little house had a yard. The houses had been conceived thoughtfully, because these architects are humane and decent and care deeply about their work and its consequences. But the planned neighborhood, for all its trees and bits of green space, looked stripped down and bare, unadorned, un-Haitian in some way. Maybe it's that my old Haiti eyes can't see the value for Haitians of things made or built for them without their input. I was to be the Haitian input on this project; this gave me an interior laugh.

It's even better, I was thinking, when Haitian things are built by Haitians, with their own investment and planning. Then those things reflect Haitian character, culture, and imagination—those things may turn out not to be modern or sleekly Scandinavian, but they will reflect Haitian living habits and Haitian norms. They won't be planned by Heather and Gerson Nozea.

I told my architect friends that the units should be built so that Haitians living in them would be able to turn several of them into a family courtyard with a shared outdoor area. That was the best counsel I could offer for their nice, green-roofed housing development. The land where this project was going to be built was also in an outlying area north of Port-au-Prince, a Corail-like hillside. The map the architects showed me made it clear to me that the land belonged to an elite family, one of the richest in

Haiti. I wondered what the Haitian government and the international donors were planning to pay the family for their land; I wondered how much
money was to be made in this little corner of the earthquake disaster.

After we finished with the housing, one of the architects' assistants
got up and made a little presentation about a tree they think will be
good for construction and other purposes in Haiti. Oh, I have seen this
tree before; I've seen it so many times, I thought, as I drank an espresso
prepared for me on the office machine. This tree, the young man said,
grows really fast. It needs little care and little water. When it matures, in
virtually no time, it can be cut down. (It will spring up again; no worries.) It can be used for construction; its wood is strong, flexible in an
earthquake, and heat resistant. But, equally, you can make clothing out
of it, *and* it's nutritious. You can eat its leaves. Its seedpods are natural
antibiotics; if you make a tea out of its bark, it gives you more calcium
than three glasses of milk. Or some such.

I drum my fingers and close my eyes, because I have heard about
these trees from development people for more than three decades but
have never seen a single person in any developing country I have visited
pick one of its leaves, build a house out of it, or make school uniforms
from it. I'm sure they do, somewhere, maybe even somewhere in Haiti.
But for me, the all-purpose tree, whatever its species, embodies the im-
pulse of so many good-hearted people from the developed world who
would like very much to find a simple solution to the complicated problems of the developing world (let's call it the starving world).

The smartest people often begin their work in development by believing a quick fix is possible: that technology, know-how, nature, and
their own good-hearted spirit will fix things. It's the Sean Penn theory of
development work, and if you're Penn, and working in a small enough
sphere, you can get a few good things done.

On the website of a group called Miracle Trees (www.miracletrees.org)
is a tribute to the amazing and multiple wonders that can be performed
by a humble shrub called *Moringa oleifera,* another tree that is a lot like the
one the architects' assistant was touting. The all-purpose tree always sounds

like a children's book to me. And there happens to be a children's book like this, called *Weslandia*. It's by Paul Fleischman. I used to read it to my sons.

In this book, Wesley, a boy who is rejected and bullied by all his classmates, rakes up the earth in his backyard, and overnight, miraculous seeds sent by the wind plant themselves in it. When the plants grow, Wesley picks a fruit from them and finds it's sweet and delicious. He makes cups and bowls from its skin. The plant's roots are like potatoes. The leaves of the plant are highly aromatic. Wesley starts to wear clothes made "from strips of the plant's woody bark." He uses the bark to make paper. He takes the seeds and pounds them into an oil that "served him both as a suntan lotion and mosquito repellant." He begins selling this oil to his former tormentors at ten bucks a bottle. He makes a flute for himself, fashioned from a stalk. He mixes the oil with soot and makes ink. He calls the world he's built from this plant Weslandia, after himself, of course. It's a utopia.

It's also a fantasy. I'm surprised the architects' assistant did not mention ink and musical instruments.

Why don't these trees save the world? I have often wondered. But after years of considering the question, I think I have figured out the answer. Which is that we live in a world where people have been living for a long time, doing things like building civilizations, cultures, and traditions, along with simply surviving and reproducing. You can take a *Moringa oleifera* into a Haitian village and the villagers may drop a couple of leaves in their soup, but really, they don't eat leaves; they eat rice and beans, and chicken when they're lucky. The only leaves they eat are thyme; they love to cook with thyme—it's the French background. They eat cornmeal with sauce. They eat canned sardines with tomato and onions over rice. They simply don't munch on leaves. They prefer mangoes and bananas. The *houngan* who practices traditional medicine doesn't know the leaves of the *Moringa,* and he, too, will turn away and go back to the leaves and bark he has always used for antibiotics, wounds, and medicinal draughts.

Here's the thought experiment: If a bright-eyed relief worker came to *you* and told you that these leaves were better for your child than a glass of milk, would you substitute the leaves for the milk? Would your child eat them with his Oreos? There is one woman in Mill Valley, California, who would probably try this out with her kid—she lives in a perfect, environmentally correct house. There are probably several people in Hollywood who would try it. But other than that no one will. Not even if your kid hasn't had a glass of milk in a week. You'd still try to figure out a way to get a glass of milk, because that's what you want for your kid, and that's what your kid wants—not leaves.

What if your house fell down, and that bright-eyed relief worker told you that if you'd just grow these trees in your backyard, like Wesley, you could build your next house from them for free? Well, you just wouldn't do it. Not even if the house you lost was a shotgun shack or a trailer home. You'd still want to build back what you'd lost; people in fact do not easily see the value in "building back better," because that "better" is subject to interpretation. Bill Clinton's better may not be Filibert Waldeck's better, and my better might not be René Préval's better. In any case, most—look into your own heart—want to build back the same. Or, you could say, the same but better. That's how it is. You want *two* glasses of milk, maybe. Two glasses of milk is the same but better. You want your same house, but with one more room: the same but better. But a bunch of leaves, while it may be "better" according to the relief worker, is not better to you. It's worse. It's inedible. And you know that the relief worker himself is not eating those leaves, either.

A house built by my architects and slapped up on some rich guy's barren land—while it may be better than your old unfinished overheated cinder-block apartment in Belair, according to the standards of Los Angeles—is most likely not better to you. It's worse. It's not in your old neighborhood. There's no place to buy sugar down the street. There's no *borlette*. There's no domino game going. It's a roof, sure, but it's unlivable in the long term for you as the person you are, a person with both an individual history and a national and cultural history, as opposed to the desperate, unhuman blank slate that the people who are fixing your life imagine you to be.

People in Haiti—even after the earthquake—don't see themselves as desperate in the way one would have to be desperate to start munching on *Moringa* leaves instead of scrounging for the food one likes (as Megan Coffee points out, if the rice doesn't have *sòs,* her patients won't eat it). They don't see themselves as so desperate for housing that they're willing to spend a month or so growing some tree recommended by some young American, and then beating its bark into panels and building with that.

They are not Wesley, a rich, entitled suburban boy with the leisure to dream a new world. They'd rather go scrounge up some rubble rebar, and get together some cash with help from neighbors and family to buy some cinder blocks, or build with mud and daub the very kind of place they lived in before on the very spot where they used to live—with perhaps some extra bolting of some kind for the next earthquake; they'll take that into consideration. The roof will be tin, not cement, this time.

I've said many retrospective things about Haiti here. Now it's not unusual to cast a look backward in order to move forward more safely and efficiently. All those commentators after the earthquake who predicted the grand finale of the country analyzed the place according to their ideas of Haiti's past; as the novelist Madison Smartt Bell says, they believe that what they call Haiti's "backwardness and primitivism causes all its problems, yak, yak, yak . . ."

But what we all are seeing today in Haiti is instead, perhaps, a look forward in keeping with Haiti's exceptional and counterintuitive modernism. Haiti was before its time with its unique (one could say premature) revolution. It was before its time with its guerrilla-style freedom-fighting rebellion against the U.S. occupation. It was before its time as a practice ground for later U.S. foreign policies of regime change. Perhaps Haiti today is in the throes of another modern convulsion. Sometimes it pays to look at it in fast-forward instead of in fast-reverse.

Especially after the earthquake, Haiti has seemed more than ever like a postapocalyptic dystopia; its deforested countryside and overpopulated,

crumbled urban landscape, with its smoke and stench, seem like plausible sets from one of the darkly pessimistic movies of the early years of
the new millennium. Maybe, I sometimes fear, this could be the future
for all of us: trees uprooted, water gone, the soil sinking into the sea,
the land filling up with plastic waste and too many people, epidemics
surging, and everyone starving and dying. As Bell says, "there's a fascination in looking at that, especially if you don't quite understand just *what*
you're looking at . . . I mean, your own future . . . or your children's . . ."

Maybe those people who go down so anxiously and generously to
repair Haiti and build nice houses and move people from one camp
to another, and put in sanitation systems and recycling programs and
provide AIDS cocktails and prenatal care and rape kits and write books
about the place are all unconsciously hoping that in trying to save Haiti,
they'll be able to save themselves, setting the scene for a future rescue of
humanity.

I spent one of my last evenings in Port-au-Prince in Toussaint Camp. It
was the rainy season, and it was raining. Not just raining, but doing what
it does in Haiti when it rains. The water sluices down out of the red and
black skies at sunset; the wind blows it first horizontally and then at a fine
forty-five-degree angle, then right straight down, while lightning shoves
open a door through the dark, then slaps it shut, and the thunder blasts.
The best place to be in Port-au-Prince in one of these tropical storms is in
a strong house with a tin roof, so you can feel and hear the glory of nature
without experiencing soaking or flooding, or too much awe.

But I foolishly had made an appointment via cell phone (answered by
Black) to meet Jerry and Samuel at the youth center. They weren't there
(surprise!) and the house was locked. My shoes were already soaked. No
one was around. The night was growing darker, and wetter. My poncho,
though fully as ridiculous as ponchos can be, also wasn't doing me much
good, because much of the water seemed to be flowing under it and
somehow in an upward direction. I was feeling defeated, soaked through,

and bedraggled. I wondered whether it was really worth hunting down the two guys who'd stood me up. No, it wasn't.

Instead, I decided to go look for Jésulà and her husband, whom I'd met months earlier and then had never been able to find again. I was always surprised at how hard it was to orient myself in this camp, the one camp I knew fairly well. It wasn't on such a big plot of land, and it had—if you included the adjacent Constitution Camp and Christophe Camp—a few landmarks, like a former fountain, a former amphitheater, the youth center. I was always lost here, but in the rain I was more lost. Is that possible?

No one over the age of sixteen was out, except for me. The shacks were as closed up as shacks can be, cardboard doors hinged shut, sheets let out to cover shack entryways. Tarp roofs were flapping in the wind like trapped wings of giant, dangerous birds. But all along the open concrete spaces where no tent or shack could be pitched, kids in shorts and T-shirts the gray-brown color of poverty were having the time of their lives. Flashes of lightning and one streetlamp illuminated the scene. Toussaint Camp was a children's camp now. They'd taken over. These tiny shrimps of energy were knocking a soccer ball around near the fountain, making it skip over the river of water flowing massively down through the camp. Lightning flashed nearby, too close. This new strongly rushing river looked capable of carrying ball, boys, tarps, tents, and everything, including me, away. Thunder clapped again. But the kids were not afraid. Kids rarely are. Two boys were riding pieces of cardboard box down the stream, one munching on an already much-munched mango pit. A few girls practiced their cartwheels in the vast puddle that had collected in a depression.

As the rain increased in ferocity, I found myself running, poncho flapping, from corridor to corridor, trying to find Jésulà. I must have looked like a deranged *loup-garou* in my outlandish getup of poncho, soaked jeans, crap shoes, with my wet hair hanging down, witchlike, over my shoulders. Finally I just stood, at a loss, rain pouring down me, as if I myself were an abandoned tent. Even the children had disappeared now, because the rain was so fierce. I was desperate for shelter. Across the way, a woman squatting beneath a small protective awning that extended from her shack beckoned me in. I wanted to kiss her.

It turned out, of course, that it was Jésulà. I'd ended up where I meant to be, by accident. This is the rule rather than the exception in my experience of Haiti. You'll be stuck on the side of a highway during a general strike with a person who needs medical attention, and eerily, down the empty highway, the one ambulance in the whole country will happen to be approaching, as if directed by Tarantino. You'll be crossing a dry riverbed in your jeep when the water starts to rise up beneath you, and miraculously, from the distant shore where before there was no one, ten peasant men in shorts will emerge, wade through the cresting river, and carry you and your things *and* your jeep in their strong arms to safety.

Inside Jésulà's shack it was dark. Her boyfriend, Wilner, had managed somehow to string a small flashlight from the roof of the tent by knotting a wire around a short stick of rebar. That was our only source of illumination. Jésulà and Wilner sat me down in their one chair. The shack was the size of a closet, and their one bed was more a cot than a twin-size bed; this they had put on two boxes and shoved up against the back wall, a wall made of wood frame and tarp.

Jésulà (it means "There's Jesus") was trying to cook some dinner in the rain. Her two little aluminum pots were roasting on top of a small bright red charcoal fire she'd made under the little awning just outside the tent. Wilner had sat the feverish baby on his lap. It made me remember Samuel's fever; maybe that's why he hadn't shown up.

Jésulà's fire cast an orange glow over Wilner and the baby. Walness, their three-year-old son, stood next to his father and let his small head rest on the mattress. He was watching his mother cook. He seemed to have an intensity of focus on the aluminum pots themselves, as if he could make them rise up from the fire and personally lay a feast for him. Roselaure, Jésulà's eight-year-old daughter from an earlier relationship, also had her eye on the pots. Roselaure was as skinny as a bean, in her red skirt and her red T-shirt, with the cheerful Digicel logo across her narrow chest. Her hair was done in a dozen or so tiny pigtails, each ending with a red rubber band.

Beyond the fire, the rainy season's river was still running, higher than before. This was to be the family's first meal of the day. Roselaure was bouncing in anticipation. She watched her mother's every move. The spoon going into the pot. The opening of the sardine tin with the family's knife, the knife's scoop of tomato paste (not ketchup), the knife's scoop of the perennial mayonnaise, a pat of butter (actually margarine), a stalk of fresh thyme, and—using, as ever, whatever is handiest—half a cup of rainwater (free of charge!) that they had been gathering in cups and buckets since the storm began. Then, last, the onion being cut and the red pepper—and into the pot. The rice was already ready.

We chatted as the sauce cooked. We were snug inside the damp, crowded shack as the storm raged. The cooking fire was like a hearth; the storm had cooled things down, so the shack wasn't sweltering. Jésulà and Wilner talked in a desultory way about what they wanted right now. The sauce bubbled. Jésulà said she wanted honest elections. "No violence," said Jésulà; Roselaure's father had been killed in earlier political unrest. She stirred the pot. It smelled so good. I realized I was hungry. Without question, I was the last person in this shack to come to that realization.

Wilner shifted the limp baby from one spot on his lap to another. He said what he wanted was for everyone to leave the camps—not that he had a plan for where they all should go. But he thought it was wrong for Haiti to have camps like Toussaint right outside the presidential palace, Haiti's grandest building. The camps were bad for Haiti's image, he said. He skipped over the fact that the palace, too, was mostly rubble, pebbles, and dust. He and Jésulà both wanted Roselaure back in school and out of the camp. It was too dangerous for a little girl here, Wilner said. Roselaure did not seem to be listening. One day, they would be out of the camp, we all knew—the camps would be cleared out. And where would

Wilner and Jésulà end up? They wanted someplace clean and safe. And cheap.

More immediately, Wilner wanted a television. Jésulà wanted a gold locket you could open and shut. She described the locket intimately, as if she had had one like it and lost it, and when I questioned her more closely, I found that this was so. She had lost hers, along with everything else she possessed, in the earthquake. A locket would make her feel more like her former self. So many people in Haiti right now were trying to become their former selves.

Ah, the food was ready. Now I wanted it very badly. From one plate, with one spoon, the family ate its meager helpings of rice and fish sauce. They passed the plate and spoon from person to person—Roselaure feeding Walness rice with sauce by the spoonful—and, along with a clean fork conjured from a damp cardboard box, they offered their dinner also to the strange lady in the strange getup who was sitting in their one little chair like some kind of awful dark-haired Goldilocks.

But I declined.

ACKNOWLEDGMENTS

First, thanks to my friend Loune Viaud, who arranges things, puts up with things, is stoic in the face of disaster, and has patience for the most important things and sometimes the least important, too. Though she's a woman of few words, those few are precisely chosen. In Haiti I owe her everything.

I thank profoundly, too, Rénald Clérismé, who survived the earthquake in spite of my public speculations to the contrary, and who for decades has beamed the light of his intelligence and humor over the whole Haitian scene, to my great benefit.

Thanks also to Maryse Pennette, and Daniel Kedar, as well as Gary Victor, Laurent Dubois, and Madison Smartt Bell. Richard Miguel helped me get around town and gave me the benefit of his singular experiences in Haiti, as did Jean-Robert Viaud.

Toni Monnin, Chantal Regnault, Kathie Klarreich, and Richard Morse each added to my store of knowledge about Haiti.

Thanks, too, to the seasoned and venerable team: the photographer Maggie Steber and the elder statesman of Haiti journalists, Greg Chamberlain, as well as Trenton Daniels and Pooja Bhatia. Thanks to Kati Maternowska, former worker in the Haitian trenches.

Thanks, thanks, thanks, to WikiLeaks, Kim Ives, Victor Navasky, Katrina vanden Heuvel, and *The Nation*. Thanks to Bob Corbett for his invaluable Haiti email list.

Thanks also to Ira Lowenthal, anthropologist, development expert, humanist, and complicated comrade.

I also want to thank Mengfei Chen for her help in researching parts of this book, Rachael Greenberg for her corrections, and Barry Siegel, head of the Literary Journalism program at UC Irvine, for his example and his help.

My students at UCI also helped me think about Haiti and the limits of revolutionary change.

Alison Humes and Klara Glowczewska, my editors at *Condé Nast Traveler,* sent me back to Haiti just before the earthquake, for which I owe them deeply. Rick Stengel at *Time* and David Remnick at *The New Yorker* did the same after the earthquake, and I'm very grateful. Thanks also to David Shipley, Sue Horton, and Dorothy Wickenden. I cannot forget, either, how Tina Brown sent me to Haiti so many years ago. Thanks, Tina.

As ever, Loida Adriano has provided invaluable support. Sally Craven boosted my self-respect.

Many thanks are due my cousin Elizabeth Williams Moore, who helped me understand Liberia, a country involved in a development crisis similar to Haiti's, as well as my brother James Wilentz, the doctor, whose experience as a cardiologist and health-service provider in Haiti after the earthquake opened my eyes to various medical issues, and also gave me Dr. Megan Coffee.

Thanks to Flip Brophy, my agent, who took me seriously when I said I wanted to write another book about Haiti, and to Alice Mayhew, my loyal editor, whose faith in my work has been unfailing and absolutely crucial to me. Thanks also to Karyn Marcus for her many useful ideas and suggestions and to Jonathan Cox for pushing the project along.

Thanks especially to those who talked to me in the camps, and helped me understand their trials and tribulations; to Jerry (who spells it Diery), Samuel, and Black Rouge.

Thanks also to Kate Manning, reader as well as writer.

My life as a writer and just my plain old life would have been profoundly impoverished had I not had the great good luck to know the late Ben Sonnenberg, the late Christopher Hitchens, and the late Alexander Cockburn. They all influenced me in different and important ways.

Thanks to my three sons, Rafe, Gabe, and Noah, who put up with their mother, the self-proclaimed drudge.

And finally, for wise, unselfish, and necessary notes on the manuscript and other aspects of my life, thanks to Nick Goldberg—my anchor, my unshakable foundation.

Los Angeles
June 2012

SELECTED BIBLIOGRAPHY

Alexis, Jacques Stephen. *Compère Général Soleil*. Paris: Gallimard, 1955.

Aristide, Jean-Bertrand. *Eyes of the Heart: Seeking a Path for the Poor in the Age of Globalization*. Edited by Laura Flynn. Monroe, ME: Common Courage Press, 2000.

Armstrong, Paul B. *Heart of Darkness: Joseph Conrad*. New York: W. W. Norton, Norton Critical Editions, 2006.

Bell, Madison Smartt. *Toussaint Louverture: A Biography*. New York: Pantheon Books, 2007.

Bruckner, Pascal. *The Tears of the White Man: Compassion as Contempt*. New York: The Free Press, 1983.

Buss, Terry F., and Adam Gardner. *Haiti in the Balance: Why Foreign Aid Has Failed and What We Can Do About It*. Washington, DC: The Brookings Institution, 2008.

Cadet, Jean-Robert. *Restavec: From Haitian Slave Child to Middle-Class American—An Autobiography*. Austin: University of Texas Press, 1998.

Clérismé, Rénald. *Main-d'Oeuvre Haïtienne, Capital Dominicaine: Essai d'Anthropologie Historique*. Paris: L'Harmattan, 2003.

Collier, Paul. *The Bottom Billion: Why the Poorest Countries Are Failing and What Can Be Done About It*. Oxford: Oxford University Press, 2007.

Danticat, Edwidge, ed. *Haiti Noir*. New York: Akashic Books, 2011.

Dayan, Joan. *Haiti, History, and the Gods*. Berkeley: University of California Press, 1995.

Deibert, Michael. *Notes from the Last Testament: The Struggle for Haiti*. New York: Seven Stories Press, 2005.

De Lacroix, Pamphile. *La Révolution de Haïti*. Edited by Pierre Pluchon. Paris: Editions Karthala, 1995 (originally published as *Mémoires pour servir à l'histoire de la Révolution de Saint-Domingue*. Paris, 1819).

Diederich, Bernard, and Al Burt. *Papa Doc and the Tontons Macoutes*. Port-au-Prince: Henri Deschamps, 1986.

Dubois, Laurent. *Avengers of the New World: The Story of the Haitian Revolution*. Cambridge, MA: The Belknap Press of Harvard University Press, 2004.

———. *Haiti: The Aftershocks of History*. New York: Metropolitan Books, 2012.

Easterly, William. *The White Man's Burden: Why the West's Efforts to Aid the Rest Have Done So Much Ill and So Little Good*. New York: Penguin Books, 2006.

Farmer, Paul. *Haiti: After the Earthquake*. New York: Public Affairs, 2011.

———*Partner to the Poor: A Paul Farmer Reader*. Edited by Haun Saussy. Berkeley: University of California Press, 2010.

———*The Uses of Haiti*. Monroe, ME: Common Courage Press, 1994.

Fleischman, Paul. (Kevin Hawkes, ill.) *Weslandia*. Cambridge, MA: Candlewick Press, 1999.

Florival, Jean. *La Face Cachée de Papa Doc*. Montréal: Mémoire d'Encrier, 2008.

Foner, Philip S. *The Life and Writings of Frederick Douglass, Volume III: The Civil War*. New York: International Publishers, 1952.

Gaillard, Roger. *Les Blancs Débarquent, 1918–1919: Charlemagne Péralte, Le Caco*. Port-au-Prince: Natal, 1982.

Girard, Philippe. *Haiti: The Tumultuous History—From Pearl of the Caribbean to Broken Nation*. New York: Palgrave Macmillan, 2005.

Greene, Graham. *The Comedians*. New York: Penguin, 1967.

Hadden, Gerry. *Never the Hope Itself: Love and Ghosts in Latin America and Haiti*. New York: HarperCollins, 2011.

Heinl, Robert Debs, and Nancy Gordon Heinl. *Written in Blood: The Story of the Haitian People, 1492–1995*. Revised and expanded by Michael Heinl. Lanham, MD: University Press of America, 1996.

Herskovits, Melville J. *The Myth of the Negro Past*. Boston: Beacon Press, 1941.

Hitchens, Christopher. *No One Left to Lie To: The Triangulations of William Jefferson Clinton*. London: Verso, 1999.

Hurbon, Laënnec. *Le Barbare Imaginaire*. Port-au-Prince: Henri Deschamps, 1987.

———. *Dieu dans le Vaudou Haïtien*. Port-au-Prince: Henri Deschamps, 1987.

James, Erica Caple. *Democratic Insecurities: Violence, Trauma, and Intervention in Haiti*. Berkeley: University of California Press, 2010.

Jenson, Deborah. *Beyond the Slave Narrative: Politics, Sex, and Manuscripts in the Haitian Revolution*. Liverpool: Liverpool University Press, 2011.

Klarreich, Kathie. *Madame Dread: A Tale of Love, Voodoo, and Civil Strife in Haiti*. New York: Nation Books, 2005.

Kurlansky, Mark. *The White Man in the Tree*. New York: Washington Square Press, 2000.

Laferrière, Dany. *Tout Bouge Autour de Moi*. Montréal: Mémoire d'Encrier, 2010.

Lowenthal, Ira P. "Ritual Performance and Religious Experience: A Service for the Gods in Southern Haiti." *Journal of Anthropological Research* 34, no. 3 (1978): 392–414.

Malval, Robert. *L'Année de Toutes les Duperies*. Québec: Editions Regain, 1996.

Maternowska, M. Catherine. *Reproducing Inequities: Poverty and the Politics of Population in Haiti*. New Brunswick, NJ: Rutgers University Press, 2006.

Melville, Herman. *Benito Cereno*. New York: Putnam's Monthly, 1855.

Métraux, Alfred. *Voodoo in Haiti*. New York: Schocken Books, 1972.

Mollien, Gaspard Théodore. *Haïti ou Saint-Domingue: Tomes I et II*. Paris: l'Harmattan, 2006.

Moyo, Dambisa. *Dead Aid: Why Aid Is Not Working and How There Is a Better Way for Africa*. Vancouver, BC: Douglas & McIntyre, 2009.

Nicholls, David. *From Dessalines to Duvalier: Race, Colour and National Independence in Haiti*. Cambridge: Cambridge University Press, 1979.

Plummer, Brenda Gayle. *Haiti and the United States: The Psychological Moment*. Athens, GA: The University of Georgia Press, 1992.

Polman, Linda. *The Crisis Caravan: What's Wrong with Humanitarian Aid?* New York: Metropolitan Books, 2010.

Price, Richard, ed. *Maroon Societies: Rebel Slave Communities in the Americas*. Baltimore: The Johns Hopkins University Press, 1973.

Price-Mars, Jean. *Ainsi Parla l'Oncle: Essais d'Ethnographie.* Port-au-Prince: Imprimerie de Compeigne, 1928.

Rasmussen, Daniel. *American Uprising: The Untold Story of America's Largest Slave Revolt.* New York: HarperCollins, 2011.

Rieff, David. *A Bed for the Night: Humanitarianism in Crisis.* New York: Simon & Schuster, 2002.

Roumain, Jacques. *Masters of the Dew.* London: Reynal & Hitchcock, 1947.

Sachs, Jeffrey. *The End of Poverty: Economic Possibilities for Our Time.* New York: Penguin Books, 2005.

Schwartz, Timothy T. *Travesty in Haiti: A True Account of Christian Missions, Orphanages, Food Aid, Fraud and Drug Trafficking.* Lexington, KY: Self-published, 2010.

Scroggins, Deborah. *Emma's War: A True Story.* New York: Vintage, 2004.

Seabrook, William. *The Magic Island.* New York: Harcourt, Brace, 1929.

Sen, Amartya. *Development as Freedom.* New York: Random House, 1999.

Simon, Paul-Emile, ed. *Le Palais National de la République d'Haïti.* Port-au-Prince: Henri Deschamps, 2003.

Sontag, Susan. *Regarding the Pain of Others.* New York: Picador, 2003.

Trouillot, Michel-Rolph. *Haiti: State Against Nation—The Origins & Legacy of Duvalierism.* New York: Monthly Review Press, 1990.

Vieux-Chauvet, Marie. *Love, Anger, Madness: A Haitian Triptych.* New York: Modern Library, 2009.

Von Tunzelmann, Alex. *Red Heat: Conspiracy, Murder, and the Cold War in the Caribbean.* New York: Henry Holt, 2011.

Wirkus, Faustin, and Taney Dudley. *The White King of La Gonâve.* Garden City, NY: Doubleday, Doran, 1931.

INDEX

ABOUT THE AUTHOR

Amy Wilentz is the author of *The Rainy Season: Haiti Since Duvalier, Martyrs' Crossing*, and *I Feel Earthquakes More Often Than They Happen: Coming to California in the Age of Schwarzenegger*. She edited and translated *In the Parish of the Poor: Writings from Haiti*, by Jean-Bertrand Aristide. She is the winner of the Whiting Writers' Award, the PEN/Martha Albrand Nonfiction Award, and the American Academy of Arts and Letters Rosenthal Award, and was also a 1990 nominee for the National Book Critics Circle Award. Wilentz has written for many publications including *The New York Times, Los Angeles Times, Time,* and *Condé Nast Traveler*. She is the former Jerusalem correspondent of *The New Yorker* and a longtime contributing editor at *The Nation*. Wilentz is a professor in the Literary Journalism program in the English Department at the University of California at Irvine. She lives in Los Angeles.